# IRISH DRAMA AND THEATRE SINCE 1950

**Patrick Lonergan** is Professor of Drama and Theatre Studies at National University of Ireland, Galway. Among his books are *Theatre and Globalization* (winner of the 2008 Theatre Book Prize), *The Theatre and Films of Martin McDonagh* (2012) and *Theatre and Social Media* (2015). With Kevin Wetmore he is co-editor of Methuen Drama's *Critical Companions* series.

# IRISH DRAMA AND THEATRE
# SINCE 1950

*Patrick Lonergan*

*Series Editors: Patrick Lonergan and Kevin J. Wetmore Jr*

*methuen* | drama

LONDON • NEW YORK • OXFORD • NEW DELHI • SYDNEY

METHUEN DRAMA
Bloomsbury Publishing Plc
50 Bedford Square, London, WC1B 3DP, UK
1385 Broadway, New York, NY 10018, USA

BLOOMSBURY, METHUEN DRAMA and the Methuen Drama logo are trademarks
of Bloomsbury Publishing Plc

First published in Great Britain 2019

A catalogue record for this book is available from the British Library.

A catalog record for this book is available from the Library of Congress.

ISBN:   HB:      978-1-4742-6264-4
        PB:      978-1-4742-6265-1
        ePDF:    978-1-4742-6267-5
        eBook:   978-1-4742-6266-8

Series: Critical Companions

Typeset by RefineCatch Limited, Bungay, Suffolk
Printed and bound in Great Britain

To find out more about our authors and books visit www.bloomsbury.com
and sign up for our newsletters.

*For Saoirse*

# CONTENTS

# Contents

# ILLUSTRATIONS

# ACKNOWLEDGEMENTS

In 2012 my home university, National University of Ireland, Galway, announced a plan to digitize the archive of the Abbey Theatre. That project made it possible to imagine a book such as this: one that would begin retelling the story of modern and contemporary Irish theatre by drawing on new archival material. For their work in securing an extensive archival collection about Irish theatre, I am very grateful to John Cox, Caroline Loughnane, Gearoid O'Conluain and particularly Jim Browne who, as university president until 2017, always sought to support research, teaching and practice in the creative arts.

Also at NUI Galway, Marianne Kennedy offered essential advice on Irish-language drama, and Ian Walsh's scholarship on mid-century Irish theatre has been a strong and valued influence. Barry Houlihan was immensely helpful in locating archival material and offering suggestions about its interpretation, and I am especially grateful for his help in sourcing and clearing rights for many of the images in this book. I'm also very appreciative of Charlotte McIvor's advice about theatre, the practice of writing, and much else besides. Thanks to the colleagues, students, archivists and artists who answered questions, sent unpublished material, assisted in securing important archival material, or helped in some other way. These include Beatriz Bastos, Nelson Barre, Lucy Caldwell, David Clare, Linda Connolly, Emma Creedon, John Crumlish, Bev Curran, Joan Dean, Mairead Delaney, Jill Dolan, Liz Elkinson, Paul Fahy, Lisa Fitzgerald, Nicholas Grene, Aoife Harrington, Miriam Haughton, Kieran Hoare, Aideen Howard, Erin Hurley, Garry Hynes, Margaret Kelleher, Aiveen Kelly, Michael Kenneally, Des Lally, Jose Lanters, Louise Lowe, Sarah Lynch, Emer McHugh, Trish McTighe, Chris Morash, Catherine Morris, Rachel Murray, Finian O'Gorman, Siobhán O'Gorman, Lynne Parker, Mark Phelan, Áine Phillips, Lionel Pilkington, Christina Reid, Tony Roche, Annie Ryan, Melissa Sihra, Matthew Spangler, Naoko Toraiwa, Shelley Troupe, Harry White, Willie White, Brenda Winter and Stacy Wolf.

Thanks to Mark Dudgeon at Methuen Drama for commissioning this book, to Lara Bateman for seeing it through to completion, and to the anonymous reader who provided very helpful feedback on an earlier draft.

Thanks finally to my family – to Therese, Saoirse and Cónall.

# A NOTE ON ARCHIVAL MATERIAL

For ease of referencing, the following abbreviations are employed.

**ATDA**  The Abbey Theatre Digital Archive at the James Hardiman
Library (JHL), NUI Galway

**BF NLI**  Papers of Brian Friel, National Library of Ireland

**DDA**  Dublin Diocesan Archives, McQuaid Papers

**DTA**  Druid Theatre Archive, JHL, NUI Galway

**GTDA**  The Gate Theatre Digital Archive, JHL, NUI Galway

**LTA**  Lyric Theatre/O'Malley family papers, JHL, NUI Galway

**NLI**  National Library of Ireland

**TKA**  Archive of the papers of Thomas Kilroy, JHL, NUI Galway

**TnaG**  Taibhdhearc na Gaillimhe archive, JHL, NUI Galway

I often quote from newspaper articles, but have drawn them from multiple sources: printed records, online databases and archival press files. To provide consistency of referencing, I give the date of publication of the article in parentheses after quotations.

I want to acknowledge the extensive use I have made of the Irish Playography, which provides information about first productions of every Irish play since 1904. I am grateful to Jane Daly and Siobhán Bourke for their continuing work on that vital resource. Unless stated otherwise, dates of the premieres of any Irish plays mentioned in this book are derived from the Playography. Production histories for productions at the Abbey, Lyric and Gate are taken from the above archives. Those for the Dublin Theatre Festival are from the history featured in Grene and Lonergan (2008), *Interactions*.

# INTRODUCTION

In October 2015, Fiach Mac Conghail announced his final programme as director of the Abbey, Ireland's national theatre. It should have been a moment of celebration, both for him and his institution. He had been appointed in 2005, a time when the Abbey had been perilously close to going out of business – and, during the following ten years, he had saved the theatre from collapse: restoring its finances, overseeing the renovation of its auditorium, re-engaging with established writers and premiering new plays. His last programme was therefore expected to allow audiences to reflect upon his achievements, and to wish him well as he made way for a new directorship.

Another important context was that 2016 would mark the centenary of the Easter Rising, the insurrection that had set in train events that culminated in the creation of the Irish Free State in 1922. The Abbey intended to play its part in the official state commemorations of that event: its productions would reconsider the histories of independent Ireland, and would explore how theatre and other creative arts had helped to shape that country. The programme's name was 'Waking the Nation', and the Abbey was using the verb in that phrase in at least two senses: to wake something can be to encourage it into action – but in an Irish context it can also mean to mourn something that has passed away. Mac Conghail seemed to be encouraging his audience to consider what kind of nation they might want to commemorate during 2016, to ask whether Ireland had become a genuine republic, a place in which all citizens are treated equally. But he was also leaving open the possibility that those audiences might want to kill off the Ireland they had inherited, to bury the past and create something new in its place.

His programming choices explored those ideas in many ways. Seán O'Casey's 1926 critique of the Rising, *The Plough and the Stars*, was revived in a new production – an assertion on the Abbey's part that its role in Irish society has never been to memorialize revolution but to interrogate it. Frank McGuinness' 1985 masterpiece *Observe the Sons of Ulster Marching Towards the Somme* also appeared, demonstrating the Abbey's engagement with the Unionist tradition in Northern Ireland – not to mention its willingness to create space for the expression of gay Irish identities. Ireland's troubled histories with gender and emigration were explored in a revival of Tom Murphy's 1997 play *The Wake*. And there was also a production of *Othello*, staged to mark the 400th anniversary of Shakespeare's death – an inclusion that provided evidence of the transformed relationship between England and Ireland, given that Shakespeare, as an English dramatist, had been banished from the theatre's repertoire for much of the twentieth century (for further discussion see Lonergan, 2015).

Almost completely absent, however, was work by women. Only one play in Mac Conghail's programme was written by a female dramatist (*Me, Mollser* by Ali White), and only two productions would be directed by women. This gave rise to expressions of disappointment and anger from audiences and theatre-makers as, first in the semi-private world of Facebook and then in the public realm of Twitter, several female directors, writers, actors and designers came forward to recount stories of having been neglected, marginalized, ignored and discriminated against within the Irish theatre – solely on the basis of their gender. Led by the designer Lian Bell, the movement took the name #WakingTheFeminists, a phrase that was at once a reappropriation of Mac Conghail's 'Waking the Nation' title, and also an expression of shock and disgust (the acronym WTF is a slang phrase for 'what the fuck'). The Abbey's centenary programme became the focal point for those protests, but Bell's work in curating responses from both male and female artists demonstrated that the inequalities went far beyond the national theatre – and had existed for a long time.

On 12 November 2015, the movement held a public gathering at the Abbey, where dozens of female theatre-makers presented speeches about their experiences. At that event, Mac Conghail apologized for the omission of women from his 2016 programme and spoke about his need to reflect upon his own biases and blind spots. 'We can't have true artistic integrity without gender equality,' he said, pledging that the Abbey would seek to do better in the future.[1]

As a theatre scholar and teacher, I watched these events with excitement and hope – but also with trepidation. Irish theatre, I knew, had grappled with this kind of challenge before. Shortly before the #WTF movement had begun, my colleague Barry Houlihan had discovered a list that had been compiled at the Abbey in 1975, to coincide with a revival of Teresa Deevy's *Katie Roche* (1936). It named plays by twenty other female dramatists, aiming to promote further productions of their work. The writers were Alice Milligan, Lady Gregory, Mrs Bart Kennedy, Rose McKenna, Dorothy Macardle, Sadie Casey, Elizabeth Harte, Susan Glaspell, Cathleen M.

O'Brennan, Deevy, Margaret O'Leary, Maura Molloy, Maeve O'Callaghan, Mary Rynne, Elizabeth Connor, Nora McAdam, Olga Fielden, Margaret O'Leary, Máiréad Ní Ghráda and Eibhlin Ni Shuilleabhainn (ATDA, ADM_00001093: 75) – names that usually appear in the footnotes of Irish theatre histories, if they appear at all. None of those plays was staged by the theatre.

Similar attempts would be made during the years that followed. As Eileen Kearney and Charlotte Headrick point out, the need to promote work by Irish women playwrights had been noted in the early 1980s, when the Dublin Theatre Festival and *The Irish Times* co-sponsored a competition for new plays by women: 'After examining the almost two hundred entries,' they wrote, 'the judges concluded that many were better than plays by male authors who had been produced in recent years' (2014: 15). Fewer than ten of those plays were staged.

At around the same time, in Northern Ireland, Charabanc Theatre Company was formed, aiming to redress not only the lack of work available for women in the theatre but also to challenge the quality of the roles that were being written for them. Staging more than twenty new plays between 1983 and 1995, Charabanc had a transformational impact on Irish theatre. Yet despite its influence, the position of women in Irish theatre remained fundamentally unequal twenty-two years after the company had folded. This, presumably, is what Charabanc co-founder Eleanor Methven was referring to when she declared at the #WTF meeting that she didn't need to be 'woken up' as a feminist Irish theatre-maker: 'I've been awake since 1976,' she said.

Perhaps the most infamous example of this phenomenon is the publication of the *Field Day Anthology of Irish Literature* in 1991. Prior to its launch, commentators were excited by what was expected to be a major redrawing of the Irish literary map. But that enthusiasm soon gave way to dismay, as it became apparent that the editors had excluded a very large number of female writers. Field Day subsequently published a fourth and fifth volume, focused on writing by and about women – but the impact of the original omission was lastingly damaging, both to the reputation of Field Day and the morale of countless Irish women writers. In an *Irish Times* column Nuala O'Faolain articulated a sense of outrage and a determination that nothing like this would ever happen again: 'the next time an anthologist bends to his task,' she wrote, 'he won't be able to forget that there are watchful women out there' (11 November 1991).

Two years after that debacle, Katy Hayes and Caroline Williams staged a festival of plays called *There are No Irish Women Playwrights* with Glasshouse

Productions. The title of the event was an ironic appropriation of the response that had been given to a visiting academic when she had asked a Dublin bookseller where she could find published scripts by female Irish dramatists; Glasshouse set out to show that in fact there are a great many such plays. That event was followed by a special issue of *Theatre Ireland* on women in Irish theatre, which was followed by a special issue of *Irish University Review*, dedicated to Teresa Deevy and other Irish women dramatists. With new work by Marina Carr appearing in the Abbey in 1994 alongside a revival of Deevy's *Katie Roche*, it seemed as if positive change was underway. Yet twenty-one years later, the same arguments were being made again. 'We thought we would change the world,' Hayes told me in 2014. 'But the world went back to its old tricks.'[2]

I've begun this book with the #WTF movement because it reveals at least two important things about theatre and how it is remembered.

The first is that, to repeat Hayes' remark, the world often goes back to its old tricks. In the chapters that follow, one of the arguments I'll make is that Irish dramatists usually present the development of their society as something that happens in cycles rather than in a linear fashion: history is always repeated, the past is always inescapable, and the best we can hope for is to fail better next time. The task and the challenge for many Irish characters is to break those cycles: to leave for America (as in Brian Friel's *Philadelphia, Here I Come!* in 1964), to finish telling the endless story (as in Tom Murphy's *Bailegangaire* in 1985), to escape from the legacies of a parent (as in Carr's *By the Bog of Cats* in 1998), or to accept that we must continue to wait for Godot, even as we know that he will never actually arrive. These and other examples will be explored in depth in the pages that follow.

But I also want to show how in the Irish theatre the content often mirrors the form, and vice versa. Beckett's *Waiting for Godot* (1955) was famously described as a play in which nothing happens – twice. In the brief outline above, I've discussed the recurrent attempts to call attention to the unequal status of women dramatists in the Irish theatre. It would be unfair to characterize those attempts as a pattern in which nothing happened at least five times, but it is notable that each iteration occurred as if for the first time. And on each occasion the response was the same: people in positions of power listened, they became engaged and they sometimes became enraged – but then they forgot, or allowed themselves to forget, and the status quo gradually reasserted itself.

These moments of forgetting demonstrate that anyone who writes about theatre needs to contemplate how and why some events are remembered while many are not. Just as theatre programmers can, in a sense, 'perform memory' by choosing to commemorate events in particular ways, so must theatre scholars think about the choices we make when we document the past. This book, then, is not just an exploration of Irish theatre since 1950 but an attempt to track relationships between apparently disconnected events – like those described above – so that neglected or unnoticed patterns can come into view. I make no claim to provide a comprehensive history of Irish theatre during this period (such a book would be considerably longer), but I do try to identify stories that I think need to be remembered, placing famous actors, plays and productions in conversation with events and people that deserve to be better known.

However, I also want to show how Irish theatre practitioners have succeeded at breaking negative cycles – that, through the efforts of successive generations, positive change has gradually been achieved in some areas. To return to the specific example of #WakingTheFeminists, in 2017 Brenda Donohue led the compilation of a report entitled *Gender Counts* that demonstrated how inequality runs through the Irish theatre sector in its entirety, showing that women were less likely to be commissioned to write or direct plays, and were under-represented in almost every other area of professional practice. In response, most Irish theatre companies put in place meaningful policies to promote equality, and it is likely that future state funding of the arts will be dependent upon evidence of the successful implementation of such policies. It remains to be seen if the pattern has fully been broken, but there is no doubt that #WTF has brought about substantial and positive change.

So one of the things that I want to show in this book is how Irish theatre has produced many such acts of gradual revolution, often brought about by individuals working in isolation from each other, and happening over several decades. What follows, therefore, is deliberately *not* written as a linear history but rather is an attempt to think about how our histories could be written. Rather than beginning at 1950 and working my way through to the present, I instead show the development of selected themes across the period – which means that chapters will sometimes overlap chronologically. My aim is to provide evidence of how the form has developed in cycles or waves: to capture repetition by sometimes being repetitious.

The second reason I have begun with #WTF is that the movement demonstrates that when history is made it often happens unexpectedly or even accidentally. The Abbey's 'Waking the Nation' programme set out to provoke debate and to inspire change – and it did exactly that, but only because so many people rejected its claim to represent what the nation could and should be. Instead, the Abbey's output became part of a wider conversation in the society about equality, feeding into debates about equal pay, sexual harassment and reproductive rights. This shows how the Irish theatre does more than simply hold a mirror to its society: it is often an agent not just of reflection but of change. We'll find many examples in this book of how Irish theatre-makers and companies bring about change by positioning themselves in a symbolic relationship with their society, doing so to challenge norms about gender, religion, sexuality, nationality, race and much more. I want to show that the power of theatre to act in this way has not always been well understood, largely because (to make the point again) individual events have been forgotten. A major objective will be to tie together apparently disparate strands in order to reveal traditions and continuities that might not have been sufficiently visible before.

I begin with a chapter that charts the contours of this argument by exploring Irish theatre in the 1950s, showing how the period made possible much of what followed. By considering the work of three important figures – Siobhán McKenna, Brendan Behan and Samuel Beckett – I want to identify how Irish theatre was developing new ways of thinking about place, language, authorship and nation at the century's midway point. Those three figures – alongside many others – began a process of reinventing what Irish theatre could be, showing that it need not be focused on the three themes that then dominated Irish literature: religion, nation and land.

Chapters 2 and 3 show those acts of reimagining developing over several decades, focusing on two of those three themes. I want first to consider religion, to chart how Irish theatre changed the nation's relationship with institutional Catholicism, not only by exposing the abuses that were being perpetrated by members of the clergy (as well as by the institution more broadly), but also by shifting a cultural imagination rooted in Catholicism into a more secular context. I turn then to nation, to a consideration of how international influences helped to shape Irish theatre, exploring how dramatists and audiences responded to the innovations of figures such as Brecht and Chekhov.

In Chapters 4 and 5 I adopt a different methodology, showing how playwrights and directors attempted to tackle specific issues – and thereby devised strategies that would later be used to bring about change in a variety of other areas. First I explore the work of important female dramatists, actors and directors including Mary Manning, Olwen Fouéré, Marina Carr, Garry Hynes and Christina Reid – showing how all (in different ways) used feminist strategies to change their societies' attitudes to gender, identity, space, the canon and authorship. I then want to demonstrate how those strategies created space for apparently unrelated developments, citing the example of how the career of Martin McDonagh has to be understood in the context of Garry Hynes' feminist reappropriation of the plays of John Millington Synge. This is not to suggest that Martin McDonagh is a feminist playwright (he isn't) but to show that, far from being one strand within Irish theatre practice, feminism has been centrally involved in every element of it – an involvement that has in some ways been rendered invisible or has been overlooked.

I make a similar case about how playwrights and actors responded to the Troubles by writing plays that explored the themes of difference and transformation. Change, they show, is painful – but it is also necessary; by dramatizing the lives of characters who experience transformation through interacting with otherness, Irish theatre showed that identities do not have to be permanently fixed, and showed too that it might be possible for communities in conflict to see the theatrical as offering new ways to live in the world beyond the theatre. We'll see that strategy being worked out in productions by Brian Friel, Marie Jones and Charabanc, and Frank McGuinness. But we'll also see how those innovations were adapted to other contexts: I conclude that chapter by showing how Enda Walsh drew on similar strategies in order to consider how Ireland had been transformed by inward migration. The aim in drawing that parallel is to start to explain why Irish theatre so often involves the repetition of old tropes, themes and characters: one way of understanding the new is to place it in conversation with the familiar – a dialogue that produces a creative tension that can be dramatically rich as well as socially impactful.

The sixth chapter considers Irish theatre now, showing the continuity of some of the patterns I have identified, but also pointing towards new developments. I'll consider how dramatists such as Conor McPherson, Mark O'Rowe and Deirdre Kinahan are developing the form by building on the achievements of earlier writers – but I also want to highlight the importance of figures such as Amy Conroy: practitioners who see themselves primarily as theatre-makers, and thus as free to move fluidly between the roles of acting, directing and playwriting (among other areas). The novelty of the concept of the theatre-maker is sometimes overstated in Ireland: as we'll see, Siobhán McKenna authored and acted in her own plays in much the same way that Conroy does, and from earlier times figures from Boucicault to Lady Gregory could easily have been called 'theatre-makers'. But it is certainly true that Irish theatre since 2008 has become much more open to new ways of working.

In choosing these themes, I have been influenced by practical considerations such as the availability of particular archival records. But I have also sought to make visible the fact that any historian will inevitably choose specific perspectives from which to judge his or her subject, and that in turn means that many areas will be omitted. For example, I have little to say about dance theatre and the development of physical theatre since the 1980s, in part because of the existence of important and comprehensive work by Aoife McGrath (2011) and Bernadette Sweeney (2008) on those topics. But I also believe there is much more to be said about such themes as social class, community theatre and the practice of acting (among many other topics). As a way of pointing towards other possible approaches to this era, the final chapter presents three critical perspectives, in which Finian O'Gorman, Siobhán O'Gorman and Áine Phillips explore amateur theatre, design and performance art respectively. Book-length studies of those topics could easily be produced: indeed, both Phillips (2015) and Siobhán O'Gorman (2019) have written much more extensively about their subjects. These essays are included as having value in their own right but also aim to demonstrate that the history of Irish drama and theatre since 1950 is multifaceted and must continue to be explored.

In choosing plays and productions to discuss, I have been conscious of the need to include works that readers would probably expect to see – Friel's *Translations* (1980) or Beckett's *Waiting for Godot*, to give just two examples – as well as a discussion of such major companies as the Abbey, the Gate, Druid and so on. But (thinking again of the 'Waking the Nation' programme) I am also mindful of the risks associated with reproducing the canon. While I am sure I have my own blind spots, I have tried to include writers whose work has been neglected, as well as underappreciated areas as Irish-language theatre, adaptation and the role of actors and directors. The selection of case studies is evenly balanced between male and female theatre-makers, and I have also been conscious of the need to consider theatre produced outside Dublin and Belfast. I have also been very influenced by Cathy Leeney's observation that 'women's contribution to Irish theatre continues often to be considered as a separate topic' but that 'recognizing women's work also needs to happen' (2016: 269): a balancing act that is difficult to achieve but that needs to be engaged in.

Why start at 1950? I see the emergence of contemporary Irish theatre as having happened in a context that was informed by the declaration of the Irish Republic in 1948 (coming into force during the following year) and the destruction of the Abbey Theatre by fire in 1951. The Irish state did not participate in the Second World War, though Northern Ireland did – so the use of the term 'post-war' to describe the period is inappropriate in an Irish context. But Ireland was affected by the broader post-war environment internationally, and I attempt to maintain a sense of how theatre in that country was in dialogue with broader international events.

The decision to start shortly after the declaration of the Irish Republic gives rise to questions about what I mean when I write about 'Irish' theatre. That is a term that refers to plays made in both the Republic of Ireland and Northern Ireland – but an 'Irish' play can also premiere in London, Edinburgh, New York, Paris or anywhere else. I will show in Chapter 3 that 'Irish theatre' is a term that must include productions by such figures as Brecht and Chekhov, and which must accommodate the many new forms of identity that have emerged in Ireland since the turn of the century. Given that many Irish productions deliberately play with the multiplicity of potential meanings of the word 'Irish' – sometimes using it to describe geographic origins or settings, sometimes to describe generic or formal qualities – it can be counterproductive to define it too rigidly. My hope is that the specific origins of a play or production under discussion will be obvious from context, but I am aware of the risk of appearing to obscure important distinctions, especially between plays made in the Republic of Ireland and those from Northern Ireland. Since the signing of the Good Friday Agreement in 1998, we have seen the emergence of the term 'Northern Irish' as a signifier of identity – and while that term remains both contested and provisional, it might be important to begin thinking of 'Northern Irish theatre' as a distinctive tradition that must, to borrow a term from the title of Tom Maguire's seminal book, be seen as existing 'through and beyond the Troubles' (2006), and which also moves beyond Ophelia Byrne's important designation of the history of such work as happening on 'the stage in Ulster' (1997). In this book, however, I have tended to present the term 'Irish theatre' as encompassing work produced on the island in its entirety.

Methodologically, my approach has mainly involved consultation of archival resources, coupled with (where possible) my own attendance at the relevant productions. As I hope to show, the availability of large amounts of archival information can transform our awareness of the relationship between theatre and its society. A published playscript can show us what an author intended, but a promptbook can reveal what the actors actually did on stage. A literary analysis of a dramatic text can reveal important social themes, but a consideration of box office figures can tell us how many people in a society actually went to see the play. Production photographs can show how directors sometimes seek to emphasize one feature in a play over another, and they also remind us that many plays contain ghostly traces of work that we've seen before. And, perhaps most importantly, the archive can help us to retrieve the voices and events that have been forgotten. This book considers some works that deserve to be better known, but the analysis of archival information also allows for new ways to think about canonical plays.

My overall aim is to show that Irish theatre has had a significant impact both on its society and on the development of the form internationally. I will make the (probably obvious) case that we cannot understand the development of Irish theatre without considering such phenomena as European integration, globalization, the impact of clerical child abuse scandals on Catholicism, and more. But I also want to make the (probably less obvious) argument that we cannot understand the development of Irish society without considering how it has been not just enriched but actively changed by its theatre. In these chapters, I want to bring to light some examples of how those changes were made possible – knowing as I do so that there is much more of the story still to be discovered and told. What follows, then, is an exploration of Irish theatre over a period of seventy years – one that is necessarily limited but which aims to provoke new conversations about how and why we remember this thing that we call 'Irish theatre'.

# CHAPTER 1
## 'THANK GOODNESS THAT'S OVER' – IRISH THEATRE IN THE 1950s

On 18 July 1951, the Abbey Theatre was severely damaged by a fire. It was forced to relocate to the nearby Queen's Theatre for what was intended to have been a short stay, but which eventually extended to fifteen years – causing the theatre to enter a period that is dismissed by most scholars and journalists as one of severe decline, both politically and aesthetically.

The 1951 fire signalled metaphorically what had been evident for some years: that the great age of Irish drama that had begun in 1899 with the first performance of the Irish Literary Theatre was now over, and had probably ended with the death of the theatre's co-founder W.B. Yeats in 1939. The Second World War had delayed an acknowledgement of the Abbey's decline: international conflict had meant that its actors were prevented from emigrating to London or Los Angeles, and had also prevented competition from visiting companies. But after 1945, the Abbey could no longer postpone facing its problems. Its best actors were leaving, its audiences were declining and it had produced few obvious successors to the great dramatists of its earliest years.

Those problems are movingly encapsulated by the promptbook for the play that was being performed on the night of the fire: Seán O'Casey's *The Plough and the Stars* (1926). That document, which is now held at the Abbey Theatre archive, includes the original typescript as prepared by O'Casey himself; we find his additions to the text pasted over discarded passages, together with notes by Lennox Robinson about blocking and lighting effects. That script had been used as the promptbook for the play's premiere, the now legendary opening that had provoked riots, and it continued to be used for every production of the play (of which there were at least thirty-five) that was staged at the Abbey until the 1951 fire.

The *Plough* promptbook could fairly be described as a national treasure. It bears the imprint of O'Casey and Robinson and was read by Yeats and Lady Gregory. It is a relic of one of the key moments not just in Irish theatre but in the development of independent Ireland, memorializing the Abbey's willingness to resist attempts to stifle its freedom of artistic expression – at a time when Ireland was about to enter a period of rigid censorship. But the iconic status of the promptbook also explains much of what was wrong at the Abbey: that it had been performing O'Casey's play in exactly the same way for a quarter of a century. Eileen Crowe and May Craig had appeared in the 1926 premiere; Craig was still playing the same role (of Mrs Gogan) twenty-five years later. Ria Mooney had played Rosie Redmond in 1926; by 1951 she had taken on the role of director. Even the interval music was largely unchanged (*La bohème* in 1926, *Tosca* in 1951) (ATDA, 3051_ MPG_01, 3 and 3396_MPG_01, 4). Where *The Plough* had provoked riots at its premiere, it was now being presented as a museum piece.

The Abbey's fidelity to the original staging of *The Plough* was not unusual for its era, but it shows how the theatre had lost its dynamism and drive. Indeed, that complaint had been levelled at the Abbey during a previous run of *The Plough* in 1947, when Valentin Iremonger had made a speech 'lambasting the present directorate's artistic policy, describing it as being characterized by "utter incompetence"' (qtd by Welch, 1999: 153). Together with Roger McHugh, he publicly protested that the 1947 *The Plough* was a betrayal of a great play.

Such deficiencies have usually been attributed to the management of the theatre by Ernest Blythe, who took over as its director in 1941 and occupied that role until 1967. Blythe is mostly remembered for the writers whose work he rejected, but he has not been given much credit for those whose early plays he supported (such as Brian Friel and Hugh Leonard). He is criticized for having dedicated so much attention to the promotion of the Irish language but, as I'll discuss later, that policy allowed directors such as Tomás Mac Anna to devise innovations in both theme and design in ways that might not have been permissible in English. Irish-language plays also gave important actors such as Siobhán McKenna their earliest professional experiences. Blythe did show a preference for comedies over more serious works, but towards the end of his career, he would explain that this approach meant that difficult issues such as partition could be discussed 'coolly and with an eye to the future' – an assertion that was self-serving but which should not be dismissed (1963: 21). Finally, he kept the theatre in business during a difficult period, and did so with a tiny annual subsidy from the government – one that, as an *Irish Times* editorial pointed out, would not even have covered the operating costs of the Gaiety Theatre's annual pantomime:

> For years the theatre has been operating under conditions of such difficulty that no producer from an outside national theatre could be brought to believe it possible that anything could be effectively staged

at the Abbey ... Scene 'flats' after fifty years use, had become so threadbare that they could not stand another coat of paint, but the theatre's treasury could not afford new ones. Dressing-rooms, wardrobe, and property storage space were inferior to their equivalents in the average village hall in Scandinavia

*The Irish Times*, 19 July 1951

It is revealing that this editorial saw the Abbey fire as an opportunity finally to oblige the Irish government to fund the theatre properly.

Leaving aside the funding (what theatre ever has enough money?), a further difficulty is that the Abbey was remaining static at a time when the nation it purported to represent was undergoing major changes. The Second World War had created a firmer division between the north and the rest of the island. As part of the UK, Northern Ireland had fully participated in the war, sending thousands of soldiers to fight in the British Army, and experiencing attack by the German air force. The rest of Ireland adopted a position of neutrality, and although many of its citizens left the country to contribute to the war effort anyway, its experience of the period was different from that of almost every other country in Europe.

As a further signal of Ireland's distance not only from Northern Ireland but also from Britain, the government declared the country a republic in 1948, leaving the Commonwealth and severing all ties with the British Crown when that act became law the following year. In one sense, this appeared to achieve the goal of the 1916 Rising, which had been fought to achieve an independent republic – but in fact the 1948 declaration was seen in some quarters as a betrayal of those goals, given that the state envisaged by the Rising's leaders was to have comprised the whole island. Implicit in the declaration of the Republic was an awareness that the partition of Ireland into two separate states was likely to persist for the foreseeable future. Acknowledging this likelihood in turn created the circumstances that allowed Ireland to play a more active role internationally, joining the United Nations in 1955 and, in 1961, applying for the first time to join the European Economic Community (EEC). Ireland's position in the world was therefore evolving rapidly at a time when its national theatre was homeless, underfunded and under the management of someone whose artistic outlook could not have been more different from that of Yeats and Gregory.

But if the 1951 fire diminished the importance of the national theatre, it also had the impact of inspiring new developments. The closure of the Abbey's smaller Peacock space, alongside Blythe's determination to stage commercially popular works in order to meet the higher running costs at the Queen's, meant that the Abbey was moving away from experimental practice, poetic drama and most other forms of risk-taking other than the staging of new Irish-language plays. That left a gap that was quickly filled by the theatre clubs that had been opening in Dublin and Belfast, most of which played to very small (and often very select) audiences of between forty and eighty people. These included the 37 Theatre Club, which had been established by Barry Cassin and Nora Lever in 1951, as well as the Lyric Players' Theatre, which was established by Mary O'Malley in the same year in Belfast and which would ultimately become the main producing house of Northern Ireland. As Ian Walsh points out, these small theatres did not need to be particularly iconoclastic in order to challenge Irish theatrical orthodoxies. 'Cassin and Lever did not set out to be leaders of a counter-movement in Irish theatre,' he writes. They 'simply wished to produce plays that were "interesting and unusual"' ... However, a commitment to the "unusual" was a daring act in fifties Ireland' (2012: 141).

By far the most important of these clubs was the Pike, a sixty-two-seat theatre established in 1951 by Alan Simpson and Carolyn Swift in a converted coach house in Dublin's Herbert Street. As we'll see, this was the stage that presented the world premiere of Brendan Behan's *The Quare Fellow*, as well as the Irish premiere of *Waiting for Godot* – and which would set out to do far more than simply produce work that was 'unusual'. As Walsh points out, even the theatre's title was a declaration of intent. Swift and Simpson 'named their theatre after a symbol of military Irish revolt: the pike was the weapon used in the 1798 uprising' against British rule (2012: 165). Their name expressed a desire not just to revolutionize the theatre but, by doing so, to change their society. As we'll see in the next chapter, that declaration would draw a retaliatory attack – one that would force the theatre out of business. But the Pike's legacies would be lasting.

Outside Dublin, a thriving amateur sector staged the first All-Ireland Drama Festival in Athlone in 1953. A competitive event that brought participants from across the island, it hosted productions that complicate the widely held view that Ireland at this time was wholly conservative and priest-ridden. Yes, the amateur sector was dominated by members of the clergy, many of whom directed plays or were otherwise prominent in the organization – but rather than acting as a force of censorship and repression, some encouraged the staging of experimental or provocative work from Europe and the United States.[1] The amateur sector was also (when compared to the professional sector) disproportionately driven by women, many of them university graduates who had been forced to quit their jobs upon marriage. By the end of the 1950s, the status of the amateur sector had risen to such a point that John B. Keane's *Sive* – which began life as an amateur production by Kerry's Listowel Players – was performed on the stage of the Abbey, an admission by the national theatre of the quality and significance of Keane's play (which Blythe had earlier rejected). Finian O'Gorman writes in detail about this production in Chapter 7.

The amateur sector also allowed people throughout Ireland to realize that they could act, write, or direct, and thus inspired the development of professional careers. That relationship can be seen in one of the most famous anecdotes about modern Irish theatre, which concerns the composition by Tom Murphy and Noel O'Donoghue of *On the Outside* in the late 1950s. The two men were socializing in Tuam, the Galway town that Murphy was born in, and the setting for most of his dramas. At a loss for something to do, one of them proposed that they should write a play. Murphy wondered what its subject should be; O'Donoghue replied that he didn't know. 'One thing is fucking sure,' he said. 'It won't be set in a kitchen' (qtd by Kilroy, 1992: 139).

That story is often told to exemplify Murphy's rejection of the Abbey's style of kitchen comedies; it's a way of showing how he would later help to reinvigorate Irish drama after Blythe's departure in 1967. But what is less frequently noted is that Murphy and O'Donoghue considered it possible to reject the Abbey's ethos because they felt emboldened to write and stage a play themselves. They submitted *On the Outside* 'to the manuscript competitions at various amateur drama festivals, winning for its authors the fifteen guinea prize at the All-Ireland Festival in Athlone,' writes Fintan O'Toole (1994: 47). Murphy's career as a professional dramatist began soon afterwards.

An intensification of activity at local level was matched by a growing awareness of the importance of the international. Bord Fáilte, the Irish tourism development agency, was established in 1955, aiming to target the US market. That coincided with an incipient shifting of attitudes towards Ireland's literary heritage, as a result of which state agencies proved more willing to support artistic initiatives. The first major event to benefit from that shift had been the Wexford Festival Opera, established in 1951 with the aim of staging rarely produced works; it quickly became popular with opera-lovers internationally, and remains an important event. Two years later, an annual festival called An Tóstal was initiated, its objective being to attract tourists to Ireland during the late spring. An Tóstal hosted a variety of events: its first year featured an enormous pageant about Saint Patrick, which was directed by Hilton Edwards and written by Micheál Mac Liammóir (see Dean, 2014). An Tóstal continued annually until 1958, when it was quietly abandoned in most areas (though it has continued in Drumshanbo, Co. Leitrim into the present). Yet it had a lasting influence, inspiring events as diverse as the Rose of Tralee Festival in Kerry and the Cork Film Festival.

Most significantly for the present discussion, it also gave rise to the Dublin Theatre Festival (DTF), an event created in 1957 by Brendan Smith, a producer who ran an acting academy and managed the Olympia Theatre in Dublin. The Irish Arts Council declined to fund the DTF at first; it was instead supported by Bord Fáilte. But that did not mean that its aim was to attract international audiences to watch Irish plays: Smith was also determined to host performances by high-profile international companies. Jean Vilar's Théâtre National Populaire was invited in the first year, presenting Molière's *La Malade Imaginaire* and Balzac's *Le Faiseur*. That experience was an unhappy one for the Théâtre National Populaire: Christopher Fitz-Simon recalls Vilar complaining that 'never, on their worst provincial tours, had [he] come across such a scruffy and ill-equipped *salle-de-théâtre*' as the Olympia (2008: 210). Nevertheless, the productions had a strong impact on those who saw them – not just because they displayed a level of professional and technical accomplishment that was beyond the means of most Dublin stages, but also because Smith's decision to invite the founder of the Avignon Festival was seen as an admirable expression of ambition.

By comparison, the offerings from the established Irish theatres seemed rather dull. The Gate presented the play that had made its name almost thirty years earlier, Denis Johnston's *The Old Lady Says No!* (1929). At the Abbey Ria Mooney presented *The Playboy of the Western World* (1907) and *Juno and the Paycock* (1924), while Tomás Mac Anna directed Douglas Hyde's *An Pósadh* (1902). Yet there was evidence of bravery from smaller Irish companies. Jim Fitzgerald staged seven of Yeats' plays, persuading audiences that those verse dramas could have a life beyond the Abbey. Also significant was the presentation of an adaptation of Brian Merriman's eighteenth-century poem *Cúirt an Mheán Oíche* in a late-night revue at the Pocket Theatre by the Irish-language company An Compántas. Frank O'Connor's English translation of the poem as *The Midnight Court* had been banned by the Irish censor only twelve years earlier (one of the absurdities of Irish censorship was that the Irish original remained available). Yet, according to Brian Ó Conchubhair, the company included English as well as Irish excerpts in their performance (Merriman, 2011: 111). An Compántas was apparently testing the strength of Irish censorship laws but, perhaps because they advertised themselves using the poem's Irish title, they managed to avoid trouble.

I'll discuss later how some of these developments drew a hostile and ultimately censorious reaction from the Catholic hierarchy. But as the case of *The Midnight Court* demonstrates, there is a need for a nuanced understanding of how theatre was regulated in Ireland at this time. Although the state banned magazines, films and novels, Ireland in the 1950s was unusual internationally in not having a formal mechanism for the censorship of theatre – unlike the situation in the UK, where the Lord Chamberlain's Office continued to require that scripts be submitted for approval in advance of production. This led to the curious situation whereby lines that had been cut from scripts in England were often performed in Ireland. For example, when Peter Hall sought permission to stage Beckett's *Endgame* in England in 1957, he received a letter from the Lord Chamberlain objecting strenuously to Hamm's description of God as 'that bastard!' who 'doesn't exist!' 'The Lord Chamberlain will not countenance doubt being cast on the legitimacy of the Almighty,' Hall was told, while a bemused Beckett found himself agreeing to replace the word 'bastard' with 'swine' instead (Hall, 2002). No such change would have been necessary in Ireland.

Yet, as Fintan O'Toole points out, the need for state censorship was mitigated by the willingness of many theatre people to engage in self-censorship, which, unlike legislative control, was 'all the sharper . . . and more damaging' for being self-imposed (2008: 192). So the Irish theatre made sure that it wouldn't need to be subject to state censorship by rarely producing work that might have attracted the attention of the relevant authorities. What we'll see in the pages ahead is a gradual erosion by Irish dramatists of the risk of censorship and the fact of self-censorship.

But in order to illustrate the complexity of the movements that were emerging in Ireland at this time, I want to draw now on three case studies, each significant in its own right but collectively showing how the period after the Abbey fire witnessed a shifting of boundaries – between languages, between the amateur and the professional, between the theatrical fourth wall and the auditorium, and between Ireland and the rest of the world.

## Siobhán McKenna and Shaw: from *San Siobhán* to *Saint Joan*

An Taibhdhearc na Gaillimhe was established in 1928 as the national Irish-language theatre, and its first producer/director was Micheál Mac Liammóir, who (with Hilton Edwards) would co-found the Gate in the same year. Mac Liammóir was impressed by the enthusiasm of the Taibhdhearc's founders and supporters, but concluded that there weren't enough actors who could perform theatre in Irish to a professional standard. The Taibhdhearc has thus operated as an amateur theatre for most of its life, though the boundaries between amateur and professional have always been a little blurred. There would often be movement of personnel between the Taibhdhearc and the Abbey, for example, with the playwright and actor Walter Macken being one of the best examples of someone who made a successful career in both institutions (see Macken, 2009).

In 1949 the Taibhdhearc invited Siobhán McKenna to play the lead role in her own translation into Irish of Shaw's *Saint Joan* (1923). McKenna had first performed in the theatre nine years previously, at the age of seventeen, and had used that experience as a springboard to a career at the Abbey, which she joined in 1944. Her fluency in Irish was seen by Blythe as an asset, though he also thought she might be able to do some secretarial work between rehearsals. Of the thirty roles she would play at the Abbey between 1944 and 1948, thirteen were in Irish – and whereas she tended to play small roles in English-language productions (as Sara Tansey in Synge's *Playboy* and the Woman from Rathmines in O'Casey's *The Plough*), her Irish-language roles were usually more demanding, giving her valuable experience at a relatively young age. She was also given the opportunity to adapt and translate J.M. Barrie's *Mary Rose* for a production at the Peacock in 1948, nurturing her ability to stage her own work in Irish. This is an impressive record for someone who was still very young – but even so, the Taibhdhearc was showing huge faith in McKenna by asking her not only to play such an important role but also to translate such a complex play.

Shaw was then into the final months of his life (he died in November 1950), but he had remained productive, completing *Shakes Versus Shaw* and *Why She Would Not* in 1949 and 1950 respectively. When asked for permission to produce an Irish-language version of his play, he responded with a mixture of generosity and scepticism: 'I don't see any sense in the Irish-language revival. But if anybody goes to the trouble of translating my plays into that language, I won't bother to charge a fee' (quoted by Ó hAodha, 1994: 39). McKenna's version opened in Galway in December 1950, a month after Shaw's death, where it was renamed *San Siobhán* – instantly establishing in the minds of its audience a connection between the actor and her character. In January 1951, that version was restaged for a single night at Dublin's Gaiety Theatre, where it met with an exceptionally enthusiastic response.

The importance of *San Siobhán* for the Taibhdhearc was enormous. There was an obvious declaration of artistic intent in their successful staging of *Saint Joan*, a play that is as complex thematically as it is demanding theatrically, with roles for twenty-four characters across six scenes (TnaG, T1_D_133_001). There was pride not only in McKenna's performance but also in her status as a translator: here was the Taibhdhearc showing that 'one of its own' could create work of ambition and sophistication. It was a sign of the importance of the production that its opening night in Galway was attended by the president of Ireland, Seán T. Ó Ceallaigh – though in an example of an emerging disjunction between Church and state (especially insofar as theatre was concerned), the bishop of Galway refused to attend at the same time. 'Much as his Lordship would like to honour the President of

**Figure 1** Gate Theatre, *Saint Joan* show programme at the Gaiety Theatre, 1959

Ireland, he does not think that attendance at a Shaw play would be a suitable means or occasion for one in his position,' explained his secretary in a letter to the theatre's manager (TnaG, T1/B/1372).

McKenna's script is believed to have been lost, though there are fragments of a translation of Shaw's play in the Taibhdhearc archive which may (or may not) be hers. But we know enough to be able to define the strengths of her version. McKenna had Joan speak in Connemara Irish, whereas her English characters' words were presented in the more 'official' Munster Irish – a distinction that would not have been lost upon the audiences at the Taibhdhearc, but which would be carried forward in McKenna's future performances in the role when she ensured that Joan spoke in an accent different from anyone else's. The production was also significant for McKenna's career as an actor. Her performance at the Gaiety was seen by Mac Liammóir, and he invited her to perform the play in English at the Gate. He had understood that the power of McKenna's translation was its reimagining of *Saint Joan* through an Irish sensibility – and as director of the Gate version, Hilton Edwards agreed that she should perform her role in a West of Ireland accent, 'retaining the Connemara cadenza as a leitmotif,' as Micheál Ó hAodha puts it (1994: 51).

What is significant about this and subsequent versions is that McKenna was able to perform Shaw's words in an Irish accent – without having to change the script in order to do so. This allowed audiences to discover features of the play that could be mapped onto Irish contexts. Shaw had completed *Saint Joan* in Cork and Kerry, and its composition and premiere coincided with the period during which Ireland was moving towards independence – so it is possible to read it as an exploration of Anglo–Irish relationships. Yet Shaw's 1924 preface places it in a broad international context, exploring issues of religion and gender that were certainly pertinent to Ireland but were also relevant elsewhere. McKenna's interpretation of the play worked in both directions, giving audiences a focal point that allowed them to appreciate the play's broader resonances. 'When I translated the play into Irish Joan spoke for me as if she were a Connemara girl,' wrote McKenna (Hickey and Smith, 1972: 55) – but she also recounted how those who had known Shaw saw her interpretation as an exact encapsulation of his intentions (see 55–7).

McKenna's Irishness was the defining characteristic of her subsequent portrayals of Joan. She played the role at the Arts Theatre in London in 1954 – where Kenneth Tynan would praise her 'brave Connemara twang' (quoted by Ó hAodha, 1994: 55) – and then in Paris and finally on Broadway, where her version would be seen as definitive. In part, such judgements arose due to a blurring of the distinctions between Joan and Siobhán. When the Gate's production was performed in Belfast, for example, McKenna expressed grave reservations about the proposal to play the British national anthem at the conclusion of the performance (something that, as we'll see, would later become a problem for the Lyric Theatre). Yet she won her audience over by delivering a speech in Irish after the anthem, following which she reminded them that she was a native of Belfast – to enormous cheers. That blend of plain-spokenness and assertiveness mirrors many of Joan's actions in the play. Similarly, in 1956, McKenna was featured on the cover of *Life* magazine – in full costume as Shaw's character.

She would return to the role of Joan at least twice thereafter. The first occasion was the Gate's production of Brecht's *Saint Joan of the Stockyards* in 1961, one of two Brecht productions that Hilton Edwards staged in Dublin after being inspired by visits of the Berliner Ensemble to London in 1956 (as will be discussed later). And, towards the end of her career, McKenna included Joan in her own production *Here Are Ladies*, which toured internationally and appeared at the Abbey in 1982. A compendium of speeches by Irish women in plays mostly written by men, McKenna's script includes Joan's trial scene, as well as her own version of Joyce's *Anna Livia Plurabelle* (ATDA, 0759_MPG_01). We thus find that, at both the beginning and the end of her career, McKenna was asserting her own creativity as an author by taking the words of canonical male writers and making them her own. There has been a tendency in the scholarship to dismiss adaptations as secondary to the composition of original plays, but, as San Siobhan shows, doing so not only obscures the extent to which adaptation is itself an act of adaptation but also leads us to neglect the fact that McKenna, in rewriting Joan, was also fashioning herself. We'll return to that point later.

But other conclusions must be drawn from McKenna's success. The first was that her *San Siobhán* had shown that the Irish language need not be an impediment to the success of an Irish play; indeed, her translation provided a means for audiences to form a new appreciation of Shaw's original, albeit that they mostly received it in the later English-language versions. We also see how McKenna's decision to highlight the Irish elements of Shaw's original allowed audiences to receive the work from new points of view. We'll see examples of all of these patterns recurring throughout this book, but McKenna's *San Siobhán* needs to be remembered as having taken a first step that many other Irish artists would follow.

## Brendan Behan: from *An Giall* to *The Hostage*

Writing in 1964, Mac Liammóir argued that Siobhán McKenna and Brendan Behan were 'the most remarkable individual stage figures of the fifties'. He conceded that their success internationally might ultimately tempt them away from Ireland – but he considered such an eventuality unlikely:

> Mr Behan and Miss McKenna ... are both too wise, knowing what they are, or too foolish, knowing what they could become [to sever all connection with Ireland] ... In Brendan with his warm, ferocious, slouching approach, in Siobhán with her Michael Angelo face, like some boyish Sybil that has fallen from the Sistine roof and been stricken into a bewildered grasp of a preposterous situation – I see, as I see in certain other things, some reason for a belief in Ireland's future
>
> (1964: 51–2)

Mac Liammóir's hopes in this pair would only partially be realized – but there certainly are parallels between Behan and McKenna, especially when we compare *The Hostage* with *San Siobhán*. Both used the Irish language as the foundation for a successful version in English – and both also used Irealnd as the starting point for international success, in London first and then in Paris and New York. Yet there would be crucial differences too, not the least of which was that *The Hostage* marked the high point of Behan's career, whereas *Saint Joan* was the first of many international triumphs for McKenna.

Behan's play first appeared as *An Giall* and premiered at the Damer Hall, a theatre established in 1955 to produce new work in Irish. In another example of how the Abbey fire inspired developments in the theatre of the nation, the opening of An Damer was partly caused by unhappiness about the Abbey's treatment of the Irish language. As Philip O'Leary recounts:

> The Abbey over the years produced a number of new one-act plays [in Irish] [but] many of those were put on after the main attraction in English and without any advance publicity, in the apparent hope of trapping people to stay for the Gaelic show. When the original Abbey ... relocated to the considerably larger Queen's Theatre ... it became even more financially unfeasible to produce work – and in particular full-length work in Irish.
>
> (2017: 12)

As the first director of An Damer, Riobard Mac Góráin was tasked with addressing this deficiency, and one of his earliest attempts to do so was to ask Behan if he might consider writing a play for them. This proved a smart move, similar to one made by the Taibhdhearc when they approached McKenna: the idea in both cases was to use the growing celebrity of the playwright to attract new audiences.

Behan's reputation had been growing steadily during the early 1950s. His radio plays *Moving Out* and *A Garden Party* were produced by Radio Éireann in 1952, and his journalism had become popular too. His first theatrical success was *The Quare Fellow*, premiered at the Pike in November 1954. Set in an Irish prison the night before an inmate's execution, it was well received in Dublin, and achieved international recognition when it was produced by Joan Littlewood at Stratford East in 1956.

Behan was also becoming well known for his public persona – something that Mac Liammóir was undoubtedly alluding to by referring to him as both 'warm' and 'ferocious'. A drunken appearance on British television in 1956 made Behan notorious, displaying for all to see the alcoholism that would kill him eight years later, at the age of only forty-one. Yet rather than seeing his behaviour as evidence of illness, the public instead encouraged it, viewing Behan as a stage Irish character in his own right, a person who constantly enacted the 'buffoonery and easy sentiment' (Gregory, 1972: 20) that Yeats, Gregory and Edward Martyn had railed against when they founded the Irish Literary Theatre in 1897. Behan thus became more famous for being Brendan Behan than for his literary output – a development that he sought half-heartedly to challenge towards the end of his life, but which would prove inescapable.

His reputation is therefore founded mostly on his autobiographical writing. His memoir *Borstal Boy* (1958) was filmed by Peter Sheridan in 2000, and a 1967 stage version by Frank McMahon found its way to Broadway in 1970 where it won a Tony Award for Tomás Mac Anna's direction. There was also a positive response to *Brendan at the Chelsea* when it premiered in 2008. Written by Behan's niece Janet, it explores his final days in New York, and has been staged in the UK, Ireland and the United States by the actor and director Adrian Dunbar. But interest in Behan's own plays has waned. There has been no major Irish production of *The Hostage* since 1996, while *The Quare Fellow* last appeared at the Abbey in 1984.

That decline is understandable but regrettable. As John Harrington points out, *The Quare Fellow* is a play that bears comparison with Beckett's *Godot*: 'both Dublin playwrights, at mid-century, found as their most resonant stage conception an absent character, much discussed, who never appears onstage' (2004: 175). But *The Hostage* also deserves admiration for the way in which – in both its Irish and English versions – it asks essential questions about how Irish history is experienced in the present. Behan also did much to pave the way for later productions of Irish plays in London, inspiring Kenneth Tynan's often-quoted remark that it is 'Ireland's sacred duty to send over every few years a playwright who will save the English theatre from inarticulate dumbness' (qtd by Grene, 1999: 252). Writers such as Tom Murphy would benefit from the existence of such expectations.

The reputation of *The Hostage* has also probably been negatively affected by uncertainty about its authorship. *An Giall* is in some ways a conventional tragedy, albeit that it also includes much of Behan's characteristically irreverent humour. It features nine speaking roles and takes place over three acts, and while Behan would later criticize the direction by Frank Dermody for being too close to the Abbey style of naturalism, it's only fair to observe that his script invites such an approach, setting the action in a recognizable version of the real world, giving the characters psychologically credible motivations and actions, and leaving the fourth wall largely in place. *The Hostage* opened four months later in Stratford East, where it was directed by Littlewood, with almost twice as many characters and a decided shift towards farce and musical hall. Far from being naturalistic, it willingly embraced its own absurdity: the audience was frequently addressed directly, there were several metatheatrical jokes, and the abiding mood was of chaos rather than realism.

In seeking to explain the differences between the two versions, many have been inclined to believe Littlewood's suggestion that the English-language script was completed with help from herself and Gerry Raffles. She amusingly describes how Raffles literally threatened Behan at gunpoint in order to get him to finish the play (2016: 521); she also told Irish radio in a 1974 interview that the production had deliberately been made different every night, not only because of the improvisational style that she encouraged in her actors but also because no one ever knew what Behan himself might do while the performance was underway (RTÉ, 1974). Behan expressed contradictory views about his play's composition: as Michael O'Sullivan writes, 'depending on his mood and to whom he was speaking, he alternated between cursing and rhapsodising about what Joan Littlewood had done to his play' (1999: 238). A sad possibility, of course, is that he mightn't have clearly remembered which parts of the play were his and which hers.

As John Brannigan reveals, Littlewood's account of the composition of *The Hostage* does not ring entirely true (2002: 104–5). She claimed to have given Behan the idea for writing a play about a soldier who had been taken hostage (basing the idea on a contemporaneous newspaper story), but we know that he was already writing *An Giall* by this time. And the additions made to the script – bringing new emphasis to themes of social class, homosexuality and race – were as much of interest to Behan as they were to Littlewood. Perhaps the simplest explanation is to see the play as – to use Robert Hogan's description – a 'rare and nearly perfect marriage of creator and interpreter' (1968: 203), albeit a marriage that both parties remembered differently after it had fallen apart. And maybe we should also think of the play as an early example of a form of writing that is now much more common, whereby a script is significantly developed in a rehearsal room by directors and actors – a collaborative style that would be relatively common by the time Irish theatre entered the new millennium.

In a lengthy introduction to an English translation of *An Giall*, Richard Wall argues that *The Hostage* is 'not a translation [but] a drastically modified version of the original play' (1987: 12). I'll suggest later that our understanding of Irish theatre would benefit from adopting a less rigid approach to the distinction between original works and adaptations, but I do agree that the plays are different in tone, content and form. Nevertheless there is a coherence between them that can be found in some of Behan's other works, arising from his treatment of the themes of history and performance.

Those themes are explored in relation to questions about why and how stories come to be both told and retold – or of how a political event comes to be reimagined first as history and then as myth. A tendency in Irish drama, especially in the first half of the twentieth century, had been to view history not as linear but as cyclical, as a series of heroic failures that would, at some unspecified time in the future, produce a positive outcome. That idea was most famously presented on stage in Yeats and Gregory's *Cathleen ni Houlihan* (1902), in which the history of (failed) Irish rebellions is, through a kind of poetic transvaluation of values, reimagined as a triumph. Speaking of those who fight on her behalf, the Old Woman in the play – a personification of Ireland itself – says that those rebels will:

> ... be remembered for ever.
> They shall be alive for ever.
> They shall be speaking for ever,
> The people shall hear them for ever.

> (Yeats, 2001: 92)

Yeats and Gregory thus reimagine political violence on a metaphorical plane, and in doing so transform it into something that is bloodless, noble, apolitical and amoral.

Many other writers would later become ambivalent about – if not hostile to – this approach. Five years after the premiere of *Cathleen*, John Millington Synge's *The Playboy of the Western World* would point out that there is a great gap between a 'gallous story and a dirty deed' (1982: 169). Synge wanted his audience to face the ugliness and futility of violence, and to resist the impulse to see violence in heroic terms. Seán O'Casey would make the same case in *Juno and the Paycock* in 1924, in which he has his eponymous heroine demand that young men try living for Ireland instead of sacrificing themselves to the cult of dying for it. And this tension between the imagined and the real persists into later Irish plays, finding its most personalized realization in Brian Friel's 1979 *Faith Healer*, in which we meet Frank Hardy, a character whose livelihood depends on his ability to persuade audiences to believe the impossible – that he can miraculously heal them – even as he seeks to obscure our understanding of the core realities of his own life: about whether he's married, about the birth and subsequent death of his child, about his own final days.

Behan's work thus needs to be seen in that tradition of Irish plays that explore how dirty deeds are transformed into 'gallous stories' (and vice versa), a theme that he presents in his characterization of Pat, a man who claims to have been wounded in the 1916 rebellion – and who uses that event as a moral standard against which to judge everyone else. 'Where were you in nineteen-sixteen when the real fighting was going on?' he asks Meg, his 'consort' (as Behan's stage directions put it) in *The Hostage*. When she replies that she hadn't been born yet he disgustedly complains that she's 'full of excuses' (Behan, 1978: 135). However, Meg easily sees through Pat's exaggerations. When he claims that he had been forced to capture weapons from the British Army, she reminds him of the truth: 'You told me yourself that you bought it off the Tommies in the pub. You said yourself you got a revolver, two hundred rounds of ammunition and a pair of jodhpurs off a colonel's batman for two pints of Bass and fifty woodbines' (136). We find a similar exchange in *An Giall* in which Cáit (which is the name given to Pat's partner in that play) likewise challenges his honesty: 'that's the story you always tell when you're drunk. But like a lot of the people in this land, that is the only time you speak the truth' (1981: 33, my translation).

The play therefore works through the difference between the romanticization of political violence and the brutal realities of actually killing someone. That story is explored through Behan's presentation of Leslie, a young English soldier who has been kidnapped by the IRA and who is being held hostage in an attempt to prevent the execution of a republican prisoner. He finds himself trapped in a pattern of repetition: if the republican is executed, Leslie will be killed in retaliation, which will lead to the execution of those who killed him, and so on. Leslie's demise is made inevitable not only by Behan's use of the tragic (or tragicomic) form but also by the way in which Irish politics produce endlessly recurring cycles of violence.

Indeed, the play itself can be seen as operating within a pattern of narrative repetition. In exploring how an English soldier can become humanized in the eyes of his captors – rendering all the more tragic his ultimate death – Behan was presenting a scenario that had been movingly explored by Frank O'Connor in his great 1931 short story 'Guests of the Nation'. O'Connor reportedly grumbled that Behan had stolen his idea, but it would be used again by Neil Jordan in his 1992 film *The Crying Game* – while Brian Friel would deploy elements of it in his characterization of Yolland in *Translations* in 1980. Indeed, the development of Behan's play itself enacts his theme: by moving from *An Giall* to *The Hostage*, he was exploring the idea of how history happens first as tragedy and then as farce. One of the significant features of Behan's play, then, is that it is *not* original, that it is one manifestation of a narrative that would need to be reimagined for successive generations from the 1920s to the new millennium.

This might be the reason that the play sets out to destabilize our sense of time and history. Its first spoken line in the English version is 'Thank God, that's over' (Behan, 1978: 130), while its last is 'I'll never forget you ... till the end of time' (236). That is, it starts with a conclusion and concludes with a promise that will last forever. The Irish-language version likewise concludes by looking to the future (Behan, 1981: 75). Behan's point seems to be that we are trapped in a cycle of eternal recurrence, where we must enact the same stories, and thus the same acts of political violence, forever. This might explain why *The Hostage* was seen in the context of the absurdist drama that had been emerging on the English stage in the late 1950s: one can detect in the play a sensibility that seems to suggest that life is a series of futile, meaningless repetitions.

Where Behan would differ from figures such as Beckett, however, is that his play offers the opportunity to break the cycle – and it does so by proposing that nationality and other forms of identity are not essential but arbitrary. In both *An Giall* and *The Hostage*, the stage directions sometimes refer to Leslie with his own name, but at other times he is referred to as 'Soldier' or in Irish as *An Saighduir*. It might be possible to dismiss those variations as an inconsistency caused by Behan's famously sloppy approach to stage directions – but the differences are mostly consistent in the English and Irish versions, suggesting the possibility that some decision-making informs the distinctions. By using the stage directions to draw attention to the times in which we should see Leslie not as an individual but in a public role, Behan shows that one impact of political violence is to transform individuals into emblems: it might be very difficult to execute a 'Leslie' but in war any combatant should be able kill a 'soldier'.

Other contrasts between publicly played roles and realities appear. The most prominent example is the play's most obviously Irish character, Monsewer, a pipe-playing, Gaelic-speaking, kilt-wearing Irishman who is in fact not Irish at all. Many other forms of performance run through the plays, especially in *The Hostage* where we find characters acting in disguise, appearing in drag or otherwise using costumes to present an identity that is different from their everyday persona. We also find this subversion of identity in the setting of the play, an old boarding house that has become a brothel. As Nicholas Grene explains, one of the most dominant tropes in Irish drama had been the use of the house to act as an emblem both of the nation and its potential transformation: 'A room within a house, a family within a room, stand in for nationality, for ordinary, familiar life; into the room there enters a stranger, and the incursion of that extrinsic, extraordinary figure alters, potentially transforms the scene' (1999: 52). If this house represents the nation of Ireland, Behan is making clear his views on what Ireland has become. Behan is disrupting many of the most cherished Irish tropes: the house that represents the nation is a brothel, the idealized female figure is in fact a real woman with sexual agency of her own, and the stranger in the house who can transform the country is, of all things, an English soldier.

Thus, one of the triumphs of the play, at least when it has been performed in Ireland, is that it has convinced successive audiences not only to identify with but also to (perhaps) fall in love with an English soldier (again, this is a trick that Friel would play in *Translations*). He does something similar with his English audiences, having Leslie break off from the action in *The Hostage* to criticize Behan himself: 'he doesn't mind coming over here and taking your money,' he tells the London audience (Behan, 1978: 204). There are many ways to read that joke: as the defensive gesture of a drunk who behaves self-deprecatingly because he knows that he probably deserves far harsher criticism, or as an example of the metatheatricality that Littlewood introduced. But what it also does is break the distinction between 'here' and 'there', between Ireland and England: the Ireland on stage, Leslie shows, is England – or more precisely it is England pretending to be Ireland. Any attempt by the audience to see Ireland as 'other', as different, is undercut by this moment.

What Behan is showing, therefore, is how nation and nationality are performative. Irishness can be presented in terms of the clothes we wear, the languages we speak, the stories we tell – and the same is true of Englishness. But the play is an invitation to tell other stories, to use different emblems. This explains one of the most touching moments in the final act, when a miraculous medal (an emblem of Catholicism) is found on Leslie's body after his death (this happens in both versions of the play, with an officer finding it in *An Giall* and Rio Rita doing so in *The Hostage*). This causes some confusion to the characters: was Leslie Catholic? 'I gave it to him. Leave it with him,' replies Teresa (Behan, 1978: 236/1981: 75). By answering this way, Teresa 'translates' the medal from a signifier of religion into something more personal about both herself and Leslie. She thus finds a way to tell the story differently, offering hope for the future – but also placing the onus on her audience to think about how they themselves might retell stories about their own nations.

Given Behan's own life, it's poignant that he chose to write a play in which he appears to urge his audience to search for the real people who lie behind public performances. And it's sad that he suggested that individuals could escape the roles that their societies impose upon them – something that he never quite managed himself. These features of his play(s) place in moving context Mac Liammóir's suggestion that Behan was one of the two key figures of the 1950s: after *The Hostage*, he wrote little of lasting value and died too young, leaving much of his promise unrealized. Nevertheless, we'll find that *An Giall* and *The Hostage* have important legacies, not only for how we think about language, but also for our understanding of the third great Irish figure to emerge in the 1950s, Samuel Beckett.

## Beckett: from *En attendant Godot* to *Waiting for Godot* to *Ag Fanacht le Godot*

Following the publication of scholarly works by Harrington (1991), Roche (1994), Kennedy (2010), Murray (2006), McTighe and Tucker (2016) and Morin (2009), among others, the relationship between Beckett and Ireland is well understood – in terms of Beckett's relationships with other Irish writers and artists, the presence of the Irish landscape in his works, and his use of language (among other topics).

That period has also seen the emergence of a tendency to emphasize Beckett's Irishness in performances internationally, a process given impetus by the curation in 1991 of the first 'Beckett Festival' by Michael Colgan's Gate Theatre. While Beckett had always worked with Irish actors (such as Patrick Magee and Jack MacGowran), Colgan's festival saw several key roles being played by Irish actors, who (as had happened with Siobhán McKenna) found that their use of Irish accents made the plays seem more accessible to international audiences – demonstrating the accuracy of Alan Simpson's suggestion that Beckett's 'dialogue flows best in Dublinese which, in heightened form, is the language of O'Casey and of Brendan Behan' (1962: 68). This allowed Irish correspondences to come into focus – not only in terms of language but also characterization. *Godot's* Didi and Gogo are, for example, readily identifiable in the context of the comic double act of O'Casey's Joxer and Captain Boyle in *Juno and the Paycock*, but also bear comparison to the Fool and the Blind Man in Yeats' *On Baile's Strand* (1904) and the Douls in Synge's *Well of the Saints* (1905). Hearing those roles played with Irish voices made such links all the more obvious.

The significance of the 1991 Beckett Festival was to bring to realization something about Ireland that had been only partially obvious before that time. Hence, that event saw the appearance of David Kelly as Krapp in *Krapp's Last Tape*, Fionnula Flanagan as Winnie in *Happy Days*, Adele King (better known for her work in pantomimes as Twink) as Mouth in *Not I*, Stephen Rea in *A Piece of Monologue*, and many other prominent Irish actors. By far the most important inclusion in the Festival was *Waiting for Godot* in a Walter Asmus production that had first appeared at the Gate in 1988, and which featured Barry McGovern and Johnny Murphy as Didi and Gogo respectively (GTDA, 1075_MPG_0001). That duo would play those roles in productions at the Gate until 2006, where their delivery of lines in Irish accents (working-class Dublin for Estragon, middle-class for Vladimir) would almost indelibly place Beckett's play in the 'Dublinese' tradition that Simpson describes.

Yet the production would also assert a form of authenticity in its links back to Beckett himself, with Asmus' direction being drawn from Beckett's 1975 production for the Schiller Theater (which Asmus had assisted). That blend of the local and the international would prove an important characteristic of the Gate's subsequent Beckett festivals and international tours. Famous international actors such as John Hurt and Ralph Fiennes would appear (in *Krapp's Last Tape* in 2001 and *First Love* in 2007 respectively); the Gate would also host high-profile international directors such as Karel Reisz (*Happy Days* in 1999) and the Oscar-nominated director Atom Egoyan, whose stage version of *Eh Joe* starred Michael Gambon and premiered in 2006. But in every case, Colgan would keenly emphasize – speaking to journalists in London, Edinburgh, New York and Sydney – that the Gate was rooting Beckett in his Dublin contexts.

Colgan thus deserves credit for having ensured that Beckett's Irishness is now understood by audiences and theatre-makers internationally – something that was not fully the case when Beckett died in 1989. Somewhat ironically, however, that awareness has had the unintended impact of obscuring the fact that there was always a distinctive tradition of Beckettian performance within Ireland itself, one that saw Beckett not as separate from – or even parallel to – the Irish tradition, but as an inherent part of that tradition, in much the same way as Behan and McKenna were.

Of course, there are differences too. Like McKenna and Behan, Beckett would use the composition of a play in one language as a means to international success in a later English-language version – and he too would build his reputation across an international network that included Dublin, London, Paris and New York. But there would never be any controversy in Ireland about whether his journey from *En attendant Godot* (1953) to *Waiting for Godot* in 1955 represented a betrayal of one language by the other. Nor would there be much concern about the possibility that *Waiting for Godot* was not the 'original' play (as had happened with Behan's *An Giall*). And, of course, *Godot* would go on to have so great an impact on international theatre that it has affected our understanding not only of everything that came after it but also of much that came before.

The first Irish production of *Godot* appeared at the Pike shortly after its English-language premiere in London. Given that it was a very small theatre – with fewer than seventy seats – and given that it would last for less than a decade (as I explore in the next chapter), the Pike has had a disproportionately strong impact on the evolution of *Godot*'s reputation both within Ireland and internationally. The origins of its production have frequently been recounted, including by Alan Simpson himself. He and Beckett had a mutual friend in Con Leventhal, a professor at Trinity College in Dublin who had told Simpson of the publication of *En attendant* in 1952. Simpson thought that an English translation could help to establish the Pike's reputation, and had written to Beckett to seek permission for it to be staged in Dublin.

Beckett was sceptical if not defensive, imagining that *Godot* could not appear in Ireland without fear of censorship, referring to 'certain crudities of language ... [which] remain in the English version', adding that 'I would not consent to their being changed or removed' (2009: 143). Simpson was able to provide reassurances that the Pike's status as a private club removed the possibility of government or clerical interference, though Beckett's intolerance of Irish censorship would persist (with good reason).

As has often been stated, Beckett's translation of *En attendant* to *Waiting* was not so much into English as into Hiberno-English. While he retains many allusions to French places, he also introduces Irish shops, such as Kapp and Petersen, a seller of pipes that used to be situated across the street from Beckett's alma mater Trinity College (2006: 35); Irish grammatical and syntactical constructions such as 'get up till I embrace you' appear (11); and there are also Irish pronunciations, as for example when the word 'tied' is (as often happens in a Dublin accent) rendered in two syllables rather than one (22). He also has Estragon contrast his own pronunciation of the world 'calm' with how it is spoken in England (as 'cawm') (17). To be sure, the geographical references transcend Ireland: Lucky's speech in *En attendant* includes many French place names. In the English version Beckett includes reference to Fulham and Clapham, but he also introduces a reference to a 'skull in Connemara' (43) – a phrase so evocative that it was stolen by Martin McDonagh for his 1997 play of the same name. These inclusions explain why the Gate's *Godot* was perceived by international audiences as fresh and authentic when it toured between 1991 and 2006: the play is naturally accommodating of the Irish accent, and can be listened to in the context of the stage tradition of Irish drama.

Those changes also explain why Simpson had seen the play as unambiguously Irish from the start, causing him to direct Vladimir, Estragon and Lucky in Dublin accents and Pozzo as Anglo-Irish. Indeed, he sought to emphasize these qualities by making minor changes to the play – something he did successfully with Behan's *The Quare Fellow* when the Pike premiered it in 1954. As Christopher Murray points out, this drew a negative reaction from Beckett, who 'regarded such a procedure as tampering with the integrity of his play' – even though today such recommendations 'would more likely be seen as collaboration between a novice playwright and an astute, instinctive director' (2016: xvi). In this case, as in the controversy over Behan's *The Hostage*, we see the beginnings of the shift in the relationship between director and playwright that would intensify from the 1960s onwards, causing Beckett, among other playwrights, to adopt an even fiercer hostility to any kind of directorial intervention.

Ironically, given Beckett's fears about Irish censorship, he introduced more Irishisms to the English-language version – but in response to demands made in Britain. There, the Lord Chamberlain's objections resulted in the changing of the word 'ballocksed' into the Hiberno-English 'banjaxed' – even though, as Gerry Dukes points out, the latter word means exactly the same thing as the former (2004: 527). Dukes also demonstrates how words such as 'talking' were changed to the more Irish 'blathering': 'this is strong evidence that Beckett took to heart the clear distinction Synge made' between these words, he notes (528) – a nice reminder that the only Irish dramatist that Beckett ever acknowledged as an influence was Synge.

And, again somewhat ironically, rather than attracting censorship, the Pike's *Godot* made a point to prospective Dublin audiences that it was playing the version of the script that had *not* been cut by the Lord Chamberlain. They left in place Gogo's reference to how the pair's plan to hang themselves would 'give us an erection' – a line that was cut in London. We shouldn't overstate the importance of the fact that the Pike went unchallenged, not only for including such lines but also for publicly promoting their production on the strength of having done what the Lord Chamberlain had prohibited on the other side of the Irish Sea. Nevertheless, it is important to reflect upon the success of Simpson's *Godot*, which enjoyed a long run at the Pike before transferring to the Gate, and from there went on a tour of provincial Ireland. That tour included a stop in Navan, where the play was advertised, Simpson tells us, 'con permiso ordinarii' (1962: 89). That is, members of the clergy were granted permission by their diocese to see the play, and Simpson reports that the Meath audience included many men from the nearby seminary in Maynooth. We find in that anecdote another example of the complexity of the relationship between the Catholic Church and Irish theatre during this period.

Another example of Irish enthusiasm for *Godot* can be found in a proposal made at this time by the actor Cyril Cusack to present the play in a bilingual version – his aim being to have Vladimir and Estragon deliver their dialogue in Irish while Pozzo and Lucky spoke English. The Galway professor Liam Ó Briain (who had been involved in McKenna's *San Siobhán*) prepared a translation of Didi and Gogo's lines into Irish, using the French script rather than the English one. Cusack's production never made it to the stage, but in 1971 the Taibhdhearc returned to Ó Briain's version (which was completed by Sean O Carra) and staged it entirely in Irish as *Ag Fanacht Le Godot*, in a production directed by Alan Simpson – one that transferred to the Abbey Theatre the following year, where it was very well received (see ATDA, 001175-AH_ADM_000001071-1.pdf).

While in Britain and the United States early responses to Beckett's play were polarized, his work was almost always greeted enthusiastically in Ireland from the start – and not just by the specialized audiences of the Pike in Dublin, but by people throughout Ireland, some of whom would have had relatively little experience of professional theatre. The point has sometimes been made that those rural theatregoers would not have seen much avant-garde European theatre before encountering Beckett's play, but it needs to be understood that such audiences would not have seen *Godot* as avant-garde anyway. Its language and characterization were not new to them and, as I discussed above in relation to *The Hostage*, a great deal of Irish drama had been founded upon the idea of repetition rather than linear progress, making a play in which 'nothing happens – twice' (as Vivien Mercier famously quipped) somewhat less challenging.

Beckett would ban the production of his plays in Ireland in 1958 – but once that edict was lifted, his work was staged frequently there. For example, he would be invited to lay the foundation stone for the new Lyric Theatre in Belfast in 1967 – and while he had to send regrets, he described himself as 'deeply honoured' by the invitation (LTA, T4/906). That theatre would go on to stage many of his works, often in Irish contexts – as for example when *Not I* (1972) was paired with *Dark Rosaleen* by Vincent Mahon in 1980. The Lyric made explicit the way in which Beckett's play is an investigation of the representation of women, by presenting it alongside a drama that explores how gender, sectarianism and Irish political violence have been affected by the personification of Ireland as a woman (LTA, T4/256).

The Abbey first presented Beckett when *Play* was staged there in 1967, and he became a frequent presence on its stage until the Gate adopted him as their unofficial house playwright in the 1990s. Indeed, the Abbey has the distinction of having staged the world premiere of the English version of *Come and Go* in 1968. The show programme for that premiere gives a sense of the importance of Beckett to the Abbey: 'PLAY, his first work at the Abbey, attracted keen, and significantly, **very young** audiences [emphasis in original]. COME AND GO, too, is a whole history skeletally reduced. PLAY took 40 minutes: COME AND GO tells the story of three girls who once sat on the same log, at the same school, dreaming of love and marriage, in far far less time!' (ATDA, 2478_MPG_01: 3).

As anyone familiar with *Come and Go* will know, that description of the play is both completely accurate and completely misleading. But it's notable that Beckett is presented as potentially rejuvenating the Abbey, bringing in

**Figure 2** Lyric Theatre, *Waiting for Godot*, 1975 (LTA, T4/212).

younger audiences – while those who might struggle with his work are reassured that they needn't be too impatient (even in its most leisurely performances, *Come and Go* will rarely last longer than ten minutes).

Thereafter Beckett was a regular fixture at the Abbey, appearing there in thirty productions between 1967 and 1990. No other living Irish writer was produced so frequently at the Abbey during that period (the only comparable figures are for Tom Murphy and Brian Friel, whose plays were produced nineteen and sixteen times respectively during the same years). And he was seen unreservedly as an Irish dramatist when his work was performed there. For example, in 1970 his *Krapp's Last Tape* was presented in a triple bill that featured Lady Gregory's *Rising of the Moon* and Yeats' *Purgatory* – two plays that in different ways can retroactively be seen as 'Beckettian' in their characterization and staging style. And as we have seen above, *Ag Fanacht Le Godot* appeared there in 1972.

Contrastingly, a 1969 *Godot* demonstrated the willingness to blend the national with the international that the Gate would later excel at: the Abbey cast the rising Irish star Donal McCann as Estragon alongside Peter O'Toole as Vladimir, only seven years after O'Toole had come to worldwide attention for his performance in Lean's *Lawrence of Arabia*. And in 1977 they brought the Schiller Theater to their mainstage, where they performed Beckett's own production of *Godot* in German; Rick Cluchey's *Krapp* (also directed by Beckett) would follow in 1980. But Irish productions would also be staged. Ben Barnes (who would go on to be the artistic director of the Abbey from 2000 to 2005) presented *Not I* in 1981. And Barry McGovern – who is now strongly associated with the Gate's versions of Beckett – played Clov in a 1985 production of *Endgame* in the Peacock.

What we find in this brief history is that it is possible to see *Godot* not only within an international tradition but also within an Irish one – one that is both similar to and different from the tradition occupied by such people as McKenna and Behan. It's also true that we're beginning to understand better the unique characteristics of Beckett in Ireland. But we do need to create space to tell more of the story of productions of Samuel Beckett's plays in Ireland, seeing that tradition as an example of a distinctively Irish performance practice that was in dialogue with an international tradition. As we'll see in Chapter 3, that relationship between the Irish and the international would dominate much of the drama that appeared from 1960 onwards.

We'll return to the 1950s at various times in this book – and we'll also hear again about McKenna and Beckett. But my aim has been to demonstrate the importance of the 1950s – to argue that, even if, as Fintan O'Toole argues, the 'second renaissance' in Irish drama began in the 1960s, it could not have happened without the developments that arose during the preceding decade (2000: loc. 1797). I will be taking up many of these strands in the chapters that follow. Artists such as McKenna, Behan and Beckett would succeed by placing Irishness in dialogue with international ideas and international audiences, even if those combinations were sometimes more volatile than harmonious. In Chapter 3 I explore how that international focus would continue to develop from the 1960s onwards. Chapter 4 considers how Irish theatre artists, especially women, would move to interrogate the canon, taking plays by prominent male Irish authors (as McKenna had done with Shaw) and making them their own. Yet I also aim to show that adaptation should not be dismissed as a secondary form of writing, but that – as *San Siobhán*, *An Giall* and *En attendant Godot* all demonstrate in differing ways – an important feature of the composition of Irish drama has been the way in which key plays have proceeded through different versions, including versions in different languages.

Lingering in the background of this chapter, however, has been the subject of Catholicism, and particularly the way in which it was related to censorship. We have seen how dramatists in Ireland could write relatively freely in Irish about topics that were impermissible in English – but also how lines that were banned by the Lord Chamberlain in London could be openly performed in Ireland. Yet there is no denying the impact of censorious Catholicism on Irish theatre during this period: what unifies McKenna, Behan and Beckett, after all, is that they succeeded most fully when they left their native country. The next chapter therefore shows how other dramatists had to navigate this relationship, discussing how the Irish theatre would, from the 1950s onwards, set out to liberate itself from the influence of Catholicism. As we'll discover, that was not a straightforward task.

# CHAPTER 2
## SECULARIZATION AND THE 'POST-CATHOLIC' IN IRISH THEATRE

In May 2009, a publication that came to be known as the Ryan Report appeared. It was the work of a Commission to Enquire into Child Abuse, a statutory investigation begun ten years previously to examine the treatment of children in reformatories and industrial schools, most of which had been run by the Catholic Church. Their findings were, in the worst sense of the word, incredible: more than 30,000 children had experienced systematic abuse, including sexual, physical and psychological violence, since the 1930s. The Commission found that the Catholic hierarchy had shielded clergy who had been accused of those abuses from prosecution – and also that inspectors acting on behalf of the Irish Department of Education had failed to intervene when concerns had been raised.

Around the time the report was published, the director Annie Ryan and her husband, the playwright Michael West, were working on a new work for their company Corn Exchange. They had wanted to address the economic collapse of Ireland during 2008, caused when a banking crisis had brought to a sudden halt the 'Celtic Tiger' period of economic expansion that had begun in the mid-1990s – and so they had been working on a play about a man who experiences a stroke, exploring ideas about how the fate of that everyman figure could stand for that of the nation. But the publication of the Ryan Report required them to shift their approach. As Ryan recounts, 'As the man's story began to unfold in the summer [of 2009] the Ryan Report was released . . . Ireland was overwhelmed with grief and remorse. It broke. It fell to its knees. Amidst job losses, the unknown future, the change in status, in life-style, the report was a shocking reminder of everyone's roots' (West, 2010: ix).

Corn Exchange thus created a play that 'isn't overtly about the collapse of the Celtic Tiger or the Catholic Church', Ryan states (ibid.), but which explores both. The resulting work was called *Freefall*, a nuanced and moving play that takes as its starting point the 'grief and remorse' that Ryan mentions. Hence, rather than lashing out at the Catholic Church – a 'them' upon which the audience might vent its anger – it addresses an 'us' in the form of the society that allowed the abuses recounted in the Ryan Report to happen. But it also asks how, as a collective, 'we' can move on. And it does so by asserting the dignity and simplicity of the life of an ordinary person, his love for his family, his attempts to do the right thing when possible. *Freefall* premiered at that year's Dublin Theatre Festival, and was restaged at the Abbey the following year, where it was praised for its compassionate but realistic presentation of an Ireland that was experiencing a severe crisis.

As this chapter will show, *Freefall* is just one example of how, since the early 1950s, Irish artists have responded to revelations such as those contained in the Ryan Report. We'll see how dramatists, directors, actors and producers spoke out against those abuses, but also how, like Corn Exchange, they offered their audiences new ways of thinking about the future. And they did so long before other parts of Irish society were willing to acknowledge the existence of such problems. While the scale of the revelations contained in the Ryan Report was shocking, the Irish public had been aware for some time of allegations of sexual and other forms of abuse within the Catholic Church. Revelations against individual priests had begun to appear from the late 1980s, but a turning point was the discovery in 1993 of a mass grave on the site of a Magdalene laundry in Dublin. The laundries had operated since the late eighteenth century and were essentially prisons for women who had been accused of some form of sexual 'misconduct' – often the 'crime' of becoming pregnant outside marriage, but sometimes simply for being perceived as flirtatious or beautiful. Many of those women became lifelong inmates, often sent there by their own families. They were forced to work without pay and subjected to varying degrees of mistreatment, both psychological and physical. And because many of the records about those women were destroyed by the nuns who ran the laundries, we have no way of retrieving all of the histories of all of the people who were incarcerated in them. But one estimate is that at least 11,000 women were held in the laundries during the twentieth century, with the last one closing only in 1996. The relationship between the state and the laundries became the subject of a separate government enquiry chaired by Martin McAleese, which reported in 2013. But there remains much that is unknown and unknowable.

Running parallel to these revelations has been a process of liberalization and secularization in Irish society – a development that was starting to manifest itself in the 1950s but which accelerated once Ireland joined the EEC in 1973, being only briefly inhibited by the visit of Pope John Paul II to the country in 1979. I describe these developments as 'parallel' to the growing awareness of abuse within the Church because they were caused by a variety of additional factors such as the influence of American and British television, the impact of European legislation on the erosion of discriminatory Irish laws, and the growth of the Irish middle class. That said, the revelations about abuse from the mid-1990s onwards almost completely destroyed the moral authority of the Catholic Church in Ireland, intensifying a process that may not have happened so completely or so quickly otherwise.

I'm using the word 'secularization' to describe a development that remains incomplete, and in the sense used by Charles Taylor, who sees the secular not as representing the absence of belief but rather as the development of a system of morality and ethics that provides the basis for organizing a society without being dependent upon the existence of a god. But it still allows for the possibility of religious belief within the society: 'the emptying of religion from autonomous social spheres is, of course, compatible with the vast majority of people still believing in God,' he writes, while noting that religion comes to be seen as one option among many in such societies (Taylor, 2007: 2). In other words, some people in Ireland still practise religions but the state is governed according to standards that are in most (but not all) cases separate from religious considerations and which are generally consistent with laws in other Western democracies.

What all of this means is that the status of Catholicism in Ireland is much more complex than can adequately be captured in a short discussion such as this one. But one brief comparison might help to make some of that complexity evident. In the 2016 census of the Republic of Ireland, 79 per cent of people described themselves as Catholic, a figure higher than in most other European countries. Yet in 2015, Ireland held a referendum on the introduction of same-sex marriage, and it was passed by a majority of almost two to one, making the country the first in the world to vote in favour of marriage equality. This demonstrates how many Irish people who identify as Catholic are also willing to make moral and political choices that directly contradict Catholic teaching. That doesn't mean that there has been a full separation of Church and state: the education and health sectors continue to be disproportionately influenced by Catholic teaching. But the days of Irish politicians consulting with and even deferring to the Catholic hierarchy are long gone.

It is also evident that since the 1950s the multiple meanings of 'Catholicism' in Ireland, both as a cultural force and a religious doctrine, have shifted, often in ways that are very subtle. Catholicism was a form of power, used as a way of controlling people in the country, particularly during the middle decades of the twentieth century. The most vulnerable were at risk of being institutionalized in places like the Magdalene laundries, but even the more powerful citizens – from politicians to teachers to medical professionals (and not excluding theatre-makers) – engaged in forms of self-censorship and other forms of self-policing. Yet there is also evidence that for many Irish people Catholicism was (and remains) a personal belief system that was practised sincerely and (with no pun intended) in good faith. It's also possible to identify examples of Catholic clergy who, both publicly and privately, were supportive of Irish theatre, as both audience members and practitioners, especially in amateur productions – just as there were others, especially at more senior levels, who sought to control or censor it. So when we speak of 'Catholicism' we can refer to an institution, a means of controlling people, a personal faith and a facet of the Irish cultural imagination.

Something similar is true in Northern Ireland, where the Troubles involved a clash between Catholics and Protestants but not between Catholicism and Protestantism. In other words, religion operated not so much as a matter of doctrine or faith than as a way of encompassing a range of ethnic, territorial and political fidelities. Hence, in dramas set in Northern Ireland, many characters firmly identify as Catholic or Protestant in the context of the Troubles, but for reasons that are not necessarily attributable to religious belief – and which might have little to do with institutional religion. So while secularism has been seen in the Republic as largely relating to Catholicism, the situation in Northern Ireland is more complex, since it cuts across a range of other tensions and loyalties.

In thinking about the relationship between Irish theatre, Catholicism and secularism, then, it's necessary to explore that topic from two interrelated but distinctive points of view. The first is the proposition that Irish theatre has been instrumental in moving the Republic into what is sometimes called (perhaps prematurely) a 'post-Catholic' state. As we'll see, Irish dramatists, actors and theatre-makers have challenged Catholicism not so much as a religion but as an ideology, and not so much as a personal faith but as an institution that wielded power, often unjustly, within Irish society. And the second is that Irish theatre has taken a leading role in the development of secularism within Irish society, both north and south, moving not just beyond Catholicism but also Protestantism and other forms of faith. The Irish theatre has not only sought to overcome the dominance of religion as a force for controlling society, but has also set out to imagine alternative ways of being in the world, alternative ways of wielding power, and better ways of thinking ethically. My claim here is that, just as the drama of the Irish literary revival can be seen as having involved a decolonization from Britain, so should we see that Irish theatre from 1950 onwards achieved a similar kind of withdrawal and renegotiation. That withdrawal was both cultural and political: it involved a transformation not only in personal beliefs but also in the exercise of power.

This chapter thus charts that development, focusing on plays that are individually important while also acting as examples of how Irish theatre more generally helped to bring about the changes mentioned above. But before doing so, I want to explore what those writers were reacting against, and how their innovations became possible.

## The Righteous Are Bold, 1946–63

As we've seen, the 1950s are remembered by scholars of Irish drama mainly for the innovations of Beckett and Behan – yet if a theatregoer in those years had been called upon to identify the dramatist most likely to be famous decades later, he or she may well have named Frank Carney, whose *The Righteous Are Bold* was the most successful Irish play of its era. Premiering at the Abbey in 1946, it enjoyed multiple revivals in Dublin during the 1950s; it also had a successful run in London in 1948, and was quite well received in the United States when it appeared there in 1956, a year that also featured McKenna's *Saint Joan*, O'Casey's *Red Roses for Me* and the New York premiere of *Waiting for Godot*. In all of those locations, the play was spoken of with admiration, as an example of the ongoing vitality of the Irish play.

To an audience today, however, *The Righteous Are Bold* would seem irredeemably old-fashioned – for at least two reasons.

One is its portrayal of women. The play presents a young woman called Nora who has emigrated from Ireland to Britain. Upon her return home she exhibits behaviour that her family find alarming: independence, wilfulness, sexual awareness. 'I've discovered that I have a mind of my own. I've learned to think for myself. I never believe anything now unless my reason tells me it's true', she says, before spitting upon and then smashing a statue of the Virgin Mary (Carney, 1951: 28–9).

The choice of name makes Carney's intentions obvious. Like the heroine of Ibsen's *A Doll's House* (1879) and Synge's *The Shadow of the Glen* (1903), Carney's Nora leaves the safety of a conventional domestic setting for an environment that allows her to define herself on her own terms. But whereas

Ibsen's and Synge's plays concluded with a person called Nora exiting both the stage and the home, Carney focuses on the aftermath of such a departure. The freedom that his character thought she would gain through emigration has corrupted her, his play suggests, and she can be saved only by reintegration into the Irish family home and thus the rigidly policed Irish social system.

This characterization reveals an apparent desire on the part of Carney – and, by extension, the Abbey and its audiences – to define and reinforce gender roles. It also reveals the high level of socially conservative alarm that had built up in Ireland in the post-war years about the issue of emigration: the fear was that living abroad would erode Catholic values in young people, especially women. When Nora's family learn about her illness, they blame it on her departure from home: 'whatever [the cause of] it is, I hope it isn't for want of keeping an eye on herself and going to the Sacraments regular,' says her father, who is quick to refer to the authority of his local priest: 'Father O'Malley is right to warn the young people against going to England at all' (Carney, 1951: 8).

The second reason for the play's fall from fashion is that its third act involves the performance of an exorcism upon Nora. It is revealed that the cause of her behaviour is not that she has been corrupted by England but that she has been possessed by a demonic spirit – though, again in keeping with the mores of that time, there is some slippage between the categories of the Satanic and the foreign in the script. Father O'Malley successfully performs the ritual upon her, but the effort of doing so causes him to die – which means that he has sacrificed his life in order to save Nora's soul. To anyone who has seen William Friedkin's 1973 film *The Exorcist*, Carney's conclusion will suffer by comparison. But – as we see elsewhere in this chapter – the use of martyrdom as a trope would recur many times in Irish plays about Catholicism.

But even if the play would struggle to find an audience today, it was popular in its own time, running at the Abbey for a record-breaking sixteen weeks upon its premiere, and being revived on ten further occasions between 1947 and 1963. It would also become a mainstay of the amateur movement until the 1970s, and appeared in a commercial production at the Olympia as late as 1987. We cannot assume that its popularity meant that its audiences always shared the values being promoted by the play. In a subtle reading, Mary Burke points to the ambiguity of both its title (who is the 'righteous' person being described?) and its conclusion, in which the priest's death can be seen as a defeat by the evil spirit rather than as a form of martyrdom (2009: 136–51). Nevertheless, the fact that the play's values went mostly unquestioned tells us something about Catholicism in Ireland during this period.

Yet there is evidence that the play's popularity arose not only from Irish conformity but also from audiences' love of sensationalism. There was, for example, the scene in which a statue of the Virgin Mary is smashed, prompting some walk-outs in New York but generally registering with reviewers elsewhere as a refreshingly shocking act of (literal) iconoclasm. But also important was the implicit presentation of Nora as a sexual object. When examined by her doctor, she is asked if she got 'into any trouble' while in England – a question that produces bafflement in her mother. Nora knows exactly what the doctor is getting at, however – that she had become pregnant and either miscarried or terminated the pregnancy. 'It's all right mother; I know what he means,' she says, demonstrating a sexual awareness and worldliness that her parents cannot even comprehend (Carney, 1951: 37). In that scene, Nora is asked to remove her blouse while the doctor examines her; later she writhes uncontrollably on the ground while the male characters hold her down. The play thus imagines and presents Nora's body as an object to be studied and controlled: by medical science, by a father or would-be husband, by religion – and thus by the audience too. While the purpose of those representations is to reinforce the importance of male power (and the male gaze), it seems reasonable to propose that these acts would have been viewed as titillating by at least some audience members. This explains Roger McHugh's anecdote about overhearing a young woman in the audience at the play in 1946: 'it's all right, mother,' she said. 'I have my eyes shut tight. I'm not looking at it at all' (qtd by Murray, 1999: 10).

These sensational qualities are evident from Figure 3, a publicity still from the 1963 revival at the Abbey – which would be the last time *The Righteous Are Bold* was performed there. The exaggerated gestures and expressions demonstrate the melodramatic quality of the actors' performances, just as the relative position of the priest and Nora – not to mention the placing of the nun and Nora's mother – reveal much about attitudes to religion and gender at that time.

The production was by then almost twenty years old but had retained its original director (Frank Dermody) and its original star, Maire Ni Dhomhnaill, who had created the role of Nora in 1946 to acclaim. The photo provides an example of the intensity of her performance – something that reviewers praised wherever the play was staged. But it also seems fair to suggest that her bared shoulder and unfastened dress would not have gone unnoticed by the prospective audience members to whom this image was directed.

**Figure 3** Abbey Theatre, *The Righteous Are Bold*, 1963 (ATDA, 3857_PH_0003). Courtesy of the Abbey Theatre Archive.

But by then the play was beginning to show its age. Material in the Abbey archive shows that changes had gradually been introduced, presumably to make it more appealing. A line in which Nora claims to have been possessed by Beelzebub is cut from the 1963 promptbook, perhaps for seeming too fantastical. We also find the introduction of a new scene – which appears on three handwritten pages in the promptbook – involving an argument between the priest and the doctor about how best to treat Nora (ATDA, 3867_PS_0001: 80–2). Almost twenty years after its premiere, the Abbey felt the need to intensify the play's staging of the debate between religion and science, between faith and reason – a theme to which it would return two years later, when Tomás Mac Anna directed Brecht's *Life of Galileo* there.

Even so, religion triumphs in the 1963 production, just as it had done in all previous stagings. While Carney's original script calls for the priest to die alone, the 1963 production leaves most of the other characters on stage for his final moments, ensuring that the audience sees their reactions to his death. We can probably attribute this alteration to a desire to heighten the play's melodramatic qualities, but one result of leaving the actors on stage would have been the removal from the audience of the freedom to interpret the conclusion themselves: their responses would instead have been prompted by the reactions of the characters. We cannot say for certain that this change indicates a desire to impose more control over audience response, but all of these additions and alterations indicate that attitudes to Catholicism were not quite what they had been when the play was premiered.

When *The Righteous Are Bold* is mentioned in Irish theatre histories, it is usually deployed as an example of how Catholicism manifested itself in Irish culture during the mid-century period. Clair Wills sees it as 'an extreme version of the clergy's panicky attitude to English irreligion' – but one that also 'chimed with paternalistic attitude to Irish women away from home' (2007: 322). Paul Murphy views it as representing 'the apotheosis of theatrical endorsement of Catholic gender ideology' (2009: 208), while for Pilkington it was a manifestation of the Abbey's adherence to the values espoused by the Fianna Fáil governments of the 1930s and 1940s (2001: 149). So when critics have explored the play, they have done so to consider it as a product of its own time – and one best left in that context.

Such interpretations are certainly valid. *The Righteous Are Bold* demonstrates how Irish religious values had become entangled with a determination to discipline the bodies and sexual identities of young women. And in the death of the priest at the conclusion we see something of how the central image of Christianity – the passion of Christ – was being appropriated as a means of normalizing suffering and self-sacrifice in Ireland generally. What we must recall, however, is that these images of control and self-sacrifice were being promulgated at precisely the time that the Catholic Church was most vigorously incarcerating women in Magdalene laundries, while also enthusiastically accepting male and female children to its orphanages, reformatories and industrial schools. The play's exploration of attitudes to sexuality, religion and suffering – and the relationship between those three things – thus becomes disturbing when viewed retrospectively.

To watch or read *The Righteous Are Bold* from a contemporary perspective is to be reminded how Irish theatre holds a mirror to its society, even if the mirroring is often uncritical or unconscious. In the plays discussed in the rest of this chapter, we find in Irish dramatists and directors a willingness to critique rather than reproduce the values that Carney's plays leaves so troublingly untroubled.

## Catholicism on the Irish stage in the 1950s

We saw in the last chapter how a new generation of theatre-makers emerged after the Abbey fire, aiming to transform Irish society by first transforming its theatre. But the firmest and most public challenge to Catholic hegemony would be offered not by a young firebrand but by a senior dramatist – Seán O'Casey, then into the final decade of his life. Like most Irish writers, O'Casey was a firm opponent of censorship, not least because it impeded his ability to make a living. But from the relative safety of his home in England it was perhaps easier for him to directly attribute the problems in Irish society to the influence of Catholicism – and he dedicated a great deal of attention to this problem in his autobiographies, essays and letters.

His plays also began to criticize Catholicism more trenchantly. His 1949 *Cock-a-Doodle Dandy* included a character with the thoroughly unsubtle name Father Domineer, a priest who carries out an exorcism that was probably an attempt to mock *The Righteous Are Bold* – which O'Casey claimed not to have read but later called 'absolute rubbish' in a 1958 letter to Paul Shyre (1975: 632). Unsurprisingly, the Abbey rejected the play (indeed, it would not appear there until 1977).

However, in an example of how theatrical self-censorship was not just a problem in Ireland, Christopher Murray points out that American producers also refused to stage *Cock-a-Doodle Dandy* because of the fear of a 'certain onslaught from the catholic [*sic*] church' (2004: 304). O'Casey would probably have savoured the battle, but his play simply went unproduced. That willingness to criticize Catholicism would cause him further problems in the United States. 'As the cold war intensified the influence of the catholic church [in America] grew,' writes Murray. 'In California the legislature anticipated Joe McCarthy by establishing a fact-finding Committee on Un-American activities which denounced O'Casey's plays' (ibid.).

Nevertheless, O'Casey persisted, writing a play called *The Bishop's Bonfire*, for which Cyril Cusack arranged a production at Dublin's Gaiety Theatre in

1955, with direction by Tyrone Guthrie. As Murray explains, the production had been widely attacked by Catholic newspapers in advance of its appearance, but somewhat ironically that aggression actually seemed to provoke curiosity in local theatregoers, who crowded to the opening night (2004: 355–63). Contemporary accounts suggest that many of those people had gone expecting a riot, hoping for a theatrical occasion that would match the premiere of *The Plough and the Stars*. They were to be disappointed, however, not only by the failure of that protest to materialize, but also by the play itself, which, while considered O'Casey's best for many years, was criticized for a lack of coherence. Nevertheless, it proved a success, and its run continued for several weeks.

*The Bishop's Bonfire* might not have been as great a success as O'Casey's first Abbey plays, but the attempts to shut it down by people associated with the Catholic Church were certainly a failure. It is possible that some Irish theatre-makers might thereby have formed the belief that they could risk staging plays on controversial topics. Yet it also seems likely that the forces that had attempted to suppress O'Casey's play were determined to reassert their dominance. A further confrontation therefore seemed likely. The staging of *The Bishop's Bonfire* thus provides important context for the next major clash between the Irish theatre and the Church, which was the production by the Pike of Tennessee Williams' *The Rose Tattoo* as part of the first Dublin Theatre Festival in 1957.

It is difficult now to appreciate the extent to which the presentation of Williams' play would have been perceived as a provocation, as a clear challenge to Irish censorship. As Joan Dean explains in *Riot and Great Anger* (2004: 155–7), two of Williams' plays – *Cat on a Hot Tin Roof* and *The Roman Spring of Mrs Stone* – had already been banned in published form in Ireland, though *The Rose Tattoo* itself had not been. Internationally, Williams had gained notoriety: the Lord Chamberlain had three times refused to license *Cat on a Hot Tin Roof* in Britain, while the film version of *A Streetcar Named Desire* had been far from uncontroversial in the UK and United States. Most importantly, in Ireland itself, the film version of *The Rose Tattoo* had been banned in 1956 – a clear sign that a staging of the play would have been unwelcome.

Nevertheless, in his personal account of the staging of the play, Alan Simpson writes of his surprise when members of the public objected to the proposal to stage the play, which he saw as 'deeply and subtly complimentary to Roman Catholicism' (1962: 142). He goes on to suggest that some of the subsequent attacks on the Pike were the work of 'people prejudiced against the Theatre in general, and Tennessee Williams in particular' (143). Yet, without wishing to doubt the sincerity of Simpson's account, he cannot have been too surprised by the reaction. As Gerard Whelan points out in a book co-written with Carolyn Swift, the theatre had been 'taken very severely to task' by the Catholic newspaper *The Standard* in 1955 over some of the material presented in its late-night revues:

> At the time Swift and Simpson had actually taken legal advice on the article. The advice they received says a great deal about Ireland in 1955: they were told that the article was plainly libellous, but were advised not to sue since no jury – whatever its members' private feelings – would dare to find publicly for a theatre in a case against a Catholic publication
>
> (Whelan and Swift, 2002: 53)

They must have understood that their work was being placed under scrutiny and that, in the case of any conflict, their chance of securing a just outcome was limited. That they determined to push on with the production of Williams' play demonstrates their refusal to be cowed – but it also explains how subsequent events transpired.

The first sign of trouble occurred when, shortly before the play's opening, Brendan Smith received a letter from a group called the 'League of Decency', complaining that the play 'advocated the use of birth control by unnatural means' (qtd by Simpson, 1962: 142) – a development that Simpson and his colleagues dismissed as a bad joke. But as soon as the run began, the Pike was formally accused of obscenity when the Irish police claimed that a condom had been shown on stage – which would have been a serious offence at the time, given that contraceptives were banned. In their separate accounts, both Swift and Simpson deny having used a real condom, but it did not matter. The accusation that they had behaved in an obscene fashion led to their isolation, and their list of subscribers fell quickly from 3,000 members to just under 300.

Thomas Kilroy, then a university student, had been working at the theatre's box office when the controversy broke – and he soon came under pressure to leave the Pike, even being advised that his association with it might result in his not graduating from university. 'When I went to talk to Alan [Simpson] he told me to go home,' writes Kilroy. 'To my lasting embarrassment, I did' (2008: 12). But even established figures would abandon the Pike. Lord Longford had promised to lease the Gate to the Pike company so that *The Rose Tattoo* could play for an extended run in a venue large enough to allow them to recoup their costs. But once the police shut down the production, he told Simpson that he would no longer be able to make the space available.

The controversy also affected people outside the theatre. As John Devitt recounts, the policeman who claimed to have witnessed the appearance of the condom on stage was being put under severe pressure by his superiors. He was 'frigid with embarrassment and didn't know whether he had seen the condom or not,' says Devitt; to admit to knowing what a condom looked like would risk social disgrace, but to deny that he had seen one would collapse the case, risking professional problems instead (2012: loc. 550). Ultimately, the legal action fell apart when the judge was harshly critical of the evidence presented by the police. But the damage had been done: the Pike closed, and under the strain of the controversy Simpson and Swift's marriage broke down.

As Pilkington (2001), Whelan and Swift (2002) and Dean (2004) have shown, the case against *The Rose Tattoo* resulted from clerical subversion, carried out surreptitiously from the office of the then-archbishop of Dublin, John Charles McQuaid. Perhaps encouraged by this success, the Dublin hierarchy would engage in a further act of interference in the theatrical world in 1958, when the second edition of the DTF was programmed.

Despite what had happened to the Pike, the first year's Festival had been considered a success, and Brendan Smith had moved to programme a second event, announcing in early 1958 that he would stage an adaptation of Joyce's *Ulysses* by Allan McClelland, a new play called *The Drums of Father Ned* by O'Casey, and short plays by Samuel Beckett. McQuaid objected to the inclusion of Joyce's and O'Casey's work, and refused to allow an opening mass for the Festival to go ahead. Learning of McQuaid's objections, the Irish Jesuit Provincial instructed that the St Francis Xavier Hall was to withdraw permission to stage the Beckett plays at that venue, while Dublin Corporation threatened to withdraw its grant of £3,000 to the DTF. Local trade unions soon threatened a boycott, and the Festival's plans were in ruins.

This Irish controversy would have an important international aspect. Members of the Catholic hierarchy in the United States were approached by two Irish bishops, who asked their American counterparts to use their influence with American senators to persuade the Irish government to extend censorship laws to include the theatre. The Irish government refused to accede to this demand and, in retaliation, the Catholic Church internationally 'encouraged a boycott of pilgrimages to Ireland', states John Cooney, who points out that this would have represented 'a tremendous blow to the tourist industry of an ailing economy' (2003: 330).

As this controversy grew, O'Casey withdrew his play from consideration for the Festival, partly because he suspected that the organizers were frightened of producing it and would be tempted to remove some of its more inflammatory material themselves. But, being O'Casey, he did not stop there: he also withdrew permission for the professional staging of any of his works in Ireland. The normally more measured Samuel Beckett made a similar choice. 'After the revolting boycott of Joyce and O'Casey I don't want to have anything to do with the Dublin Theatre "Festival"', he wrote in a letter to Alan Simpson (qtd by Knowlson, 1997: 447–8). He soon reversed that decision, but remained disgusted by the slight against Joyce.

Smith soon bowed to pressure, and the 1958 Festival was 'postponed' – which is to say that it was cancelled: the productions of Joyce's and O'Casey's works never happened. But Smith's choice of word would prove important. The reaction of the Catholic hierarchy to Smith's programme shows that the Irish theatre was perceived by both sides as a battleground for control over Irish culture. A letter from McQuaid to one of his subordinates made his views on this clear: 'I shall feel obliged to take very definite action if either *Ulysses* or O'Casey's play be chosen by the [Festival]', he wrote. '*The Rose Tattoo* ought to have been a lesson to [them]', he revealingly added (DDA, AB/8/6/XXV). In such a context, Smith's choice of the word 'postponement' rather than 'cancellation' showed that he was acceding to the demands of McQuaid and others – but only temporarily. The Festival returned in 1959, and soon established a reputation for the production of new Irish work, including, in 1961, another adaptation of work by Joyce by Mary Manning – something I'll return to in Chapter 4.

Those controversies – the case of *The Rose Tattoo* and the cancellation of the 1958 Festival – are sometimes presented as examples of what was wrong with Ireland at that time. And that is entirely appropriate. But they must also be seen as representing important acts of resistance which, although damaging to those involved, ultimately helped to bring about positive change. Terence Brown explains the significance of what Simpson and Smith had achieved: 'Had the judgement gone against Simpson subsequent directors and theatre managements would have been forced to exercise an inhibiting caution in all doubtful cases … The judgement meant that adventurous experiments could be embarked upon' (2004: 218). Kilroy makes a similar point about the 1958 Festival: 'I truly believe that this incident strengthened rather than weakened the Festival. The absurdity of it was one further step towards the dismantlement of Irish censorship' (2008: 14).

## Catholicism in court: Máiréad Ní Ghráda's *An Triail*, 1964–5

The accuracy of Kilroy's words would be evident from the early 1960s onwards, when Irish theatre artists began to say things that might not have been possible even a few years previously. Catholicism itself was changing: Archbishop McQuaid would feel compelled in 1962 to write to his parishioners to reassure them that the Second Vatican Council (then getting underway in Rome) would have no measurable impact on their religious practice. This of course would prove incorrect.

Nevertheless, the Church remained powerful, both culturally and politically. For that reason, the appearance of two plays that directly sought to question that power was notable. Both would be presented in the form of courtroom dramas, establishing a contrast between the law and Catholic morality. Both would focus on the status of young women; both would be very well received by audiences and critics alike – and both have been given very little attention in histories of Irish theatre. The first is Richard Johnson's *The Evidence I Shall Give*, which I discuss briefly – but my primary focus here is on Máiréad Ní Ghráda's *An Triail* [*The Trial*], which appeared at the Damer during the 1964 DTF.

*The Evidence I Shall Give* opened at the Abbey in 1961, where it staged a court case concerning a decision to remove a girl who had broken the law from a reformatory run by nuns. As stated earlier, the Abbey under Blythe has been repeatedly (and deservedly) accused of conservativism and an unwillingness to challenge authority. This renders all the more impressive its willingness not only to produce *The Evidence I Shall Give* but to revive it five times during 1961 – giving it a high-profile slot in that year's DTF, which by then was attracting international critics and visitors.

The Abbey archive holds three scripts for those productions, one of which has been extensively cut and edited, though it is not clear how much of this work (if any) was done by Johnson himself. While many of those changes can be explained by the need to make the play work better on stage, there is also evidence of an attempt to make the main nun in the play seem *less* sympathetic than she had originally been rendered by Johnson. The status of its author as a respected district court judge may have emboldened the theatre to make such decisions, but it is surprisingly frank for its time.

Decades later, the Ryan Report would refer to Johnson's work: 'Far from being controversial, the message of the play was well received by the audience and its success reflected the readiness of the public to hear the criticisms made by [it]' (2009: 1.173). The Commission was also informed of a Department of Education memo that attributed to the play a shift in attitudes towards reformatories. The memo, prepared in 1963, suggests that the Catholic Church had complained repeatedly about its difficulty keeping reformatories open. 'There are insufficient commitments to make their schools economical', states the memo. 'There is a strong prejudice against certified schools and this prejudice has been strengthened to some extent by District Justice Johnson's drama entitled *The Evidence I Shall Give*' (qtd in CICA, 2004: 107, 108). That document demonstrates that Johnson's play had an impact on its society – that it was judged to have created a situation in which people who might otherwise have been placed in a reformatory were not sent there. It is impossible to estimate how many people might have been saved from that fate by Johnson's play – and the Abbey's decision to stage it – but whether they number in the tens, hundreds or thousands, we need to have an awareness that its production was seen in its own time as a challenge to Catholic authority.

Rather like Johnson, Ní Ghráda was by the early 1960s a well-established figure in Irish society. She had had five of her plays produced at the Abbey since 1945, while at the Gate Mac Liammóir had also been a strong supporter. All of her Abbey plays had been in Irish and most were one-acts designed to act as curtain-raisers or afterpieces for other (more commercially viable) productions – and perhaps for those reasons they have not received much critical attention. Yet, as a figure in the history of the Abbey, Ní Ghráda stands with Lady Gregory and Marina Carr as one of only three female playwrights to have had her work produced consistently over a long period there. Even without the success of her next play, she would therefore merit sustained and serious attention.

But that next play would represent a watershed in the history of Irish theatre, going much further than Johnson did in exposing the hypocrisy of Catholic morality about women's sexuality – and doing so in a staging style that represents one of the earliest examples of Brechtian techniques being employed in an Irish context. Both thematically and formally, the play was doing things that simply had not been done before.

*An Triail* premiered at the Damer during the 1964 DTF – the year when that Festival in many ways came of age, falling into a well-balanced rhythm of producing new Irish plays alongside international work. Even though it gained less attention than English-language works by male playwrights, *An Triail* was well received. Harold Hobson, the critic for the British *Sunday Times*, saw it twice, confessing that even if he had not understood it fully, he found it deeply moving. And in *The Irish Times* it was described as 'entitled to rank as the most important offering [by] the Theatre Festival', mainly due to its exploration of the theme of what the critic (reluctantly) called 'illegitimacy' (23 September 1964). It subsequently became the subject of a debate in the letters page of that newspaper, with most correspondents seeing its production as an important moment for Irish culture.

The story can be seen as offering a variation on – or, strictly speaking, a corrective to – the fable of the fallen woman that had informed plays like *The Righteous Are Bold*. Its lead character Maire is a young woman from rural Ireland; her 'crime' is that she falls in love with a married man who abandons her when she becomes pregnant. Her own family also reject her and she is forced to raise her child alone in Dublin. She is placed in a Magdalene laundry. When the married man is reintroduced into her life – but has married someone else, following the death of his first wife – Maire considers herself to have no option but to murder her child and then commit suicide.

This story is presented to the audience in the form of a trial, which means that we know from the outset what Maire has done: 'I killed my child because she is a girl. All girls grow up to be women. But my daughter is free. She is free. She won't be a soft or compliant person for any man. She is free. She is free. She is free' (Ní Ghráda, 2003: 19, my translation). We learn that this is not so much a criminal case as an inquest, one that sets out to attribute responsibility for the death of Maire and her child. But whereas we might expect the play to condemn the young woman, it instead points to the failings of her family and the broader society – not just of her mother, who neglected to provide her with any knowledge of sex, but also her brothers, who are more concerned with their social status than their sister's plight. There is also a priest who insists that Maire break off her relationship, quoting the biblical injunction that we should cut off our right hand rather than allow it to offend God (34), but who otherwise has no guidance or comfort to offer. And others are brought forward to show their own culpability: a social worker, a landlord, a factory manager. And then there is the married man himself, a schoolteacher called Padraig who, we learn at the end of the play, had boasted to his friends about his seduction of Maire. These events suggest that, like an Irish Tess of the D'Urbervilles, Maire is doing the best she can under impossible circumstances – but she falls victim to a combination of powerlessness, poverty and a lack of education.

From a formal point of view, what makes the play remarkable for its time is that the audience is placed directly in the position of being Maire's jury. As the final scene opens, one of the lawyers addresses the audience to state that the verdict of murder and suicide cannot be denied – but also to demand that we determine who is guilty of those crimes (Ní Ghráda, 2003: 89). One by one, the characters attempt to justify themselves: to suggest that Maire's actions were shameful and that they had no choice but to disassociate themselves from her in order to avoid being similarly disgraced. Maire, we must acknowledge, is killed not by her own hand but rather by her society's hypocrisy in blaming women for actions that they have not been sufficiently educated to understand – and in simultaneously failing to condemn the men who are responsible for the conception of 'illegitimate' children.

By insisting that we judge these actions, Ní Ghráda ensures that we cannot absolve ourselves, that we too must take responsibility. It has sometimes been asserted that Ní Ghráda was able to grapple with this topic because the play, being in Irish, would not have been seen by a wide audience. However, it is important to say that Ní Ghráda wrote an English-language version and it was staged only six months after the Irish-language premiere, again directed by Mac Anna, and in the larger theatre of the Eblana. That version was staged by Phyllis Ryan, a producer who had a huge impact on the development of new Irish work – so it must have made an impression upon her audiences when Ryan told *The Irish Times* that Ní Ghráda's play had so impressed her that she'd decided to try to improve her Irish (3 October 1965).

There were changes to the Irish original: the married man's name is changed from Padraig to Kevin, and some of the language used to describe Maire by her brothers is more aggressive. But it is no less insistent upon Irish audiences' complicity in what happens to young women.

And once again it was well received. In contrast with the attempts by Archbishop McQuaid to shut down the DTF in 1958, the play met few clerical objections, either in its Irish- or English-language versions. Indeed, an *Irish Times* profile of Ní Ghráda reported that:

> there was some anxiety ... about whether the action and characterization might not give offence in clerical circles – an anxiety that was not fully dispelled until it reached the author's ears, by devious means, that a priest who moved in official circles had been to see it and had thoroughly approved of its message. Further, an equally unexpected endorsement came from another source. Miss Ní Ghráda

picked up the telephone at home one evening to hear a Jesuit say that he had just been to see the play: he had no criticism to make; but thought that one line if added to the confession scene . . . well, might give it a greater degree of authenticity

(19 April 1965)

Hence, the Church still saw its role as endorsing Irish dramas on controversial topics, and it's remarkable to consider the playwright being contacted at home by a Jesuit with unsolicited feedback. Nevertheless, we must acknowledge that Ní Ghráda had determined to write and stage the play regardless of whether there were clerical objections.

In 1965, the play was broadcast in Irish on RTÉ television, with Fionnula Flanagan taking the lead role, and again it was well received. This demonstrates that it was seen and discussed throughout the society – and that, far from being offended, audiences were excited not only by Ní Ghráda's willingness to grapple with a difficult issue but also by her use of the Irish language.

## Tom Murphy's *The Sanctuary Lamp*, 1975

*An Triail* was a turning point, but the moment that most decisively marks the transformation of the relationship between theatre, the state and the Catholic Church in Ireland was the staging at the Abbey in 1975 of Tom Murphy's *The Sanctuary Lamp*.

Murphy's first solo-authored play, *A Whistle in the Dark* (1961), had been rejected by Blythe when it was submitted to the Abbey, so the staging of *Famine* there in 1968 was both a literal and figurative homecoming, bringing Murphy not only back from London to Dublin but also establishing him as a key playwright for the national theatre. That status grew steadily, with the Abbey premiering five of Murphy's plays in quick succession, while also inviting him to sit on its board of directors. Those works differ from each other in terms of both form and content: for example, *The Morning After Optimism* (1971) is set in a fantastical realm, while *The White House* (1972) is deeply suspicious of the tendency towards the fantastical in Irish life. But collectively they established Murphy as a leading Irish playwright, a dramatist whose impulse towards formal experimentation was balanced by a radical commitment to truth-telling.

Yet despite Murphy's reputation for innovation and honesty, *The Sanctuary Lamp* came as a shock to Irish audiences when it premiered as part of the 1975 DTF. The action takes place entirely in a church and, although published editions today make clear that the setting is England, the original script was less specific: many reviewers assumed that the setting was Ireland. Into that sacred space three characters arrive, whose presence might have been considered inappropriate by devout Irish audience members. One is a teenage girl called Maudie who is intellectually disabled and appears to have suffered some form of sexual abuse. Another is a circus strongman called Harry, whose Jewish background gives him a kind of anthropological curiosity about Catholicism – a device that Murphy presumably intended as a subtle estrangement effect that would cause his mostly Catholic audience to think anew about their Church's practices and images. And the third is an Irish juggler called Francisco: a man who, though raised Catholic, is now alienated from and hostile to that religion.

In the play's first production, Murphy's opening scene included a vacuous sermon by a Catholic priest, who recounts the story of the immaculate conception from the point of view of the Virgin Mary; he concludes by taking up his guitar to sing a folk song (ATDA, 2544_PS_0001.pdf). That scene was cut from subsequent versions, probably because it delayed the appearance of Murphy's core characters and thus inhibited the development of dramatic momentum. Yet the inclusion of that sermon did have a balancing effect, because the play concludes with a kind of anti-sermon, delivered from the pulpit by Francisco: 'I have a dream! I have a dream: the day is coming. The not too distant future. The housewives of the capitals of the world – Yes, the housewives of the very Vatican itself, marching daily to the altar rails to be administered of the pill at the hands of the priest himself' (Murphy, 1994: 155).

It's striking to consider that these lines were spoken in the national theatre only eighteen years after *The Rose Tattoo* had been shut down due to the (non-)appearance of a condom on stage. And because audiences in 1975 were able to place Francisco's words in direct comparison with the priest's sermon about the conception of Jesus – which had been delivered from the same pulpit – Murphy's play was provocative in a way that couldn't even have been imagined in the 1950s. He had shown that the anti-clerical rage of a Francisco would be far more passionate (and dramatic) than the flaccid piety of a priest.

But Murphy does not so much reject Catholicism as reappropriate it for dramatic means. In that same speech, Francisco presents a devastating critique of the Catholic Church as 'the great middle-man industry', an institution staffed by 'predators that have been mass-produced out of the loneliness and isolation of people, with standard collars stamped on'. As shown in the original promptbook, his language becomes particularly vivid and visceral. Priests, he says, are 'black on the outside but, underneath, their bodies swathed in bandages – bandages steeped in ointments, preservatives and holy oils! – Half mummified torsos like great thick bandaged pricks!' The subsequent two lines are placed in square brackets, creating uncertainty about whether they were delivered in the original production: 'Founded in blood, continued in blood, crusaded in blood, inquisitioned in blood, divided in blood'. But what follows was certainly spoken and is no less shocking: 'And *they* tell *us* that Christ lives! … They arrive at their temporary sated state, these violence-mongering furies, and start verily wanking themselves in pleasurable swoons of pacifism, forgetting their own history and forgetting who caused the trouble to start with' (ATDA, 2544_PS_0001.pdf: 77–8).

This is a rejection of Catholicism that is steeped in Catholic imagery – but with many of the key ideas inverted, so that Francisco's sermon becomes a kind of anti-consecration, with the symbol of blood being used to evoke images of destruction rather than creation and resurrection. And, anticipating later revelations about sexual abuse by Catholic priests, Murphy's linking of sexuality, violence and religion contrasts with the play's allusions to the virginity of Mary and the celibacy of priests. Maudie operates as an ironic manifestation of the Virgin Mary: we learn in the play's second act that she had conceived and given birth to a child who had been taken away from her. And even in the choice of three characters, we have a reimagining of the Trinity, with Harry's Judaism operating as the Father to Francisco's Christianity, while Maudie's unworldliness might be seen as an analogue for the Holy Spirit. In these and other examples we find *The Sanctuary Lamp* carefully rethinking the meanings of Catholic iconography and ritual.

The premiere reinforced the play's most provocative elements. The design by Bronwen Casson refused the audience any possibility of imagining the play as a fantasy, metaphor or allegory, instead presenting a naturalistic recreation of a Catholic church that includes realistic statues of the Sacred Heart and the Virgin Mary (ATDA, 2544_PH_0001). The smashing of a statue in *The Righteous Are Bold* had shocked audiences in 1946, but what is shocking here is that these Catholic icons remain undisturbed during Francisco's blasphemous speech.

Of further interest is that the play's premiere was used to mark the fiftieth anniversary of the Abbey's receipt of a state subsidy. In 1924, the newly independent Irish government had made the Abbey the first subsidized theatre in the English-speaking world, a decision that brought with it the threat of government interference in its programming (a tension that came to a head in the debate about whether to stage *The Plough and the Stars*). It is telling that they chose to mark the anniversary of the awarding of that subsidy by again asserting their rights to present images and ideas that many Irish audiences would find unpalatable. This is not to suggest that they were looking for a fight – but they certainly were not avoiding one either.

Unsurprisingly, the play was controversial. In *The Irish Times* Seamus Kelly reported that it has been immediately condemned as 'the most anticlerical Irish play ever staged by Ireland's national theatre' (8 October 1975) and Murphy was called upon to defend himself. 'It doesn't re-affirm anything about faith,' he said of the play:

> You have the three people knocking at the door, the feeling of being lost, adrift, cut off from something – call it Nature or God, whatever. They are locked inside this metaphorical monster that is a church, and what does a church stand for? Stability, civilization. But religion merely provides the venue for the people to do their own thing ... So really, *The Sanctuary Lamp* hasn't anything to do with religion.
>
> (ATDA, 2544_PC_0001: 10)

The word 'really' in Murphy's final sentence is being asked to do a lot of work in the above passage. It's true that, when considered as a metaphor for society generally, the church where the action happens might not be seen as representing religion generally. And we must always be cautious about attributing to playwrights the views of their characters. But whatever the play is 'really' about, Murphy must have known that his audiences would see it as anti-clerical. A public debate about it was soon scheduled and – again thinking of the history of riots at the venue – many commentators predicted that a rough night lay ahead for Murphy.

But that debate was attended by the then-president of Ireland Cearbhall Ó Dálaigh who, invoking the privileges of his office, took to the stage to speak before anyone else – and he strongly defended Murphy. 'The play,' he was quoted as saying in *The Irish Times*, 'ranks in the first three of the great plays of this theatre: *The Playboy of the Western World*, *Juno and the Paycock*, and *The Sanctuary Lamp*' (12 October 1975). Murphy was present at the time, though sitting out of sight in the theatre's sound and lighting booth.

The president's comments were 'very flattering to me', Murphy told Alexandra Poulain. 'But it killed the debate. Had he gone instead of staying throughout, there might have been better chances for people expressing their wishes' (2008: 96).

His play remained controversial, but a clear marker had been set down: the Irish theatre was free to express its views on Catholicism without fear of censorship, state-led or otherwise. The Abbey would remain cautious for some years – for example, a production of Kilroy's *Talbot's Box* in 1976 was accused of being prejudiced against Catholicism, and it seems that the Abbey board was nervous about its reception. Nevertheless, they still agreed to its production, and change came quickly from that point onwards.

## Stewart Parker's *Pentecost*, 1987

The theatre in Northern Ireland had also experienced controversy over attempts to stage dramas that directly addressed religious issues, though usually such plays concerned sectarian division rather than matters of doctrine, faith or institutional malpractice. An important example is the collapse of the Ulster Group Theatre (founded in 1940) when its board cancelled a production of Sam Thompson's *Over the Bridge* only two weeks before it was due to open in 1959, saying that 'the Ulster public is fed up with religious and political controversies' (qtd by Byrne, 1997: 47).

As Connal Parr shows, the board's decision to withdraw support for Thompson's play was made on religious grounds: he quotes from an interview with Thompson, who explained how the chair of the board 'wanted [a] mob scene cut and the language curtailed. In his opinion the religious references in the play were blasphemous. [The chair] told me in forceful terms that if the play went on in full, the guns would be out, the blood would flow and the theatre would be wrecked by mobs' (2017: 88). That prophesy proved incorrect, however: *Over the Bridge* was staged in 1960, after the Group had disbanded, and although its treatment of sectarianism in a shipyard was indeed viewed as contentious, it proved one of the most popular plays ever staged in Belfast. It later toured to Dublin and Glasgow before being filmed for British television.

However, as political and sectarian violence intensified from the 1970s, theatres became more reluctant to address religion directly. Writers such as Christina Reid and Marie Jones did tackle the cultural legacies of Protestantism (as I discuss later), as would Graham Reid and Gary Mitchell, among others. But there was little appetite to explore faith in itself as Murphy had done in *The Sanctuary Lamp* (indeed, I could find no record of that play ever having been professionally produced in Northern Ireland). Nor was there much appetite to criticize institutional Catholicism or religious hypocrisy, as Ní Ghráda had done with *An Triail*.

When viewed from this perspective, Stewart Parker's *Pentecost* seems all the more courageous. A 2014 revival of that play by Lynne Parker (Stewart's niece and the artistic director of Rough Magic) demonstrated that it can successfully be staged beyond the context of the Troubles, but at its heart it can be seen as a deliberate intervention into that conflict, by suggesting that one way of overcoming sectarian division might be to reinvent Christianity into a form that could be shared by Catholics, Protestants and non-believers alike. As Marilynn Richtarik states, 'those who view the play solely in [political] terms often see its religious themes as tacked on rather than intrinsic . . . For Parker himself, however, the play's spiritual dimension came to supersede the political in importance' (2012: 310). Parker sought to present a third way between belief and unbelief; perhaps we could therefore see *Pentecost* as a play in which the religious and the political are deeply intertwined.

He achieves that combination by using a strategy employed by many writers who sought to tackle the Troubles, which is to make a case for societal renewal by reinventing theatrical tropes. Like *The Hostage*, the action of *Pentecost* is set in a house that represents a national space (here the space is Northern Ireland, though Parker is clearly in dialogue with the broader Irish dramatic tradition). Into that house come four characters: two men (one Catholic and one Protestant) and two women (again, one Catholic and one Protestant). The Catholic woman, named Marian, is haunted by the former occupant of the house, a Unionist called Lily who is deeply affronted by the presence in her house of an 'idolater' like Marian (2000: 181). Marian is joined by her estranged husband, Lenny, who is also from a Catholic background; as the action unfolds we learn that their marriage has collapsed under the strain of the death of their only child, Christopher. They are accompanied by a college friend called Peter who, though originally from the north, has moved abroad, and by Ruth, who – in another common trope in Northern Irish drama – has left her husband (a Royal Ulster Constabulary policeman) because he has become violent towards her. Much of the action concerns a debate about what to do with the house. Marian initially proposes turning it into a museum of working-class Belfast life, before deciding that 'what this house needs most is air and light' – that is, to be lived in (238). The point of the metaphor is clear enough: if Northern Ireland is to have a future it must open itself to outside influences.

In addition to the use of the house as a metaphor for Northern Ireland, the other major tropes are the ghost and the death of the child. Dead children haunt Irish drama, usually operating as symbols of thwarted futures, or as evidence that the society is doomed. We see some of this in *The Sanctuary Lamp*, in which both Harry and Maudie have lost children; it is also a major presence in Murphy's *Bailegangaire* (1985) and *A Thief of a Christmas* (1985), in which the central trauma is the necessity for a parent to bury first her children and then her grandchild – and those plays are in turn in conversation with Synge's *Riders to the Sea* (1904). The trope is a presence also in Brian Friel's *Faith Healer*, in which Frank denies that he and Grace had a child who was stillborn. And Marina Carr has dedicated extensive attention to rewriting this image, both in her early play *Low in the Dark* (1989) as well as her adaptation of *Anna Karenina* (2016) – though she would also reproduce it to powerful effect in *By the Bog of Cats* (1998).

Likewise, ghosts often feature in Irish drama. In some cases, this is simply because of the influence of Gothic forms in Irish culture: Ireland, after all, is the country that produced Stoker's *Dracula*, so there are times in the Irish theatre when the audience is intended to believe that a character is literally interacting with a supernatural force (as we've seen with *The Righteous Are Bold*). But more frequently the ghost is used as a metaphor for memory – specifically for a traumatic memory that needs to be faced so that it can be forgotten or otherwise laid to rest. As we'll see in Chapter 6, many of the plays of Conor McPherson work as straightforward ghost stories, but they are at their most impactful when audiences see those ghosts as a dramatization of both personal and historical traumas, something that is particularly evident in *The Weir* (1997), *Shining City* (2004) and *The Veil* (2011) – the first and third of which also feature dead children, incidentally. But we find ghosts or spirits being used in this way in the plays of Sebastian Barry (*The Steward of Christendom* from 1995 and *Hinterland* in 2002), and Stacey Gregg in *Lagan* (2011), among many other examples.

It might be tempting to view the presence of these overfamiliar tropes in Parker's play as evidence of a lack of originality. But that would be a mistake. In his earlier *Northern Star* (1984), Parker had demonstrated a deep awareness of the history of Irish drama, writing a play that pastiched the work of Boucicault, Synge, Wilde, O'Casey and Beckett (among others) to suggest that Irish history can best be understood through the lens of performance, just as Irish drama must be understood in the context of the island's histories. Parker is using these tropes in *Pentecost because* they are overfamiliar: he is attempting to show that images from the past can be reinvented – that, just as Teresa in *The Hostage* rechristens a miraculous medal as a symbol for her love for the English soldier, it is possible for old images to be given new life. This starts to answer a central question about reconciliation in Northern Ireland, which is how two communities in conflict can remain faithful to their defining images and symbols while also changing sufficiently to be able to coexist peacefully.

In using theatre as a neutral space that could reimagine potentially incendiary images and symbols, Parker's plays can (and indeed should) be seen as accommodating the broader Field Day objective of using theatre as a 'fifth province', a deterritorialized space that can allow for the invention of new ways of living. Parker does so most powerfully in the final scene of the play, which stages a ritualistic rechristening of the tropes that had driven the action to that point. The ghost of Lily is laid to rest when she confesses to an infidelity and to the 'loss' of her own child; the house is saved from the fate of becoming a museum. Likewise Marian recreates the story of the death of her son, having been enabled to do so by Ruth and Peter's recitation of the story of the Pentecost from the Acts of the Apostles. 'I called him Christopher. Because he was a kind of Christ to me, he brought love with him . . . the truth and the life. He was a future. Until one day I found him dead' (Parker, 2000: 244). Ruth views Christ not in Catholic or Protestant terms but in relation to concepts that are shared by both religions: humanity, love and the spiritual value of communion. 'We have got to love that in ourselves', says Ruth. 'That's the only future there is. Personally I want to live now. I want this house to live' (244–5). The play then concludes with the two men coming together to perform 'Just a Closer Walk with Thee' – playing the music but not singing the words – as Ruth opens the windows.

Here the theatre again becomes a space of ritual, in which the creation of art – music by the characters, theatre by the actors – offers the possibility of transcendence: of history, politics and religious division. The Pentecostal ritual itself is reimagined, with its images of communication and understanding being shifted from the spiritual realm to the theatrical – and from there into the social and political. Parker thus finds a way to move beyond those elements of religion that trap people in a state of fealty to unchangeable absolutes. The religious, the political – and indeed the theatrical – can and must be renewed and reinvented, allowing the future to be created anew.

## Patricia Burke Brogan's *Eclipsed*, 1992

While *Pentecost* was premiering in Derry, another dramatist was finishing a draft of a play that was asking similar questions about religion – about how to leave behind the elements of Catholicism that were damaging, without losing its positive characteristics. The play was called *Eclipsed* and was written by Patricia Burke Brogan, who based it on her own experiences as a novitiate nun who had worked in (but subsequently left) an order that had run a Magdalene laundry.

Her willingness to ask those questions is an example of how much of the energy that drove criticisms of the Irish Church came from people who were practising Catholics. The 1975 public debate about *The Sanctuary Lamp* at the Abbey, for example, had been chaired by the priest and playwright Desmond Forristal, whose 1974 play *Black Man's Country* at the Gate had provided an exploration of the role of Catholic missions in the Biafran War. But despite (or perhaps even because of) her former role within the Church, Burke Brogan attracted a considerably more hostile response than Ní Ghráda, Murphy or Forristal did when her play premiered in 1992.

The first 'public' outing of *Eclipsed* was in 1988 when she presented an early version of it to friends at her home. Later it was read by Fintan O'Toole, who knew immediately that *Eclipsed* was saying something that hadn't been said before: Ní Ghráda's *An Triail* had exposed the hypocrisy and misogyny that had sent women to the laundries, but *Eclipsed* revealed how badly the women there had been treated. He urged Burke Brogan to submit the script to the Abbey and other Irish theatres without delay. She followed O'Toole's advice – and the rejection letters were quick to arrive. As she recounts:

> One well-known theatre director asks if I realise what I am saying in my script. He suggests that I change the dialogue of the Magdalen characters. His mother, who had worked in a Magdalen Laundry, told him that the women wouldn't speak like that . . . A letter-writer advises me to send *Eclipsed* to European theatres, as it could never be produced in Ireland.

> (2014: 125)

*Eclipsed* finally appeared in Galway in 1992, when it was produced in a disused garage by a small local company called Punchbag. It was greeted with enthusiasm by almost everyone who saw it. The local member of parliament (and later president of Ireland) Michael D. Higgins stated that

*Eclipsed* 'changed everything' (qtd in Burke Brogan, 2014: iv), and he led a standing ovation on the opening night. But it also provoked serious negativity. There were protests outside the theatre as a result of its presentation of nuns, and Burke Brogan encountered some hostility personally, including abusive letters.

Matters were made more complex by the revelation later that year that the bishop of Galway, Eamonn Casey – who was also a patron of Punchbag and had donated old robes to be used as a costume in the play – had fathered a child with an American woman called Annie Murphy in the 1970s. When Irish newspapers published this story, Casey stepped down from his position as bishop and fled to America – and although Murphy was vilified by sections of the Irish media (the implication repeatedly made was that she had 'seduced' Casey, and that he would otherwise never have transgressed), his resignation became one of the first of a series of scandals that would undermine the authority of the Catholic Church. This meant that *Eclipsed* was seen by many as offering a timely consideration of Catholic attitudes to women and sex – but it also meant that sections of the Church and its followers were feeling particularly defensive. With *The Sanctuary Lamp* Tom Murphy had had the backing of the president of Ireland – not to mention the status of having his play staged at the national theatre. But Burke Brogan was obliged to fight for her play largely alone.

*Eclipsed* draws strongly on her personal experiences, with the character of Sister Virginia acting as a surrogate for the author herself. We also encounter four of the 'penitent women' of the laundry who, despite their differences in background and personality, share a sense of bewilderment and despair about how they have been abandoned by their family, neighbours and friends. Making up the group is a seventeen-year-old orphan called Juliet who has been sent to the laundry to work, showing how the nuns exploited the labour of children who had been placed in their care. Burke Brogan is clear in demonstrating how poorly educated Juliet is, especially about men, sex and sexuality: she entirely lacks confidence and is thus very vulnerable to exploitation, both by the nuns and by the men who visit the laundry. Finally we have the aptly but ironically named Mother Victoria, who ensures that everyone in the institution – not just the inmates but also the nuns – carries out her work according to the strictest possible precepts.

The laundry was just one location in Ní Ghráda's *An Triail* but most of *Eclipsed* takes place in that setting. Its story happens in 1963, but the action is framed by a narrative in 'the present' (1992), which means that audiences could not distance themselves from what they were seeing: the prologue and epilogue forced them to confront the laundries' continuing legacies. In those framing sections, we meet the child of one of the inmates, a person who had been taken from her mother as an infant and sent to America for adoption. She returns to Ireland as an adult to find out more about her parents – but, tragically, discovers that few records have been kept: she knows that her mother was a 'penitent' but learns nothing about her father except his first name. Here Burke Brogan is tackling an issue that would later come to international awareness in Stephen Frears' Oscar-nominated film *Philomena* (2013) – which is how institutions like the Magdalene laundries sold children that had been born there to wealthy families in America and Britain. She's also highlighting the misogyny upon which those institutions were founded, the hypocrisy that led to the imprisonment of women while leaving men unpunished.

Burke Brogan's aim, then, is to force her audiences to think about their own culpability, both individually and as a society. As she writes, the play aims to show that 'the nuns did not go out with grappling hooks to capture the Magdalen women. Society and the state colluded with the sisters in charge in order to rid themselves of those outcasts, those unmarried Irish mothers' (2014: 129). Carol Hunt, who played Mandy in the original production, elaborates on this point: 'In the majority of cases the women had been signed in by their own families and official Ireland didn't just collude in what was, in many cases, illegal imprisonment, it actively supported it by lending the sisters the services of the local gardaí [the police] anytime some poor soul would try to make a break for freedom' (*Irish Times*, 21 July 2017).

Hence, at the start of the play Burke Brogan has one of her characters (Nellie Nora) read from the laundry's records, where it's shown that most of the inmates were sent there by their parents, and in Nellie Nora's own case by 'her employer' (2008: 17–18) – which implies that she was made pregnant by someone she was working for, and that he evaded his responsibilities by sending her away.

Burke Brogan also challenges her audience by attributing the Church's treatment of these women to patriarchy – and it is noteworthy that the character most responsible for maintaining misogynistic power structures is not a man but Mother Victoria. She is all-powerful in the laundry but derives her authority from men: speaking of the local bishop, for instance, she declares that 'His Lordship must be looked after first. Remember, he's a Prince of the Church!' (2008: 40). Later there is a debate between Sister Virginia and Mother Victoria about Saint Paul, the man who gives his name to the laundry. This choice of name, as Virginia points out, is a supreme irony: Paul 'hated women', she says, arguing that he was unlike Christ, who 'had many women friends' (59). Virginia is calling for a Christianity that would be based on the life of Christ rather than the ideas of Paul, one that sees men and women as equal to each other. Her own journey during the play will lead her to declare that she can – and must – 'think for myself' (80), and she means that both ethically and spiritually. Hers will be a Catholicism that is not about blindly following rules but is based upon questioning, creativity and taking responsibility.

Burke Brogan also alludes to the story of Jesus in the presentation of one of her four imprisoned women. Within Christian faiths, the passion of Christ is intended to use the suffering of one figure emblematically to represent the redemption of an entire community. I've discussed earlier how that representation of suffering as redemptive informs the characterization of the priest in *The Righteous Are Bold*, with his death operating as a form of martyrdom. Here, however, it is not a member of the clergy who dies but one of the inmates – Cathy, who is smothered in a laundry basket when she attempts to escape. When Virginia learns of this death she gives the keys of the laundry to the inmates, but only one of them (Brigit) leaves, showing how the institutionalization of these women had not only taken their freedom of movement but also their confidence in themselves.

As the action concludes, the stage directions call for the playing of 'He Was Despised' from Handel's *Messiah*. This displays the parallel between the suffering of Christ and the death of Cathy. Christ, Burke Brogan shows, was 'despised', just as the Magdalene women were: he too suffered violence and imprisonment and he too lost his life. The play is therefore proposing that the character who is most like Jesus is not a bishop or a nun, but (we might almost say 'on the contrary') someone who has been imprisoned for her 'immorality'. One of Burke Brogan's most successful strategies, then, is her use of Christian values and ideas to hold the Catholic Church in Ireland to account. So *Eclipsed* must be seen as a feminist reimagining of some of the core concepts of Christianity – one that aims to tell stories that had never been told, one that forces its audiences to acknowledge truths that they had ignored for many years. But it does so within an aesthetic that is strongly influenced by Catholicism.

The play has continued to be well received internationally, becoming one of the most frequently produced Irish plays since 1990 – though it remains unproduced by any of Ireland's prominent professional theatres. *Eclipsed* must thus be seen as one of the last genuinely revolutionary Irish plays about Catholicism, telling people something that they did not know or would not acknowledge. This exemplifies how the Irish theatre – or, more frequently, individuals working within the Irish theatre (often in relative isolation) – led the way in exposing truths that would only later be acknowledged, first by the media and then by the state.

## From *Eclipsed* to ANU's *Laundry*, 2011

Five years after the premiere of *Eclipsed* another play about Catholicism would open in Galway. It would feature a self-professed 'shite priest' who commits suicide (McDonagh, 1997: 4), and included jokes about clerical child abuse and a scene in which dozens of statuettes of saints would be smashed to pieces – an act that recalls *The Righteous Are Bold*. That play was Martin McDonagh's *The Lonesome West*, appearing as part of *The Leenane Trilogy*, which was directed by Garry Hynes for her company Druid Theatre. It is a sign of how much Ireland had changed in a relatively short period that its irreverent treatment or religion went mostly unchallenged.

*Eclipsed* had been essential in bringing about that change. After its premiere, the Irish radio talk-show host Gerry Ryan had run an item about the Magdalene laundries, with former inmates calling in to recount their experiences. Originally intended to last only for one programme, it was extended to a whole week, so great was the number of women who wanted to tell their stories. The journalist Mary Raftery was also highly influential in revealing important truths: her documentary *States of Fear* and her book *Suffer the Little Children* (both 1999) provided harrowing evidence of what had been happening in Ireland's reformatories and industrial schools, something that she had been reporting on for many years. She would later draw on that material when the Abbey Theatre invited her to write a verbatim play called *No Escape* in the wake of the Ryan Report.

But the need for plays like Burke Brogan's was also evident in the ongoing treatment of Irish women. In the year of the play's premiere the family of a fourteen-year-old girl who had been raped by a neighbour sought the advice of the Irish police: the girl was suicidal and the family intended to bring her to Britain for an abortion (which was illegal in Ireland), but wondered if DNA evidence could be taken from the foetus and used to prosecute the rapist. The Irish Attorney General sought an injunction to prevent the girl from leaving the country, reasoning that the ban on abortion in Ireland entitled him to do so. A subsequent Supreme Court judgment – now known as the X-Case – overturned that decision. But, understandably, it gave rise to a divisive and bitter debate in Ireland about the right to travel, abortion and the impact of religious doctrine on legislation and human rights. The fact that the girl was treated as a criminal while her rapist remained at large displayed the way in which moral standards were applied differently according to gender, as Burke Brogan had so clearly pointed out. The self-evident inhumanity of the Irish state's actions towards the girl created further momentum towards a widening of the gap between Catholic morality and Irish law.

But the country was changing as a result of its growing openness to other cultures too. Ireland's membership of the EEC (reformulated as the European Union in 1992) had brought about important legislative change in a variety of areas, including the decriminalization of male homosexuality in 1993. That change was imposed upon Ireland from the outside (albeit that the EU was acting in response to court cases that had been taken by Irish campaigners such as David Norris). But the citizens of the country would themselves display a willingness to go against Catholic teaching when they voted in a 1995 referendum to remove the ban on divorce – though by a very narrow margin, with 50.28 per cent in favour.

Those changes were evident culturally too. In 1995, the British TV station Channel 4 began broadcasting *Father Ted*, a comedy about three priests on a remote Irish island. The star of that show, Dermot Morgan, had already demonstrated that it was possible to satirize the Irish clergy, having created a character called Father Trendy for *Scrap Saturday*, an Irish radio show that was broadcast in the early 1990s. But *Father Ted* would go considerably further than anything ever done before, directly tackling such issues as clerical celibacy in a style that was surreal, irreverent and very funny. Although produced by a British company, it was warmly and speedily embraced in Ireland, and was soon broadcast on Irish TV too.

This in turn created space for the production of plays – most of them in the form of comedy – that would seek to undermine the power of the Catholic Church by laughing at it. This had been done even as early as 1987 when Roddy Doyle's comedy *Brownbread* imagined the kidnapping of an Irish bishop. But from the late 1990s onwards those comedies became more darkly satirical in their treatment of religion. There were sometimes minor objections to those works. In 2002, for instance, I attended a rehearsed reading at the Peacock of a play by Hilary Fannin called *Doldrum Bay*, which concerns two advertising executives who are hired to devise a recruitment campaign for the Christian Brothers – an order that had been the subject of complaints of violence and sexual abuse. At a post-reading discussion with

Fannin, one audience member told her that he hoped her play would 'sink without trace' because he was offended by its plot. But despite such intolerance, Fannin's drama proceeded to a full production at the Peacock in the following year.

But there were also desperately serious accounts such as Mannix Flynn's autobiographical *James X* (2003), which not only explains what it was like to be a child in a Catholic reformatory, but also dramatizes the way in which its inmates were given no support in coping with the abuses they had experienced there. James invents a persona and history for himself in an attempt to forget the abuses that were inflicted upon him. His gradual revelation of the truth of what was done to him becomes a form of personal liberation that has national consequences.

Also hugely significant was *Laundry* by Louise Lowe and ANU Productions. This site-specific immersive performance was set in a building in Dublin's inner city that had been used as a Magdalene laundry, a location that increased the audience's understanding of what life there had been like. As with most productions by ANU, the audience were required not just to passively watch the action, but also to contribute to it. This meant that they had to interact with any inmates that they met as they walked through the building – thus obliging them to make ethical decisions about how to react to those characters. By forcing us to respond, Lowe and the actors highlighted powerfully how easy it had been for audiences to ignore the residents of the laundries in the past.

Many very difficult encounters are staged. One character reads out the names of some of the actual inmates who had been incarcerated in the building and asks the audience member/participant to remember just four of those names. Another seeks the participants' help to escape. And in another scene, the participant is asked to hold bandages that have bound the breasts of one of the inmates. Lisa Fitzpatrick recalls her experience interacting with this performer:

> Naked, she steps into the tin bath and sits, shivering. Beyond the room a baby howls and her body convulses in response. The room is full of the buckets of whitish liquid that I have been told before was breast milk. Women in the Laundries often developed mastitis but were denied medical attention. The young woman emerges from the bath and gestures to me to hold the cloth, and she winds her body until she is bound once more

> (2012: np)

The impact of this scene is made compellingly evident by the final sentence in Fitzpatrick's description: 'I do not know what to do.'

We see in such responses how the Irish theatre has consistently asked questions of its audience. Máiréad Ní Ghráda did so directly, putting her audience in the role of jury. Murphy and Parker involved their audiences in a ritual, seeing theatre as a form of communion that could be transformative in secular contexts. And Patricia Burke Brogan combined all of these approaches, using Christian aesthetics and values to encourage her audiences to follow the example of Sister Virginia – that is, to think for themselves.

The power of *Laundry* was its appeal to the decision-making capacity of the individual audience member. The participant who says that she does not know what to do in *Laundry* has been confronted with questions of agency, morality and community. She has, in other words, been provoked into action; she has been given what Brian Singleton calls a 'will to remember' (2016a: 52).

As I hope to have illustrated in this chapter, the journey from *The Righteous Are Bold* in 1946 to *Laundry* in 2011 is one in which a series of Irish theatre artists have sought to persuade their audiences that change is possible, that there might be other, better ways of living. But the starting point for such change must always begin with the admission of our own vulnerabilities and uncertainties.

There are important differences between all of these works, of course, including how gender determined where they were staged and how they were received. *The Evidence I Shall Give* and *The Sanctuary Lamp* were both written by men and staged at the national theatre; *Pentecost*, also written by a man, was staged by Field Day, a company that had strong national ambitions but which never produced a play by a woman. Ní Ghráda had staged many plays at the Abbey before *An Triail*, but that play would be premiered at the Damer instead, and Burke Brogan's was rejected both by the Abbey and Field Day. While Louise Lowe's ANU is now celebrated as one of the most innovative companies in the contemporary Irish theatre, it is notable that *Laundry* emerged from a then-underfunded independent company rather than the Abbey. In later chapters, we'll see more examples of these kinds of divergences in the careers of male and female theatre-makers.

But we've also seen how theatre-makers sought to use international influences in order to bring about change in Ireland. For the Pike, this meant staging the work of Tennessee Williams; for Ní Ghráda and Mac Anna, it meant using the staging style of Brecht; for Lowe, it involved drawing on the practice of companies like Punchdrunk. When Tom Murphy needed to defend *The Sanctuary Lamp* he did so by stating that he was working in an English dramatic tradition rather than the Irish one. And within both *Pentecost* and *Eclipsed* we find characters who return to Ireland from abroad, using their experiences to transform their home country. All of this exemplifies how changes like the ones outlined above were inspired and made possible by engaging with traditions outside the country. In the next chapter, I explain how that international engagement helped to transform Irish theatre.

# CHAPTER 3
## INTERNATIONALIZING IRISH THEATRE

### *Philadelphia, Here I Come!* (1964) and the 'Second Renaissance'

Many histories of Irish drama trace the beginnings of the contemporary period to the early 1960s, when a new generation of writers emerged, many of them finding success in New York and London as well as in Ireland (see for example Murray, 1999 and Roche, 2009). Tom Murphy's *A Whistle in the Dark* had premiered at Stratford East in 1961, transferring from there to the West End. Friel's *Philadelphia, Here I Come!* moved from the 1964 Dublin Theatre Festival to Broadway in 1966, where it was nominated for a Tony Award for Best Play. As we saw in Chapter 1, an adaptation of Behan's *Borstal Boy* found its way to New York in 1970, playing for a respectable 143 performances in the Lyceum. And Hugh Leonard's *Da* ran on Broadway from 1978 to 1980, winning four Tonys, including Best Play.

Those dramas explore a range of traditional Irish themes such as emigration, memory, the relationship between fathers and sons, and the place of Ireland in the wider world. But what set them apart from earlier work was their authors' commitment to formal inventiveness and, especially in the case of Murphy, to revealing unpalatable truths about Ireland's past and present. Those international successes – together with the emergence of such figures as John B. Keane and Thomas Kilroy – have led many scholars to assert that this period should be seen as representing a 'Second Renaissance' in Irish drama, one that followed the Irish dramatic revival of roughly 1897 to 1939 (see Fintan O'Toole, 2000).

As I've shown in Chapter 1, there are some unintended problems with the notion that the 1960s represented a rebirth, one of which is that the dominance of that idea has caused us to overlook important figures, events and theatres from before that time. As Lionel Pilkington points out, 'cultural commentators have become used to the idea of 1950s Ireland as a "lost decade" and as existing in negative contrast to what [followed]. That theatre history hails the 1960s for its resurgence of dramatic writing ... renders all the more compelling this view of the 1950s as culturally deprived' (2016: 286–7). Since 2000, that view has come under scrutiny – and has largely been rebutted – in books by Dean (2004), Paul Murphy (2009), Ian Walsh (2012) and indeed Pilkington himself (2010). The combined impact of that scholarship has been to demonstrate that the 1960s should be seen as representing a kind of opening up, with trends and tendencies that had already been evident being given more space to develop.

That change in Irish theatre coincided with a new openness to the outside world, especially the United States, and also what would become the European Union. The Irish government published T.K. Whitaker's *Programme for Economic Expansion* in 1958, arguing for the need to attract foreign investment into Ireland. A free-trade agreement with the UK followed in 1965, paving the way for both countries to join the EEC together eight years later. The election of John F. Kennedy as president of the United States was also a key moment for Ireland internationally, showing that the descendent of an Irish immigrant to America could rise to that country's most powerful office.

This gradual move towards economic globalization was matched by an increased openness to international culture, especially in its popular forms. The Irish TV station RTÉ was established in 1961, with the Taoiseach Sean Lemass declaring on its first broadcast that 'the Irish people are citizens of the world as well as of Ireland', and adding that 'the reasonable needs' of the population 'would not be satisfied by programmes of local origin' (qtd by Morash, 2010: 171). Consequently, programming from Britain and the United States quickly made an impact on Irish life.

Radio also had an important role in promoting pop music and the nascent celebrity culture that went along with it. In the early decades of the twentieth century, the Irish public had rioted in response to *The Playboy of the Western World* and *The Plough and the Stars*. In 1963 they rioted to the Beatles, whose two Dublin concerts in November of that year created such a frenzy that more than a dozen people had to be arrested when the Irish police lost control of the crowds that had gathered to see the band. Two years later the Rolling Stones also toured Ireland, and they had to abandon their second Dublin concert when fans stormed the stage. Such scenes were, of course, also taking place in Britain and the United States, but it can be worthwhile to think about them in the context of Irish audiences' history of riotous behaviour at public performances.

And while censorship of the cinema continued to exist – leading to the banning of such films as *Ulysses* (1968), *A Clockwork Orange* (1971) and Monty Python's *Life of Brian* (1979) – there was a gradual decline in the willingness of the censor to cut or ban movies, and that meant that Irish attitudes were more likely to be influenced by values from overseas. Similarly, the Irish government's *Censorship of Publications Act* of 1967 signalled a growing reluctance to ban books and magazines – though even in subsequent decades some publications would continue to be prohibited or restricted, especially if they dealt with contraception or abortion, or featured pornography.

The play that probably best captures the development of Irish drama in the 1960s – and the open spirit of those times more generally – is Friel's *Philadelphia, Here I Come!* In the early 1960s, Friel was best known as an author of short stories, some of which had been published in the *New Yorker*; he came to writing plays professionally at the relatively late age of thirty. His first produced play was *A Doubtful Paradise*, which opened in Belfast in 1960; it was one of the last dramas ever staged by the Group Theatre. It was followed by *The Enemy Within* (1962) at the Abbey, where it was directed by Ria Mooney and designed by Tomás Mac Anna who, as we'll see, later directed the premiere of Friel's *The Freedom of the City*. Friel's third play followed in 1963, when Phyllis Ryan staged *The Blind Mice* – and although Friel later spoke disparagingly about that play, he did allow it to be revived in Belfast in 1964, where it was well received (LTA, T4/88).

To read those early plays is to form a sense of a writer who was not only attempting to understand how dramatic action could work on stage but who was also searching for a sense of thematic direction (BF NLI, MS 37,043 /1, MS 37,046/1). Many other people in the Irish theatre had a similar sense of wanting to break free from a claustrophobic social environment by doing new things on the stage, a need memorably articulated in a 1959 article by Thomas Kilroy:

> In our search for a new Irish theatre we are probably looking for premises with a clear view from every window. Too often the view from our modern Irish windows is cluttered-up with distracting monuments to the dead and glorious past of politics and art. If we ever do come to house a creative theatre for a new generation, many of these idols will have to be demolished so that the interesting faces of modern Ireland may crowd at every window of the theatre
>
> (1959: 192)

Irish theatre, Kilroy felt, could only liberate itself from the past by opening up to new influences, especially those from abroad.

I'll discuss later how Kilroy set about realizing that ambition in his own work, but Friel showed that he was thinking along similar lines when, in 1963, he took up an invitation to spend a six-month residency at the newly opened Guthrie Theater in Minneapolis, where he observed Tyrone Guthrie at work. As he later recounted:

> I found myself ... almost totally ignorant of the mechanics of play-writing and play-production apart from an intuitive knowledge ... [At the Guthrie Theater] I learned a great deal about the iron discipline of theatre [and] these months in America gave me a sense of liberation – remember, this was my first parole from inbred, claustrophobic Ireland – and that sense of liberation conferred on me a valuable self-confidence and a necessary perspective so that the first play I wrote immediately after I came home, *Philadelphia Here I Come!*, was a lot more assured than anything I had attempted before
>
> (Delaney, 2000: 104)

Friel doesn't say so explicitly, but his time in Minneapolis also illustrates the existence of a pattern in Irish drama – which is for the creation of new Irish plays to be stimulated by dramatists' engagement with non-Irish work. The plays that Guthrie was directing during Friel's visit were Chekhov's *Three Sisters* and Shakespeare's *Hamlet* – and the influence of both can be detected in *Philadelphia*.

Friel's title captures well the antic enthusiasm of his protagonist, a young man called Gar O'Donnell who intends to emigrate from Donegal to the United States. We meet Gar in the days before his departure – though we're never completely certain that he will actually leave Ireland: the play's final lines see him being asked why he has to go, and his response is 'I don't know. I – I – I don't know' (1996: 99). His idea of America is drawn from popular cultural forms such as westerns (34) and from the stories of returning Irish immigrants (60–6). So the Philadelphia of the play's title is not a real place that he experiences or that the audience encounters; it is a manifestation of Gar's hopes, fears and ambitions. In that respect, Gar's Philadelphia is not unlike the Moscow imagined by the Prozorov sisters in Chekhov's play.

Echoes of *Hamlet* can also be detected. Friel's chief innovation in *Philadelphia* is to split his character into two personae, a Public Gar and a Private Gar, who are played by different actors. Shakespeare's play is also about a young man who is in constant dialogue with himself, and there's a discernible distinction between the Hamlet who talks to the audience and the Hamlet who interacts with other people – between, that is, his public and private selves. Friel finds a new way to capture the sense of Gar's development as an individual by presenting an interior monologue between two versions of himself. Like Shakespeare – and like Chekhov – Friel manages to generate great drama from a situation in which someone constantly talks to himself about doing something, rather than actually doing it.

Friel's emphasis on waiting also points to a resemblance to Beckett's work. As we've seen, *Waiting for Godot* is a play in which nothing happens (twice), and *Philadelphia* also gives us a character who anticipates events that are never realized on stage. Gar imagines marriage with a local girl called Kate; he wishes for an open and honest conversation with his father; and he fantasizes about a new life in America – but none of those things happens during the play. So all he is really doing is, in Beckettian terms, passing the time: waiting for Philadelphia, or perhaps just waiting for his life to start. But in an epilogue included in the original production (and preserved in Hilton Edwards' promptbook), Gar's family housekeeper, Madge, suggests that a rather bleak future lies ahead for him:

> When the boss was his age, he was the very same as him: leppin' and eejitin' about and actin' the clown; as like as two peas ... And you'll find that when he's the age the boss is now he'll turn out just the same. [the following sentence is crossed out in the promptbook: And although I won't be here to see it, you'll find that he's learned nothin' in-between times.] That's people for you – they'd put you astray in the head [crossed out: if you thought long enough about them]. Goodnight.
>
> (GTDA, 2071_PS_0001: 82)

And with those words, the curtain came down. Here we again find an example of Irish life being symbolized in terms of a series of repetitions, and although Friel later moved this passage to a different part of the scene, it's worth being reminded that his first Irish audiences' reactions were informed by this finale.

Friel also displays a mildly Beckettian preoccupation with the theme of memory, presenting a scene in which Gar recounts a fragmentary image of seeing a blue boat with his father (1996: 83). The resemblance to the recollections of a boat trip in *Krapp's Last Tape* (Beckett, 2006: 220–1) may be coincidental, but it demonstrates how Friel and Beckett were both concerned with the way in which memory is used to construct character. In a 1967 lecture called 'Theatre of Hope and Despair', Friel would speak out against the way in which modern drama 'depicts man as lost, groping, confused, anxious, disillusioned, [and in doing so] is expressing the secret and half-formed thoughts of all our heart' (1999: 33). For Stephen Watt, these words should be seen as evidence of Friel's 'antipathy toward Beckett' (2009: 61), but although Friel disliked Beckett's bleakness, the resemblances between the two writers shouldn't be ignored (a point Watt also makes). Whether deliberate or not, such similarities demonstrate that Friel was grappling with themes that were being explored internationally in the kinds of plays that Martin Esslin would dub the 'Theatre of the Absurd'. This is not to suggest that Friel's play should be categorized in that way, but instead to show how his ideas were anything but parochial.

What is now often forgotten is that *Philadelphia, Here I Come!* was not particularly successful upon its premiere at the 1964 Dublin Theatre Festival – and, ironically in the light of the discussion above, one of the criticisms against it was that it seemed to be 'too Irish'. It was praised for its comical elements, and Friel's decision to split Gar in two was admired without being seen as notably innovative. But *Philadelphia* was also thought to be a straightforwardly Irish play. 'One wondered', wrote the *Irish Times* critic, 'why [everything] hadn't all been said years ago, and at the Abbey, which is . . . its proper place?' (29 September 1964). That question was not intended as a compliment.

In fact, the play that everyone was talking about at the 1964 DTF was Eugene McCabe's *The King of the Castle* – and as we've seen in Chapter 2, Ní Ghráda's *An Triail* was also attracting notice. In contrast with Friel's work, both were discussed in the context of how they drew on international influences: Brecht in the staging of Ní Ghráda's play, and Tennessee Williams in the composition of McCabe's. Set in rural Ireland, *The King of the Castle* presents a rigorous exploration of Irish sexuality, gender and the acquisition of land – but it also attracted controversy for its frankness about those matters. At a symposium dedicated to new Irish writing, McCabe was forced to defend himself against the accusation that his play was 'pornographic', even as he acknowledged that it was 'ugly and unlikeable'. 'It refers to basic facts and functions', he said, glumly adding that 'I would imagine that my play would have a very dampening effect on sex' (*Irish Times*, 30 September 1964).

Key figures came to his defence. Niall Montgomery, alluding to McCabe's exploration of Christianity and sex, as well as his indebtedness to Williams, described him as a 'Catholic on a hot tin roof', while Mac Liammóir said that

McCabe had made the 'terrible discovery' that 'Kathleen Ni Houlihan had legs under her skirt' – by which he meant that he had attempted to insert the sexual into the nation's conception of itself (*Irish Times*, 30 September 1964). Those remarks probably reveal more about their speakers' desire to say something witty than they do about McCabe's achievement, but both were trying to praise *The King of the Castle* for bringing a new frankness to the representation of Irish sexuality. Crucially, they attributed McCabe's candour to his exposure to international writing: not just to Williams, but also to Eugene O'Neill and Harold Pinter.

Put simply, critics of the day liked McCabe's play because they saw the international influences in it, and were less impressed by Friel's because it seemed too conventionally Irish – which is to say that its international features were less legible to them. Friel's fortunes began to shift when his play drew international attention, however. In a sign of the DTF's burgeoning reputation abroad, many London critics had come to Dublin in 1964, and Harold Hobson had praised *Philadelphia* warmly. 'It is immensely desirable that the play should be seen in London', he wrote. 'The best drama is rooted in the soil from whence it sprung and this play is all Ireland' (qtd in *Irish Times*, 5 October 1964.) Again we see a critic focusing on the Irish elements of the play, but for Hobson that was an unambiguously positive thing, because (as Tynan had done with Behan) he was imagining how Friel might contribute to the vitality of the English theatre. A British production of *Philadelphia* would indeed by staged in 1967, but in the meantime Friel's play had made its way to Broadway where, as we've seen, it was a commercial and critical success. And from then onwards, the reputation of the play and its author quickly changed within Ireland: the lukewarm reaction to its premiere was forgotten and *Philadelphia* quickly established itself as one of the best-loved of Friel's works.

This discussion illustrates that the 'international' as a concept informed the development and reception of Irish theatre at this time in at least three ways. *Philadelphia, Here I Come!* showed how Ireland was being affected by international culture, giving us a character who could at one moment dance along to an Irish ceilidh while at another listen to Mendelssohn, before copying an Al Jolson song and then quoting Edmund Burke. Other Irish dramatists (Seán O'Casey especially) had demonstrated the hybridity of Irish culture before, but what was different about Friel's play was the sense of liberation offered from 'inbred, claustrophobic Ireland' by the international.

The second way of thinking about the international relates to the fact that the turning point in Friel's early career was his engagement with work outside Ireland: not just the fact that he left the country (which was important) but also that he was exposed to productions of plays by non-Irish dramatists. Of course, he had read those plays before, but what mattered was the exposure to the live experience.

In these two conceptions, then, we see the international being imagined first in cultural terms and then spatially. The final point is that we can detect in Ireland at this time the dominance of the idea that the international had inherent value: that a play should be praised for drawing on international influences (as McCabe's *The King of the Castle* did explicitly) – but also that Friel's *Philadelphia, Here I Come!* came to be seen as a classic Irish play not because of how it fared in Dublin upon its premiere but rather because it was liked in New York. Hence we find Irish drama mirroring developments in the wider society, which after the 1958 *Whitaker Report* had abandoned the idea of economic self-sufficiency in favour of international investment. My aim in this chapter, then, is to show how those conceptions of the international should inform our understanding of Irish theatre since the 1950s, both for good and ill.

## 1956 and all that

One of the dominant narratives about British theatre is that 1956 was a turning point in that country's stage history, and for several reasons. The first was the opening of the English Stage Company at the Royal Court, and its inauguration of a series of 'angry young men' plays led by John Osborne's *Look Back in Anger*. Those works were seen as revitalizing theatre in England in terms of language (through the use of everyday speech), character (by the inclusion of people who had not previously been seen much on the English stage, such as those from working-class backgrounds), and a willingness to challenge the censorship of the Lord Chamberlain by including themes that might have been blocked on moral grounds in the past (such as infidelity, promiscuity or domestic violence). While in an era of Twitter we might feel that there are probably more than enough angry young (and old) men in the world, we can't underestimate how influential this movement was at its time, and for Ireland as well as England.

A second important development was the increased openness to international productions, one major example of which was the enthusiasm that greeted the visit in September 1956 of the Berliner Ensemble to London, where they performed *The Caucasian Chalk Circle, Mother Courage* and

*Trumpets and Drums.* But there were many other influences. As Dan Rebellato points out, 'in the early fifties, probably the most successful playwright in Britain was Jean Anouilh' (1999: 128). And the work of Cocteau, Artaud and many others also had an impact.

Irish theatre played an important part in these developments. It is highly likely that Brendan Behan's and Tom Murphy's successes in London owed something to the vogue for angry young men plays there. Take for example Kenneth Tynan's review of *A Whistle in the Dark* in 1961, when he declared that although he had never met Murphy he felt sure that he was 'the kind of playwright one would hate to meet in a dark theatre.... Something whispers that he might unnerve me' (qtd by O'Toole, 1994: 9). But another Tynan remark is also relevant here: the one quoted in Chapter 1 about how the 'sacred duty' of Irish dramatists was to reinvigorate the English theatre every generation. In making that quip Tynan was putting forward the serious point that national traditions are regenerated by bringing in work from other cultures. And while Irish drama was not perceived as 'foreign' in London in the way that was true of Brecht's theatre, English theatre at this time displayed a willingness to look for new ideas from outside its own borders and traditions.

It needs to be understood that developments in London had an influence on the Irish theatre too – not just because many Irish writers and actors worked in London, but also due to the circulation of ideas about theatre in newspapers and journals that were read on both islands. Irish practitioners travelled to England to encounter new work – but new British theatre also toured or was produced in the country. Peter Brook first travelled to Ireland in 1957, for example, bringing Dürrenmatt's *The Visit* to Dublin – and while audiences did not display huge enthusiasm for his work, it was still seen (see Brook, 1988: 36). But Osborne's *Look Back in Anger* was as popular in Dublin as it had been in London, playing in Ireland three times between 1958 and 1960.

Even at the Abbey, Ernest Blythe showed himself willing to set aside his usual antipathy to the staging of international work in English when he permitted a production of *Long Day's Journey Into Night* by Eugene O'Neill in 1959. During the 1920s, O'Neill had been seen by Yeats as part of the Irish tradition, and in 1932 he and Shaw had included O'Neill in their Irish Academy of Letters. That sense of inclusivity was reflected in the Abbey's programming: they staged six of O'Neill's plays between 1926 and 1934, including *The Emperor Jones, Anna Christie* and *The Hairy Ape.* But his work had been banished during the years of Blythe, which meant that the theatre's decision to stage *Long Day's Journey* – presenting one of the first English-language performances of that play – was all the more surprising. As Vincent Dowling, who played Edmund in that production, concedes, Blythe's willingness was based on an underestimation of the play: 'We heard that he had informed the Board of Directors that as the new [John] McCann Play, *I Know Where I'm Going*, was clearly in for a long run, and as there were only five in the O'Neill cast, we could be spared to do this "harmless rubbish"' (Dowling, 2001: 204). The regular Abbey audiences seemed to agree, flocking to nine separate productions of the McCann play between 1959 and 1964. But despite all of that, the Abbey did produce *Long Day's Journey* and then revived it in 1962. This would be one of the first signs of its re-engagement with international drama.

Having said that, the perception that the Abbey staged no foreign work during Blythe's years overlooks the importance of translations into Irish of European plays during the 1940s and 1950s. These included versions of plays by Henri Ghéon, Erckmann-Chatrian, Jacinto Benavente, Pierre Jalabert, Harold Brighouse and François Coppée. One of Tomás Mac Anna's first jobs as director at the Abbey was in an Irish translation of Chekhov's *The Proposal*, which was renamed *Cursaí Cleamhnais* by its adaptor Muiris Ó Catháin (ATDA, 2056_PS_0001: 10). Premiering in 1947, it was performed alongside a production of George Shiels' *New Gossoon*, while its revivals in 1950 and 1956 saw it being paired with popular plays by Louis D'Alton and Lennox Robinson respectively. In all of those cases, we find Blythe supporting Irish translations of international plays by pairing them with plays that seemed likely to draw an audience. That willingness might have been begrudging – if there had been suitable original plays in Irish, Blythe would undoubtedly have put them on instead. But they were staged and so they need to be remembered.

The theatre most strongly associated with staging international work in Ireland was then – and remains to this day – the Gate, which was founded in 1928 by Hilton Edwards and Micheál Mac Liammóir. Referring to the fact that Edwards and Mac Liammóir were partners both in life and in the theatre – as well as the Abbey's predisposition to stage hokey peasant dramas – a joke soon emerged that the Gate and Abbey should be seen as 'Sodom and Begorrah' respectively. But while such remarks also suggested a distinction between the internationalist Gate and the nationally focused Abbey, in reality the differences were more subtle. The Gate saw itself from its inception as having a national remit, one that certainly involved producing original Irish drama; especially in its first decade, the Gate discovered and staged new plays by many Irish writers including Denis Johnston, Mary Manning and Christine Longford. But it also held the conviction that a truly national theatre should engage with non-Irish work, both as a way of developing the craft of Irish theatre artists and enriching the experience of Irish audiences. The national and international were not seen as mutually exclusive categories at the Gate.

Edwards and Mac Liammóir had kept faith with their ethos, but by the early 1950s their company was in need of rejuvenation. With the end of the Second World War, the duo therefore increased their engagement with new international playwriting and stagecraft. In 1950, only a year after its New York premiere, they staged Miller's *Death of a Salesman* in Dublin, for example. They had intended that the role of Willy Loman would be played by Orson Welles, whom Edwards and Mac Liammóir had known since 1931 when they had given him his stage debut at the Gate. Welles had to withdraw from that production at short notice but did return to Ireland in 1959 when he conceived *Chimes at Midnight* with the assistance of Edwards, staging it in Dublin and Belfast during the following year (see Callow, 2015: 287–311). A reimagining of Shakespeare's Henriad, *Chimes* presented Welles in the role of Falstaff – which, as the 1965 film of the same name demonstrates, was one of his great performances. Irish audiences had the privilege of first seeing that performance on stage, and it was so well received that it prompted the *Irish Times* critic to remark, rather wistfully, that 'Schoolchildren in Ireland now abed will boast of seeing [*Chimes at Midnight*], I hope, when Elvis is long forgotten' (1 March 1960).

Mac Liammóir's career took on a new energy in the 1960s due to the international success of his *The Importance of Being Oscar*, a celebration of the life and work of Wilde. But for Edwards, the most important source of inspiration during this period was the production of Brecht's work in London in 1956. This inspired him to try new things: as we've seen, he staged Brecht's *Saint Joan of the Stockyards* in 1961 with McKenna, but he had also produced *Mother Courage* in 1959. He was also encouraged to write what would become one of the best books of Irish theatre criticism from this (or any other) era, *Mantle of Harlequin* (1958). In it, Edwards declared that twentieth-century theatre had reached a stalemate: 'it has been subjected to too many influences alien to itself. It has suffered loss of identity by confusion with similar forms of entertainment and a too intense preoccupation with realism.' He went on to outline his difficulties with finding writers who have a knowledge of stagecraft, with reconciling theatricality with realism, and with the limitations of scenic design. But he had a solution: 'The more I learn about Berthold Brecht the more I feel his may be the influence that could lead us out of the wilderness'. Brecht's strength, he felt, was that he evolved a type of theatre that could not be confused with any other form of dramatic expression, an austere beauty that he suggested Yeats would have approved of (1958: 129).

These remarks show that Edwards had understood Brecht's objectives as a dramatist and director, but they also help to explain his subsequent decisions about producing new Irish plays. As Anthony Roche explains, Tyrone Guthrie was first offered the chance to direct *Philadelphia, Here I Come!* but he passed on it (2011: 149). Edwards, however, agreed enthusiastically. As Friel would later write, 'I like to think I came into [Edwards and Mac Liammóir's] lives at a point when they were ready for something new. I know they came into my life at a point when their practical skill and their vast experience and their scholarship were of most value to me' (Luke, 1978: 21). Friel's play repeatedly draws attention to its artificiality and theatricality; it finds a way to reconcile the demands of realism with a commitment to a most playful form of stagecraft. *Philadelphia* is not a Brechtian play, but Edwards' engagement with Brecht explains why he was so keen to direct it: Friel was the 'something new' that would allow Edwards to explore these new ideas.

As the contemporary period began to take shape from the 1960s onwards, we find Irish theatre-makers looking to the outside world. The Dublin Theatre Festival had established the principle that Irish work is best seen when staged alongside international work (and vice versa). The Gate and the Abbey were regenerating themselves. And throughout the island, we find people looking abroad for new ideas: to Beckett in Paris, to Tennessee Williams and Miller in the United States, to Brecht (via London), to Osborne and the Royal Court. And we find international artists performing in Ireland too: Brook, Vilar, Welles and many others. Far from diluting Irish theatre, those engagements helped to give it new energy and direction. And this would become most evident at the newly rebuilt and reopened Abbey Theatre from 1966 onwards.

## Towards a Brechtian Irish theatre: Tomás Mac Anna, Murphy and Friel

From the mid-1960s, the influence of Brecht would become more evident in Irish playwriting and directing. As we saw in Chapter 2, the impact of Ní Ghráda's *An Triail* was heightened by the style of direction employed by

Tomás Mac Anna. That allowed him to emphasize important features: Ní Ghráda's use of an episodic structure, for example, together with her metatheatrical estranging effects such as direct address of the audience. And the play deliberately demands not only that its audience thinks but also that it acts: it is an exercise in forcing decision-making upon an audience. Over the subsequent decade, Mac Anna would have opportunities to bring this style of direction to two other major new Irish plays, Tom Murphy's 1968 *Famine* and Friel's 1973 *The Freedom of the City*.

Mac Anna's interest in staging international drama dominated his career, such that when he died in 2011 Fintan O'Toole described him as the 'Gorbachev of Irish Theatre', as a 'crucial figure in Ireland's cultural glasnost, opening the Abbey up both to European theatre and to the energies of a new generation of playwrights, actors and directors' (*Irish Times*, 19 May 2011). This had been evident from the beginning of his career when, as we've seen, he directed an Irish-language production of Chekhov. By 1965 he was ready to stage Brecht at the Abbey – which was still under the control of Ernest Blythe and still at the Queen's, though it would move to its rebuilt premises during the following year.

The theatre's decision to present Brecht for the first time is impressive in the context not only of Blythe's attitude to international work but also in relation to Brecht's left-wing politics. The Cold War was well underway at that time and, although Ireland was militarily neutral, the Catholic Church was fervently anti-communist – so much so that in 1952 Archbishop McQuaid successfully brought about the cancellation of a proposed international football match between (Catholic) Ireland and (Communist) Yugoslavia. Brecht's politics had for similar reasons drawn some negative attention, prompting one letter-writer to *The Irish Times* to draw a parallel between the treatment of Galileo by the Church and Brecht's capitulation when the government of East Germany insisted that he rewrite parts of *The Threepenny Opera*: 'This may not be a classic example of what is known as alienating one's audience,' observed the correspondent snidely, 'but it must be of interest in any comparison of Brecht's theories with his practice' (19 September 1956). In that same newspaper, Desmond Fennell dedicated several columns during the 1950s to arguing that Brecht's communism could be disregarded because his ideas about theatre were so important; the fact that Fennell kept returning to that theme demonstrates that he wasn't agreed with universally. Staging Brecht at the Gate was permissible given that theatre's commitment to the avant-garde. And Brecht himself had visited Ireland in 1953 when he attended the congress of PEN in Dublin (see

Brady, 2017: 128). But putting him on the stage of the national theatre was another matter.

Of further importance was the choice of play. Brecht's *Life of Galileo* presents the Catholic Church in a most unflattering light, as an institution more dedicated to preserving its power than responding to evidence; Galileo's submission to the Church's threats shows what happens when religious faith is wedded to political power. This was a potentially risky theme for Ireland in the 1960s, a country that was beginning to enjoy some economic prosperity but which was also wondering how many of its traditions it would need to dispense with in order to modernize fully. And, as we've seen, there were any number of Galileos in the country's Magdalene laundries and reformatories. Brecht's play could not have been more relevant, even if few people would ever have said so publicly.

In 1966, the Abbey finally opened a new theatre, designed by Michael Scott, on its former site. That building has been much disliked by actors and audiences ever since for its poor acoustics and uninviting façade. But, inspired by the new space, Mac Anna, as newly appointed 'artistic advisor', would play a major role in broadening the Abbey's approach to both Irish and international works. This included a re-engagement with Lady Gregory's plays (including an Irish-language version of her *Gaol Gate* by Ernest Blythe). But the national repertoire would be broadened to include Boucicault – whose *The Shaughraun* premiered there in January 1967 – as well as Beckett, whose work appeared there for the first time when *Play* was performed in the Peacock, also in 1967. But there were also major productions of international dramas, such as Lorca's *Yerma* (1966) and Genet's *The Maids* (1968) – plays that spoke directly to Irish attitudes to gender, reproduction and the imprisonment of women.

But in another demonstration of how international productions stimulated new developments in Ireland, one of the major new plays at the new Abbey was Tom Murphy's *Famine*, which appeared on its Peacock stage in 1968. This was Murphy's first play at the Abbey, and in his biographical note he mischievously introduced himself to his audience as having been educated by nuns, priests and brothers who 'taught me no end about celibacy' (ATDA, 2481_MPG_01: 2). But, much more seriously, Murphy also presented an essay in the show programme in which he outlined his vision for the play.

On the surface his aim might seem to have been to dramatize the period of the Great Irish Famine of 1845–50, an event that led to the death of a million people, and the emigration of at least the same number. But as he indicated in his programme note, he wanted to broaden awareness of that event both geographically and temporally:

> I found when I researched Famine that European countries had experienced similar calamities at that period. Ireland was by no means the only country that had experienced it . . . When I started to write the play I started to wonder if I was a student or a victim of the famine. It is said that it takes nine generations before the racial memory of a people is killed.
>
> (ATDA, 2481_MPG_01: 2)

His suggestion was that he – and everyone else still living in Ireland at that time – was 'suffering a hangover that had lasted over a hundred years': they might no longer lack food but they were victims of other 'poverties', including a poverty of thought. That is why the play is called *Famine* (an ongoing state) rather than *The Famine* (an event in Ireland's past). He was also keen to relate Ireland's past to the world's present:

> Continuing my research I learned that in this prosperous modern age over half the population of the world is underfed, that famine exists in several areas. And two years ago, that a high ranking member of the Indian Government could state to the press that contrary to what the rest of world believed, and much as it might disappoint us to know it, Bihar was not starving. The appalling thing is not the question of whether there is or is not famine in Bihar, but that there should be any doubt about it.
>
> (ATDA, 2481_MPG_01: 2)

Commentators of the day also made a connection between Ireland's past and the largely man-made famine in Biafra that killed two million people between 1967 and 1970. These moments of empathy and identification with two other former British colonies are examples of how Ireland found itself reflected in the outside world.

The use of programme notes was a new practice at the Abbey, having been introduced only two years previously, so it was unusual to find an author being given the space to articulate these kinds of political views. In the play itself, Murphy's focus on his characters' decision-making, together with the play's episodic structure, demonstrate how *Famine* is influenced by a Brechtian sensibility – which meant that those politics would be clearly evident to Murphy's audiences.

His primary protagonist is John Connor, the head of a family that will be destroyed as the play unfolds. The action starts with the funeral of one of John's children – a death that causes him to ask a question that is faced by so many of Murphy's protagonists, in so many of his plays: 'how am I to overcome it?' (ATDA, 4002_PS_0001: 4). Many of the world's great dramas set their characters on pathways to a tragedy that is inevitable and inescapable. But Murphy usually begins his plays after tragedy has happened: he imagines characters not as powerless victims of an indifferent fate, but as individuals whose agony gives them dignity and agency – but which also imposes upon them a responsibility to act.

So, like Brecht, Murphy shows his audience how decisions are made and forces us to consider how we might react in similar circumstances. We watch as starving villagers see their corn being taken away from them while their government fails to offer them any relief, citing the need to prop up an economic system based on free trade. Equally sobering is one character's observation that the government would be much faster in providing money if they were dealing with a military crisis rather than the starvation of the country's poorest citizens. Murphy also shows how the Irish peasantry suffer while their social superiors squabble self-interestedly, competing with each other in terms of religion, land ownership and political influence.

In an elaboration of Murphy's idea that Ireland in the 1960s remained a victim of famine, the hunger experienced by his characters is metaphorical as well as literal. We see evidence of how hunger changes John's daughter Maeve in the play's fourth scene. At its commencement, Maeve is described as a having a harshness that would be 'suited to a bitter old hag' (ATDA, 4002_PS_0001: 42), yet by eating she progressively 'becomes a sixteen-year-old girl again' (43). In staging that transformation, Murphy appears to be drawing on Gregory and Yeats' *Cathleen ni Houlihan*, in which the old woman who personifies Ireland is transformed into a beautiful young woman through the blood sacrifice of a young Irish Nationalist. But in *Famine*, the transformation is caused not by political violence but by food.

By the end of the play, John makes a decision to kill his family – not from violence but love: he gives them a speedy and thus merciful death. Murphy is causing us to look past our inherited moral precepts – beyond the edict that 'thou shalt not kill' – to show that, moment by moment, we must make our own choices, devise our own moralities. As a conclusion, this is undoubtedly bleak, but it shows that the solution to our problems will not be found from our rulers or our gods or our environment – but from ourselves. This was a new kind of play for the Abbey.

Mac Anna would be responsible for an even more provocative intervention into contemporary Irish politics in 1973, when he directed *The Freedom of the City*. *Famine* had used the past to consider the present, but Friel's play was a direct analysis of a then-recent event, the murder by members of the British Army of thirteen civilians who had been participating in a civil rights march in Derry. Dubbed Bloody Sunday, this 1972 massacre badly inflamed the situation in Northern Ireland, bringing to international prominence the conflict that became known as the Troubles.

That conflict is the subject of a longer discussion in later chapters, but it should be evident that Friel was straying into contentious territory. Looking back on the production, he would write that '*The Freedom of the City* was a more reckless play and a much more ill-considered play because it was written out of a kind of anger at the Bloody Sunday events in Derry. I don't say I regret it but I certainly wouldn't do it now' (1999: 125). Those words have sometimes been misunderstood as a repudiation, but as Anthony Roche has pointed out (2011: 84), Friel had been working on the basic scenario before Bloody Sunday – suggesting that although its production was 'reckless' it was not thoughtless.

In the play, a trio of protesters inadvertently find themselves in Derry's Guildhall when they take shelter after a civil rights march turns violent. The security forces determine (falsely) that the trio are occupying the building for political purposes, and when they emerge they are shot – executed, we should probably say. The conflict between inner and outer worlds that we'd seen in *Philadelphia, Here I Come!* is given political heft here, as Friel juxtaposes the real motivations of the protesters inside the hall with the motives attributed to them by everyone outside – from academics to news media to maudlin republican balladeers to the British legal system. This difference between interior and exterior, or private and public, is not just thematic or political; it also functions spatially on the stage, determining where characters are placed, how the set is designed and who stands where. Hence, there was something mildly subversive in Mac Anna's staging of *The Freedom of the City*, which placed the three protesters (literally) centre stage while locating those who judge them on the margins – a direct reversal of the power relations that functioned in Northern Ireland at the time of the play's premiere (as seen in the promptbook, ATDA, 4579_PS_0002).

Again, the production has a clear indebtedness to ideas that corresponded to Brechtian precepts, in that it doesn't just dramatize the situation of the

**Figure 4** *Life of Galileo*, directed by Tomás Mac Anna, Abbey Theatre, 1981 (ATDA, 0767_PH_0011.pdf). Courtesy of the Abbey Theatre Archive.

characters but also shows how their story is interpreted and appropriated by those around them. This places the audience in the position of observing the action, gathering evidence, making decisions about what has happened. And because Friel makes clear from the start that the trio will be murdered, the audience does not become immersed in the development of a plot that must reach a conclusion but is instead encouraged to focus on the course.

The importance of Mac Anna to both of these productions is that as a director he understood how to use techniques that would do justice to what each author was attempting to achieve. And he had, furthermore, helped to make audiences more receptive to them by staging *Galileo*. For his success with such works, Mac Anna would become artistic director of the Abbey Theatre in 1973, staying in that role until 1978. During that tenure he would return to Brecht, staging *Arturo Ui* in 1973 – a play that he also produced for the Lyric in 1974. But he would also use his interest in European drama to reintegrate O'Casey back into the story of the Abbey, staging many of his later expressionistic works such as *Purple Dust* in 1975, *Cock-a-Doodle Dandy* in 1977 and *The Star Turns Red* in 1978.

He would return to Brecht in 1981 upon the invitation of the recently appointed artistic director Joe Dowling, when the Abbey presented *Life of*

*Galileo* again – this time in a new version by Howard Brenton. Once again the Abbey was using a production of Brecht as a statement of intent. Brenton was at that time the subject of accusations of indecency in Britain following the production of *Romans in Britain* in 1980. Dowling's decision to stage his translation of Brecht made clear where the Abbey stood on that matter.

## 'I feel so extraordinary': Lynne Parker's Rough Magic

By starting to explore international influences from the late 1960s onwards, the Abbey was in many ways falling into line with the wider Irish theatre sector. Both the Lyric and the Gate had always had a tradition of mixing Irish with non-Irish works and, as we've seen in the example of Osborne's *Look Back in Anger*, there were regular commercial and visiting productions of plays from Britain and the United States too.

Also very influential was the last of the great Dublin small theatres, the Focus, which was established in 1967 and continued hosting performances in its tiny auditorium (a converted garage) until 2011. It emerged from a Stanislavski Studio that had been set up in 1963 by Deirdre O'Connell, an American performer who had worked with Lee Strasberg at the Actors' Studio. Under her leadership the Focus staged international plays and introduced Stanislavskian acting techniques into the Irish performance tradition. The Focus thus became the theatre where many Dublin audiences and actors first encountered Chekhov, Ibsen, Anouilh, Strindberg, Pirandello, Albee and O'Neill. But of equal importance was the fact that so many great Irish actors came through the Focus and the Stanislavski Studio, with notable examples including Tom Hickey, Gabriel Byrne and Olwen Fouéré. And in the production history of the Focus we can again find evidence of how producing international plays acts as a stimulus for new Irish writing: the Focus soon moved to producing work by Tom MacIntyre and Mary Elizabeth Burke Kennedy, among others.

The Dublin Theatre Festival also continued to stage international work, and that too fed into the development of new Irish performance styles, especially from the 1980s onwards. As Fintan O'Toole writes:

> With the visit of companies like the Wroclaw Contemporary Theatre from Poland (who came to the Festival in 1981 and 1982) you could see Irish audiences being profoundly disturbed by what they were

seeing, but profoundly engaged too. They realized that theatre could function in a largely non-verbal and physical way, using image, movement and light. This has a profound effect on audiences. I remember strongly at the time that practitioners were also talking about these developments: you could actually overhear conversations between actors and directors about how interesting these productions were. There was a real sense of a connection being made

(2008: 199)

Other influential visits included the Moscow Art Theatre with Chekhov's *The Seagull* in 1989, Footsbarn's *A Midsummer Night's Dream* in 1990, Robert Wilson's *Woyzeck* in 2001, Anne Bogart's *Radio Macbeth* in 2007, and Ontroerend Goed's *The Smile Off Your Face* in 2010 (see Grene and Lonergan, 2008; Lowe, 2013: 57–9).

International performances were also staged outside Dublin. The Galway Arts Festival was established in 1978 and has now become a leading producer of new Irish work, premiering plays by Enda Walsh, Olwen Fouéré, Conall Morrison and many others. But even it its earliest years it showed huge ambition. Robert Lepage's *The Dragon's Trilogy* – one of the key international productions of the latter half of the twentieth century – was performed in a tiny school hall in Galway in 1987. And two years before that, in 1985, the Spanish street theatre company Els Comediants brought their show *Devils* to the city, directly inspiring the foundation of Macnas, which has now become one of Europe's leading street performance companies.

Indeed, the 1980s would prove a crucial period for the deepening of the relationship between Irish and international work. That link is encapsulated by the foundation in 1984 of Rough Magic, a company led by Lynne Parker that has since gone on to present Irish premieres of work by David Hare, Caryl Churchill, Michel Tremblay, Michael Frayn, Timberlake Wertenbaker, Anne Washburn, Lucy Prebble and many others. Speaking in a 2001 interview about her company's foundation, Parker explained that 'we felt very strongly that we were of a generation whose main influences were British and American television and American film as well, and that we were definitely being influenced by other cultures' (qtd in Chambers, Fitzgibbon and Jordan, 2001: 394); staging international work was a way for them to name and explore those influences.

What was especially important about Rough Magic, however, was that they eventually sought to develop original dramas that would reflect those international influences. Their staging of Irish plays had begun with an engagement with the work of Thomas Kilroy, whose *Talbot's Box* and *Tea and Sex and Shakespeare* they revived in 1984 and 1988 respectively – with Kilroy's decision to rewrite the latter play a sign of his trust in a company that was then still very young (see Woodward, 2014: 60–2; also TKA, P103/85). But it was the English dramatist Howard Brenton who pushed them to write and stage their own plays. 'He was an idol,' the company co-founder Declan Hughes told Donald Clarke. 'And he said that we really had to start doing our own stuff. He said that is when a company really starts to come into its own' (*Irish Times*, 7 February 2004).

New work from Donal O'Kelly (*Bat the Father, Rabbit the Son*) would soon follow, but the play that is now seen as the definitive Rough Magic production was Hughes' *Digging for Fire*, which premiered in 1991. Taking its title from a song by the alternative Boston rock group the Pixies, it featured music by New Order, REM, Iggy Pop, Tom Waits and the Sex Pistols, presenting a group of twenty-something Irish people who saw themselves as citizens of a global village. They debated the merits of Brett Easton Ellis' novel *American Psycho*, discussed the differences between London and New York, and even expressed relief that pornographic magazines were banned in Ireland, since they found the experience of seeing them for sale in shops abroad so unpleasant. All of this was very new for the Irish stage – but Hughes was using familiar Irish tropes too. The emotional high point of *Digging* was a scene in which a woman dances alone, an image that seemed to nod to Friel's *Dancing at Lughnasa*, which had premiered at the Abbey the year before. And in its presentation of a group of young Irish people who grapple with emigration, loneliness and alcohol abuse, it evoked many of Tom Murphy's great dramas, with *Conversations on a Homecoming* (1985) a clear influence.

But *Digging for Fire* was also innovative in one other respect: it put on stage a group of Irish people who were like the audience watching the play – young, cosmopolitan, middle class. In the theatrical cultures of England or the United States, such characters would not have been unusual, but in Ireland it remained the case that, as Nicholas Grene observed, 'On the whole, Irish drama has continued to look to social margins for its setting, whether the western country districts or the working-class inner city. It is thus typically other people that a largely middle-class urban audience watches in an Irish play, other people who speak differently – more colloquially, more comically, more poetically' (1999: 264). Hence, as Hughes explains, 'There was an active hostility to telling these stories then, because they were about suburban, middle-class people. There seemed to be a sense that they had no right to be on stage' (*Irish Times*, 7 February 2004).

The interests and skills that Hughes displayed in 1991 are apparent in many of his later dramas – he explored the Irish middle class again in his 2003 play *Shiver*, for example, while *The Last Summer* (2012) returned to the theme of how international music could express Irish hopes and fears. But the success of *Digging for Fire* must also be attributed to the direction of Parker, who displayed in that production many of the traits that would become prominent as her career developed. Hughes' play requires the ability to keep in balance an ensemble of seven, and in the years ahead Parker would often be at her best when directing large-scale productions of plays such as *The Taming of the Shrew* (2006) or Schiller's *Don Carlos* (2007). She also demonstrated an ability to fully theatricalize the music in the play, very memorably at its conclusion which featured New Order's 'True Faith'. That song is about the feeling of intense vulnerability that adulthood brings with it: it's about the loss of childhood, the sense of freedom that comes from facing the future – but also the sense of terror that goes along with that freedom. Lyrically, it therefore speaks directly to Hughes' play. But under Parker's direction it also worked musically: defiantly percussive with a strong bass, it's a song that is assertive and energetic, wistful but never sentimental – and as such was perfectly matched to the needs of the production. As Rough Magic developed, Parker would display an exceptional sensitivity to the use of music on stage. This would be evident not only in new Irish musicals such as Arthur Riordan and Bell Helicopter's 2004 *Improbable Frequency* and Riordan and Bill Whelan's *The Train* (2015), but also in adaptations of *Phaedra* by Hillary Fannin (2010) and *Peer Gynt* by Riordan (2011), both of which included new songs that were played live on stage.

Another revolutionary feature of *Digging for Fire* was its frankness about sex. Since its inception, Rough Magic has shown itself to be the only Irish theatre company consistently willing to both laugh at and openly discuss sexuality, as evident in plays such as Christian O'Reilly's *Is This About Sex?* (2007), which considers transvestism and infidelity, and Mark Cantan's *Jezebel* (2012), which is about threesomes. Of greatest significance here is Gina Moxley's *Danti-Dan* (1995), a comedy that presented teenage female sexuality with both dignity and a sense of humour – something that had never been done on an Irish stage before. Given that Moxley's play appeared shortly after the X-Case had denied an Irish teenager permission to travel to England for an abortion, *Danti-Dan* was – like all great comedies – making a point of the utmost seriousness, in this case about the right of young Irish women to sexual agency. Because so many Irish plays hinge on the denial of sex (as evident in all of Synge and much of John B. Keane, for example),

Rough Magic's willingness to acknowledge it in all its everyday messiness has often felt very liberating. And that willingness can be attributed to the company's openness to staging international plays that were similarly frank, such as Mamet's *Sexual Perversity in Chicago* and Churchill's *Top Girls* (both 1984), or even work such as Wycherley's *The Country Wife* (1986).

So my primary argument here is that Parker's significance for Irish theatre lies in her ability to bring clarity to the relationship between Ireland and the outside world. And she has done this not just through directing but also by her decisions, as artistic director of Rough Magic, to commission plays that locate Irish life in its international contexts. One of the greatest of these is Elizabeth Kuti's *The Sugar Wife* (2005), which placed the horrors of the Irish Famine in the context of slavery in the Americas. Another is Morna Regan's *The House Keeper* (2012), which placed the 2008 financial crash in Ireland in a broader context by setting the action in New York. But on an altogether more intimate scale is Sonya Kelly's 2014 play *How to Keep an Alien* (directed by Gina Moxley), which draws on well-known Irish tropes about migration, nation and identity to tell a deeply moving love story about Kelly's attempts to prevent the deportation of her partner Kate.

All of these plays are different from each other in tone, form and content, but they share a determination to break away from any sense of Irish exceptionalism. Regan uses America as a frame to think about Irish social class and money. Kuti shows an awareness of Irish class barriers, but also seeks to find a common humanity that can overcome differences of race, gender and religion, without hiding the distinctions between those forms of identity. And Kelly's play speaks directly to matters of social justice: the rights of migrants, and the need for same-sex marriage to be legally recognized. All of these plays show that Irishness comes most clearly into focus when placed in an international context, that we can best understand ourselves not as inhabitants of an island but as citizens of the world. That is what makes them typical Rough Magic plays.

From the 1990s onwards many Irish companies would follow the example of Parker. Blue Raincoat was established in Sligo in 1991, and produces rigorous physical work that is inspired by the theories of performance devised by Jacques Copeau, Marcel Marceau and Étienne Decroux. In the same year, Pan Pan Theatre Company also emerged, and has gone on to explore a variety of international performance styles ranging from the postmodern to the postdramatic, while co-producing work in Germany, Poland and China. These were followed in 1992 by Prime Cut in Belfast, which stages both Irish and international works; in 1993 by Barabbas, which drew heavily on the ideas of Jacques Lecoq; and in 1995 by Annie Ryan's Corn Exchange, which has integrated practices from *commedia dell'arte* into the Irish repertoire.

It bears emphasizing that, without exception, all of these companies proceeded from staging international work to developing new Irish plays, many of them firmly embedded in the practices that the company specialized in. Hence we find Blue Raincoat's collaboration with Jocelyn Clarke in *Shackleton* (2015), an entirely movement-based exploration of the eponymous Anglo-Irish explorer's attempt to cross the Antarctic; Corcadorca's site-specific Enda Walsh play *The Same* (2016); Michael West's *commedia*-driven plays *Dublin by Lamplight* (2004) and *Everyday* (2006) with Corn Exchange; and Gina Moxley's postdramatic *The Crumb Trail* (2008) for Pan Pan – among a great many other examples.

## Chekhov in Ireland: Carr and Caldwell

I want to conclude by bringing the discussion into the twenty-first century, with an exploration of two approaches to the work of Chekhov: Marina Carr's 2011 loosely biographical *Sixteen Possible Glimpses*, and Lucy Caldwell's resetting of *Three Sisters* to Belfast in the 1990s, which was produced by the Lyric in 2016. My aim is to highlight the importance of these plays in their own right – but also to argue that both are responding to earlier Irish approaches to Chekhov, and in particular to how those versions highlighted issues of gender and authorship in an Irish context.

Without question, the key dramatist for an understanding of Chekhov in the modern Irish theatre is Friel, who has written versions of *Three Sisters* (1981) and *Uncle Vanya* (1997), as well as stage adaptations of Chekhov's short stories in *The Yalta Game* (2001, based on 'The Lady with the Lapdog') and *The Bear* (2002). He also wrote a short original work called *Afterplay* (2002) that imagines a meeting between Andrey from *Three Sisters* and Sonya from *Vanya*. There are also strong Chekhovian features in Friel's plays, especially *Aristocrats* (1979) and *The Home Place* (2005), both of which, in focusing on the decline of a formerly aristocratic 'big house', evoke *The Cherry Orchard*. We could also point to resemblances between the five Mundy sisters (and their eccentric brother) in Friel's *Dancing at Lughnasa* (1990) and Chekhov's Prozorov family in *Three Sisters*. Where Friel has been most influential in this context, however, is in writing about *why* he chose to stage Chekhov, and in particular his explanation for the decision to present his version of *Three Sisters* as the second production by Field Day, following their premiere of *Translations* in 1980.

As we'll see in Chapter 5, although it was set in Ireland's past, *Translations* was interpreted (and in some ways misunderstood) as a direct intervention into the Troubles, as an attempt to comment on relationships between Ireland and England in the late 1970s. For the company to move from such a theme to staging Chekhov might at first have seemed to be evidence of a lack of focus or even a loss of nerve – but it would soon become apparent that Friel's decision to create a version of Chekhov for the Irish voice and ear was in keeping with his company's aims. He was, after all, following a play about translation by writing a translation (albeit that he did so by using other English-language versions of the text rather than the Russian original), and he did so with clearly defined objectives. Working on Chekhov, he wrote:

> was a kind of act of love, but after a while I began to wonder exactly what I was doing. I think *Three Sisters* is a very important play, but I feel that the translations which we have received and inherited in some way have not much to do with the language which we speak in Ireland. I think that the versions of *Three Sisters* which we see and read in this country always seem to be redolent of either Edwardian England or the Bloomsbury set. Somehow the rhythms of these versions do not match with the rhythms of our own speech patterns, and I think that they ought to, in some way ... This is something about which I feel strongly – in some way we [in Ireland] are constantly overshadowed by the sound of [the] English language, as well as by the printed word. Maybe this does not inhibit us, but it forms us and shapes us in a way that is neither healthy nor valuable for us.
>
> (Delaney, 2000: 145)

Friel's suggestion was that Ireland had yet to stage its own version of Chekhov and, in seeking to put that to rights, he was continuing to explore the questions that *Translations* had opened up: about how language helps to define our understanding of place and identity, about the relationship between gender and power, and about how the metropolis views the periphery (and vice versa). What was important was not just that he was writing Chekhov for an Irish audience but that he was showing how that

Russian writer could offer a way for those audiences to think about themes that were of immediate local importance.

While there's no denying the importance of Field Day's *Three Sisters*, it has been so influential as to have inadvertently obscured the fact that Chekhov was an important presence on the Irish stage long before 1981 – and not just in versions that had premiered in London. Plunkett, MacDonagh and Martyn's Irish Theatre Company staged Chekhov in 1914, and while they attracted small audiences and mostly baffled reviews, one measure of their impact was that in 1916 the entertainer Percy French included a spoof of their production of *Uncle Vanya* in his revue *How Dublin Does It* (see Feeney, 1984: 104–6). His skit was called 'Gloom', and was presented as if written by an author called 'I Kan Nokemoff'; it featured characters with names like 'Tileoff' and 'Orfolkoff' (the latter name presumably intended to be rendered as 'awful cough', but the pronunciation may have slipped into a more vulgar phrase in performance). To be satirized can be seen as a kind of success, if an unwelcome one; it certainly reveals something about Chekhov's status in Dublin only twelve years after his death that French was willing to make fun of him.

But Chekhov would soon become a relatively common figure on the Irish stage. The Abbey premiered *The Proposal* in 1925, reviving it three times between then and 1936. The Dublin Drama League first staged *Three Sisters* in 1929. The Gate first presented Chekhov in its sixth season (in 1932), when they produced *The Cherry Orchard* and *The Seagull*. And, as discussed above, Tomás Mac Anna had directed Chekhov in Irish many times during the 1940s and 1950s.

A particularly significant production appeared in 1968 at the Abbey when Maria Knebel of the Moscow Art Theatre directed *The Cherry Orchard*, with Siobhán McKenna playing Ranyevskaia and Cyril Cusack playing Gayev. As Ros Dixon recounts, Knebel's aim had been to 'present an authentic image of Russia', but that didn't mean that she ignored the Irish background of the actors (2008: 78). For the Abbey company, Irish attitudes to home offered a way to identify with *The Cherry Orchard*, but the play's relevance to their country was a starting point rather than a final destination. A further visit of a Russian director to the Abbey would occur in 1978 when Vladimir Monakhov presented *Uncle Vanya* there. Chekhov was also produced eight times between 1951 and 1980 at the Lyric in Belfast; and the Focus staged *The Wedding* and *Uncle Vanya* in 1968 and 1970 respectively (NLI, MSS 44.841–44.959). In short, he was a writer who was far from unknown in Ireland before Field Day was established.

Friel's point, of course, was not that Chekhov had been *absent* from the Irish stage but that his work had been framed from an English perspective, that audiences in Ireland were seeing his work at two removes: not just from Russia but also from Standard English. But while that suggestion may have been true for readers of Chekhov's plays (who could only purchase versions from London-based publishers), it risks oversimplifying the position on the Irish stage, where Chekhov was approached from many different perspectives.

Of course, this doesn't mean that Friel's version should be discounted. He leaves the setting and plot largely unchanged, aiming to have an impact primarily in his introduction of Irish idioms. Some of these are subtle, such as Irina's statement that 'you have me crying' (2008: 23) – a Hiberno-English construction that would make sense if translated literally into Irish but which speakers of Standard English might find irregular. Friel also includes many mild religious oaths: all of the characters pepper their conversation with statements like 'Lord', 'My God' or 'I hope to God' – and while such language would probably have been considered inappropriate in Ireland at the turn of the twentieth century, it was very common in the early 1980s. There are also easily identifiably Irish pronunciations such as Ferapont's dropping of the letter *t* when he asks Irina 'Wha's tha', Miss?' (19) or his use of the word 'like' as a meaningless interjection halfway through a question to Andrei in the final act (106). But the important point here is that Friel does *not* change the setting or seek to make the play more relevant to Ireland; rather he wants to show how his use of an Irish register can allow for the play's foreignness to come more clearly into view.

That approach contrasts with that of Thomas Kilroy, who in 1981 presented a new version of *The Seagull* at the Royal Court. He had been invited to do so by that theatre's director, Max Stafford-Clark: 'the idea is the play should be cast with English and Irish actors, and instead of being set in Russia, should be set in the midst of an Anglo-Irish family', wrote Stafford-Clark, adding that this was a 'crude outline' and that he was happy to consider alternatives to it (TKA, P103/115).

What Kilroy came up with was a play set in an Irish Big House – not unlike Lady Gregory's Coole Park – at the turn of the twentieth century. Constantine's name was unchanged, but his mother, Arkadina, became Isobel Desmond, a darling of the London stage and an Anglo-Irish landlord – a surprising but not improbable combination. Mr Aston – played in the 1981 production by Alan Rickman – was the name given to the Trigorin character; Nina became Lily (who was played by Harriet Walter), and most of the other characters' names were similarly altered. The plot was relatively unchanged but there were minor variations due to the Irish setting. For example, Constantine's disastrous first play was presented as a typical example of 'Celtic Twilight' drama such as Yeats was writing in the 1890s – a contrivance on Kilroy's part that displays the links between Irish national drama and European expressionism.

But the change of setting also brought new affinities into view. By having the Trigorin character become an Englishman who seduces a young Irish girl, Kilroy was presenting Aston in the tradition of Englishmen who fall for Irish women – which, as we saw in the discussion of *The Hostage* in Chapter 2, is a very familiar Irish trope. Similarly, he was working with the Irish 'Big House' genre, a group of plays and novels that chart the decline of the Anglo-Irish aristocracy, as they grumble about their distance from the metropolis of London and alternate between bemusement and hostility in their dealings with the local peasantry. Suddenly Chekhov seemed to occupy a position in a tradition occupied by writers such as Maria Edgeworth, Elizabeth Bowen, Lennox Robinson, Molly Keane and others.

But the political features of *The Seagull* also became more visible. Both Ireland and Russia had been dominated by questions of land ownership at the end of the nineteenth century. Ireland had experienced a revolution in 1916 and so did Russia in 1917 – but the fate of each country deviated thereafter. Where Friel had made Chekhov's foreignness more evident, Kilroy showed how his Russia had much in common with Ireland.

As Catherine Rees points out, the period from the 1980s onwards was marked by a 'proliferation of adaptations' of European classics in Ireland (2017: 27); most critics attribute that to Friel's *Three Sisters*, but Kilroy's importance should also be remembered. In addition to his work on Chekhov, Friel would adapt two works by Turgenev (*Fathers and Sons* for the Royal National Theatre in 1987 and *A Month in the Country* at the Gate in 1992), and the last of his works to be premiered during his lifetime was Ibsen's *Hedda Gabler* at the Gate in 2008. Frank McGuinness would adapt more than twenty international plays for Irish theatres, notable highlights including his own adaptation of *Three Sisters* for the Gate in 1990; a version of *A Doll's House* (1996) that transferred to Broadway; Ramón del Valle-Inclán's *Barbaric Comedies* for the Edinburgh Festival and the Abbey in 2000; and most of the major ancient Greek tragedies, as well as works by Racine, Lorca, Strindberg, Pirandello, Brecht and Ostrovsky. Kilroy would write a version of *Ghosts* in 1989 and of *Six Characters in Search of An Author* in 1996; these were followed by an adaptation of *Spring Awakening* called *Christ Deliver Us!* in 2010. Most of Tom Murphy's adaptations were of English-language texts by writers such as Oliver Goldsmith, Synge and Liam O'Flaherty, but he too wrote a version of *The Cherry Orchard* for the Abbey in 2004. Michael West wrote a version of *The Seagull* for Corn Exchange in 1999; in 2016, it was presented in a new version co-written with Annie Ryan that changed Constantine into a young woman called Constance. There were also two postdramatic responses to the play: Loose Canon's *Anatomy of a Seagull* in 2009 and Pan Pan's *A Seagull and Other Birds* in 2014 (directed and devised by Jason Byrne and Gavin Quinn respectively). And the younger generation of male writers have also done translations: examples include Mark O'Rowe's *Hedda Gabler* (2014); Enda Walsh's version of *The Brothers Karamazov*, *Delirium*, in 2008; and Conor McPherson's versions of Strindberg (*Dance of Death*, 2012) and Kroetz (*The Nest*, 2016).

What all of those examples demonstrate is a deep and ongoing relationship between the Irish theatre and Chekhov in particular (as well as other major writers such as Ibsen), one that is worthy of a deeper investigation than I've given here. But one facet of that relationship that needs to be considered is the extent to which it is determined by gender: almost all of the playwrights mentioned above are male – and of all of the productions named above, only one was directed by a woman: Corn Exchange's *Seagull*, which was directed by Annie Ryan. In the research I've completed for this book I have been unable to find evidence of any Irish production of any version of the works of Brecht, Pirandello or Strindberg written by a woman. Marie Jones did produce her own version of Gogol's *The Government Inspector* for DubbelJoint in 1993 – but other than that, I could find no comparable examples. Belinda McKeon and Annie Ryan co-wrote a version of Ibsen's *A Doll's House* called *Nora* in 2017, but otherwise is no adaptation of Ibsen by an Irish woman on record. This is the necessary context, then, to explain the production and, perhaps more importantly, the reception of Carr's *Sixteen Possible Glimpses* and Caldwell's *Three Sisters*.

Carr's play premiered in 2011 and provided – as the title suggests – a series of imagined 'glimpses' into the life (and death) of Chekhov. Running across fourteen scenes, the action is presented out of chronological sequence, allowing for our impressions to accumulate, rather than building towards a straightforwardly biographical account of Carr's subject. We see how Chekhov's sister, Masha, argues with Olga Knipper about his welfare; we watch as he discusses with Tolstoy the banalities of writing; we contemplate his relationships with other family members and friends; and finally we witness the last moments of his life. On the page, it is a formally inventive and moving exploration of Carr's longest-held preoccupations. These include questions about how we might escape from our origins (whether social or biological), something she's written about in *By the Bog of Cats* (1998), *On Raftery's Hill* (2000) and *Ariel* (2002). There are links too with *The Mai* (1994), *Woman and Scarecrow* (2006) and *Marble* (2009) in her consideration of the place of love in marriage (and the occasional incompatibility of the two). And Chekhov's determination to face death with courage and defiance is matched in *Portia Coughlan* (1995) as well as in *Woman and Scarecrow*, whose primary protagonist follows Chekhov's example by deciding to greet death with champagne.

However, the premiere production was – perhaps surprisingly – unsuccessful when it appeared on the Abbey's Peacock stage for the 2011 Dublin Theatre Festival. While reviewers admired the acting (especially by Patrick O'Kane as Chekhov), there was evidence of mild hostility to the style of direction employed by Wayne Jordan, who included live video projections that were seen both as a distraction and as producing an effect that was excessively similar to the style of Katie Mitchell (whose *The Waves* had visited Dublin only four years earlier). Carr's use of a supernatural figure called the Black Monk was also criticized for being derivative – though reviewers seemed unaware that she was appropriating that figure from Chekhov's 1894 short story of the same name. But the primary criticism seemed to be that the play had failed to match audiences' expectations of what a Carr play should be and do. Almost without exception, reviewers described it not as a development of her earlier work, but as a departure from it, and especially her quartet of midlands plays that had appeared between 1994 and 2000. 'When Irish writers adapt the work of Anton Chekhov, they are not simply measuring one sad, eccentric culture against another, they are measuring themselves against a master', began an *Irish Times* review that awarded the play two stars out of a possible five (7 October 2011). The implication was that Carr didn't measure up, that she had not achieved mastery of the form.

To be fair to that reviewer and to Carr herself, she had only ever claimed to have been inspired by Chekhov. '*Sixteen Possible Glimpses* is an attempt to capture, imagine and riff on those fleeting moments that make up his life and work', she wrote. 'He has been an enormous influence on me as he has on many writers before me and no doubt on many to come' (2015: ix). Nevertheless, it's notable that the male Irish authors who had been producing versions of Chekhov for more than thirty years by this time had never been questioned about their entitlement to take on the works of such a 'master'.

Carr's play can be admired for the courage it displays in asserting the strongest possible identification between the two playwrights. Her use of dialogue is defiantly Irish and contemporary, much closer to how she herself might speak. Her Chekhov uses the Irish convention of referring to family members not with personal pronouns but with the definite article: not 'my brother' but 'the brother' (Carr, 2015: 11). Characters 'clap eyes' on each other (20); Chekhov says that 'the fuckin' country's falling down with ice' (21), is accused of 'riding half of Moscow' (20), complains that people are 'taking the complete piss out of me' (27) and describes the countryside as 'the sticks' (63). In its colloquialism and its crudity, Carr's language becomes an assertion of her own authorial control over the material: this is not Chekhov as he was but Chekhov as reinvented by Carr.

Furthermore, the play is not just a meditation upon writing but can also be seen as an attempt to map out the trajectory of Carr's own career. She gives us Chekhov at the age of forty-four, when he died. The play premiered when Carr herself was forty-six and, while not facing mortality in a literal sense, she was at that time clearly trying to break free from her reputation: from the idea that all of her plays needed to be like those bog plays from *The Mai* to *On Raftery's Hill*. She had announced that intention with *Woman and Scarecrow*, a play that (as I discuss in the next chapter) attempts to kill off at least one iconic female figure, and in doing so marks a definite point of rupture from what had come before (notwithstanding the thematic coherence of her *oeuvre* in its entirety). The relationship between death and writing was also a feature of *The Cordelia Dream*, her 2008 meditation on *King Lear* and the Oedipal relationship between playwrights and their artistic father figures. And in 2009 she produced *Marble*, a play that made the case that dreams are often more meaningful than reality – and in doing so seemed to suggest that she wanted to move away from the grimly realistic plays that had brought her success in the 1990s.

*Sixteen Possible Glimpses* needs to be seen in these contexts and, I would suggest, was unsuccessful partly because audiences may not have been willing to face it on its own terms. In seeing herself in Chekhov – as she had seen herself in Shakespeare in *The Cordelia Dream* – Carr was expressing her right to define the contours of her own career: even in her use of a non-linear form to imagine Chekhov's life, she resists the idea of the writing career as teleological in favour of a more Beckettian pattern of 'failing better' through multiple attempts at the same thing. For Carr, writing Chekhov becomes a way for her to write herself.

In becoming the first woman to have a solo-authored new version of Chekhov staged in Ireland, Lucy Caldwell encountered many of the problems that had greeted Carr, especially in relation to media response:

> My *Three Sisters* garnered the whole gamut of reviews: the raves tended to be from younger critics, especially those immersed in the world of theatre and familiar with the work of Chekhov. Those from the Belfast-based critics were often of a shamefully low standard; the worst of them streaked with a viciousness and vindictiveness that should have no place in arts criticism.
>
> (Caldwell, 2017: 122)

Again, a two-star *Irish Times* review provides a good example of the negative responses more broadly. 'The elegant, poetic spirit of Anton Chekhov is but a distant echo in Lucy Caldwell's new version of *Three Sisters*', it begins, before pointing out a small number of links between the new version and the original. But its first paragraph ends with a damning summation: 'There ends the comparison' (21 October 2016). The clear implication is that the bulk of the play has little to do with Chekhov, that – once again – we are dealing with a female playwright who has 'failed' to measure up to 'the master'.

And again the negativity seems to relate to expectations rather than actual accomplishments. Caldwell's version resets the action to Belfast in the 1990s, and one of its most admirable features is her use of language that is colloquial, vivacious and often quite crude. As she explains, 'I think we misuse the term "Chekhovian language", using it as a short-hand for languid, restrained, wistful; taking our cues from the Edwardian English of the first translations, or the melancholy poetry of the 1950s versions'(2017: 118). Her version does not quite update Chekhov so much as revise our understanding of him in and through her use of Belfast English.

Caldwell's transposition to Northern Ireland sees Olga, Masha and Irina becoming Orla, Marianne and Erin; the longed-for Moscow of Chekhov's original becomes America – a place imagined not just as a geographical space but as a cultural inspiration, something that Caldwell makes clear by including references to the Velvet Underground and the Pixies, to *Star Trek* and *Little House on the Prairie*, and many other examples of American pop culture (though she is undoubtedly alluding to Friel's *Philadelphia* too). The family come from what in Northern Ireland would be called a 'mixed' background, with 'an English Catholic Dad and Ulster Protestant Mum' (Caldwell, 2016: 36); they are linked by family ties to the British Army and the Royal Ulster Constabulary, though they never express any particular affiliation to one side or the other in the Troubles. The sense of wistfulness and loss that pervades Chekhov's original is now imposed upon a five-year period leading up to the Good Friday Agreement of 1998. It's sometimes joked that a way to imagine Chekhov in an Irish context is to give *Three Sisters* the title *Waiting for Moscow*; here, Caldwell might be renaming it *Waiting for Peace*.

However, her most important change is to introduce the topic of interculturalism to the original, showing how the large number of immigrants to Northern Ireland since the beginning of the 2000s is forcing a reconsideration of the rigid distinctions between Catholic/Nationalist/Irish on the one side and Protestant/Unionist/British on the other. She does so by changing Chekhov's Natasha into a Cantonese-speaking immigrant from Hong Kong, named Siu-Jing in the script but usually called Jenny by her sisters-in-law, who can't be bothered learning how to pronounce her name properly. Caldwell contrasts the sisters' disengagement from their society with Siu-Jing's gradual development of confidence in her place there – as she masters the English language, takes control over her household (and her husband, Andy) and maps out an appropriate future for their children.

In Irish productions of the original play, Natasha is usually presented as an interloper, as someone who defies and upsets boundaries of social class and decorum, and whose ascendancy at the play's conclusion is seen as evidence of the decline of the dignified society represented by the Prozorovs. While Caldwell's script does not present her as an entirely sympathetic character, the audience is at times more likely to identify with her than with the sisters, especially when confronted with the latter's casual racism (of which there are many examples).

In the Lyric production as directed by Selina Cartmell, these characteristics were heightened not only by the performance of Shin-Fei Chen in the role of Siu-Jing but also by Caldwell's decision to include a prologue that brings that character to the front of the stage, where she directly addresses the audience (in perfect English): 'These are my sisters and this is their story', she tells us. 'It is also my story. It might not have my name on it but it is my story too' (Caldwell, 2016: 18). Rather than using Siu-Jing as a 'stranger in the house' figure (like Leslie in *The Hostage*), Caldwell calls for a more capacious understanding of what Northern Ireland might be: a place that has room not

**Figure 5** Shin-Fei Chen addressing the audience in *Three Sisters* by Lucy Caldwell, Lyric Theatre, 2015. Photograph by Steffan Hill.

only for Catholic and Protestant but also for people who identify themselves in terms of both or neither of those categories. Siu-Jing, writes Caldwell, is 'the future of the country: her mixed-race children hint at a much-needed plurality in generations to come' (2017: 118).

For Caldwell, *Three Sisters* represents an engagement with non-Irish (or, strictly speaking, non-Northern Irish) traditions in at least two senses. Her interaction with Chekhov becomes a way for her to say something new, not only about his great play but also about Northern Ireland today. But she also uses the metaphor of the 'foreign' in the figure of Siu-Jing to demonstrate the need for openness to new influences, new people and new definitions of what identity might mean in Northern Ireland today.

These productions by Carr and Caldwell demonstrate that Chekhov remains an important presence in the Irish theatre – but that there are gendered assumptions about how his work should be seen, produced and appropriated that these two writers have finally begun to break down. This is not to suggest that any negative criticisms against these pieces were motivated by misogyny, but rather to point to the apparent existence of a set of expectations about how non-Irish work can and should be staged. We'll return to this topic in the next chapter.

## Conclusion

It's often been stated in histories of Irish drama that many of the country's greatest plays involve a creative interaction between a dynamic outsider and a static Irish community – whether that is Christy Mahon in Synge's *The Playboy of the Western World* in 1907, Valerie in McPherson's *The Weir* ninety years later, or the Czech immigrant to Dublin who transforms the life of a Dublin busker in Enda Walsh's stage adaptation of the movie *Once* (2012). My argument in this chapter has been that the same kind of relationship is evident in the history of Irish theatre's engagement with non-Irish work, and not just since 1950. If we want to understand why there were great Irish plays in the 1960s, we can point to the important international plays that were produced in the country in the 1950s; if we want to understand why there were so many new Irish playwrights in the 1990s, we must look at the emergence of companies such as Rough Magic in the 1980s, showing that by bringing such writers as Churchill, Hare and Mamet to Irish audiences, they were laying the foundation for new Irish work.

What this points to is a suggestion that the meanings of the term 'Irish theatre' must be expanded. That phrase shouldn't just refer to plays that are written or devised by Irish people, but must also include plays that are staged in Ireland, regardless of their national origins. This is not to flatten out the differences between Irish and non-Irish works but, on the contrary, to start talking about the importance of those differences.

That observation in turn directs us to questions of how we think about our theatre histories. What I've tried to sketch here is a sense in which successive generations have had to discover great international works as if no one in Ireland had done so before. One of the positive characteristics of Irish theatre is its willingness to be assimilative: to take ideas that originate with figures such as Brecht and to use them until they seem characteristically Irish. But one of its negative characteristics is that those original inspirations are so often forgotten. The modern Irish theatre has never fully disengaged from European and American influences, and has sometimes looked further afield. This needs to be understood and celebrated.

My final point leads to the next chapter. There is a need to think more about what we mean when we consider authorship and the canon. How do we make space in our understanding of Irish theatre for the possibility that a list of the most important playwrights of this period must include Brecht, Tennessee Williams and Chekhov (among others)? And how can we expand our understanding of authorial creativity beyond the act of playwriting, so as to give credit for the interventions of directors such as Hilton Edwards, Tomás Mac Anna, Deirdre O'Connell, Joe Dowling, Lynne Parker and Selina Cartmell, all of whom have 'authored' Irish theatre through their decisions about what to stage and how to stage it? And finally, is the term 'Irish theatre' fit for purpose when we've seen how it can obscure important distinctions of race, gender, identity and the differences between Northern Ireland and the Republic? These are the questions that inform the next chapter.

# CHAPTER 4
## REPEAT AND REVISE – RECYCLING IRISH IMAGES, NARRATIVES AND TROPES

This book has suggested that a defining characteristic of Irish theatre since 1950 is the routine repetition of tropes, ideas and themes, such that the country's drama often moves cyclically rather than teleologically. Those repetitions partly arise because of historiography, because earlier innovations are forgotten or were unrecorded, which means that problems have to be addressed recurrently or battles must repeatedly be fought as if for the first time. But they also arise because, far from being a sign of stasis, repetition in the Irish theatre has, perhaps paradoxically, engendered enormous creative advances.

My aim in this chapter is to refine this discussion by suggesting that these patterns of repetition and revision provide evidence of a determination on the part of writers, actors and directors to rewrite and reimagine images, tropes, symbols and narratives from the Irish tradition. In the sections that follow, I want to give a loosely chronological (if often overlapping) account of how theatre artists have set out to revise our understanding of canonical Irish figures such as Joyce, Synge and O'Casey, while also renewing our understanding of other forms of culture and performance. Those revisions, I will suggest, have been presented to allow us to imagine ways of acknowledging and performing identities that had hitherto been neglected or misunderstood.

Much of what I discuss involves considering how Irish theatre has been reimagined from feminist perspectives – whether through Garry Hynes' work on canonical Irish dramatists, Christina Reid's use of feminism to critique the Troubles, or Marina Carr's appropriation of iconic female figures from the male-dominated canon. However, acts of revision have also been carried out for other reasons, by male and female authors. My intention in choosing to explore a gendered perspective in the present chapter, however, is to assert the centrality of feminist theatre-making to the development of the Irish tradition since 1950, and to show how the innovations of figures such as Garry Hynes have created space for new ways of writing plays and making theatre. For that reason, I conclude the chapter by discussing how the career of Martin McDonagh can be understood in the context of what has come before – so that although his work would not usually be seen in the context of feminist theatre histories, my suggestion is that it would not have been produced without the prior work of feminist artists. I make this argument as being important in its own right, but I want it also to stand as an example of how change happens in Irish theatre – something I develop further in Chapter 5.

## Rewriting James Joyce, 1961–2014

In Chapter 3 I drew attention to an apparent difference in the responses that greeted male and female authors when they adapted or wrote about Chekhov. Before making assumptions about the cause of that difference, we do need to clear away some potential objections. Couldn't it be argued that Carr's and Caldwell's plays were less well received than Friel's and Kilroy's not because of gender but because of other factors? Mightn't Friel's and Kilroy's versions just have been better? Does the acting or direction of the productions need to be taken into account? And what does it matter if a handful of reviewers made some throwaway comments when audiences went to the plays anyway?

Certainly, such questions deserve more detailed answers than are possible here, but one response might be to consider some statistics. The Irish Playography is an online database of every Irish play produced since 1904 – and thus it can allow for a detailed analysis of how gender affects (and perhaps even determines) what is produced. In my earlier work *Theatre and Globalization*, I used those records to show that for every year between 1990 and 2005 the proportion of new plays produced by women in Ireland was usually somewhere between a quarter and a third (2009: 29). More recently, Brenda Donohue and colleagues' *Gender Counts* report (2017) showed that women writers made up only 28 per cent of the people employed in creative roles by the ten highest-funded theatre companies in the Republic of Ireland between 2005 and 2016. The Playography shows that those patterns have been evident for decades: while there are occasional variations, plays by women have usually made up somewhere between 20 and 35 per cent annually of all new works in Ireland since 1950, averaging at slightly more than a quarter of the total. The proportion of adaptations written by women is lower again. For the period 1950–2016, the Playography lists a total of 396 English-language adaptations or translations. Of those, only eighty-one are by women: roughly 20 per cent of the total. Fifteen of those plays are co-authored, in twelve cases with male authors. This means that single-authored adaptations by women are rare indeed, averaging at less than one per year.

Also noticeable are the kinds of adaptations that female authors have been commissioned to write or, in many cases, have produced themselves. Almost half of the eighty-one adaptations are of novels or short stories, often of classics such as Hardy's *Mayor of Casterbridge*, Eliot's *Silas Marner*, Austen's *Emma* and Emily Bronte's *Wuthering Heights* – all of which were adapted for the stage by Mary Elizabeth Burke Kennedy, and all of which were on the Irish secondary school syllabus at the times of their production. The director Judy Hegarty Lovett appears on the list six times for her work in staging Beckett's fiction with her husband Conor Lovett and their company Gare St Lazarre: notable productions include *Molloy*, *Malone Dies* and *The End*; the duo also staged Melville's *Moby Dick*. Jennifer Johnston, Edna O'Brien and Cecilia Ahern have adapted their own novels for the stage. And we also find Caldwell's *Three Sisters*, adaptations of Lorca's *Yerma* by Lynne Parker and Ursula Rani Sarma, and Carr's *Phaedra Backwards* and *Hecuba* – but there are otherwise few examples of women writers producing adaptations of European classics. Furthermore, in the list of plays just given it is notable that Parker's and Caldwell's plays were staged in Belfast, Carr's *Hecuba* and Rani Sarma's *Yerma* in England, and Carr's *Phaedra Backwards* in Princeton – showing how such work happens mainly when writers are commissioned by theatres outside the Republc of Ireland.

These figures support the suggestion that women dramatists appear to face barriers when they adapt works by prominent male authors. Something similar can be said of Irish theatres' willingness to hire female directors for plays by major world dramatists. The Abbey, for example, staged or hosted twenty-seven productions of Shakespeare between 1970 and 2016. Of those, only one was directed by a woman, Selina Cartmell, who presented *King Lear* in 2013 – and this despite the fact that Cartmell had directed *Macbeth* and *Titus Andronicus* for her own company, Siren Productions, winning the Irish Times Theatre Award for best director in 2006 for the latter. Meanwhile, at the Gate Theatre during Michael Colgan's tenure (1983–2017), there were five Shakespeare productions: all were directed by men. Yet in other contexts, both of those theatres engaged readily with female directors such as Ria Mooney, Garry Hynes, Lynne Parker, Cartmell and many others. The accumulation of evidence is such as to suggest that these patterns can't arise from coincidence, but that there are underlying biases, presumably unconscious, that merit further exploration.

But there is one exception – and because it stands out, it helps to explain the broader problem. Since the 1950s, a series of Irish women have written, staged or performed in adaptations of the works of James Joyce, a writer who – certainly in an Irish context – is rivalled only by Shakespeare in terms of his status as a canonical figure. The pattern begins with Mary Manning, a playwright whose first works were produced by the Gate in the 1930s, and whose *Youth's the Season?* (1932) is an unjustly neglected tragicomedy about Dublin's bright young things. She also edited the Gate's magazine, *Motley*, using it to formulate many of that theatre's ideas about the relationship between national and international plays. And from there, her career expanded rapidly: she was the screenwriter of a 1935 adaptation of Frank O'Connor's *Guests of the Nation* (directed by Denis Johnston), and wrote a well-received novel called *Mount Venus*, published in 1938. However, as Cathy Leeney explains, 'in common with many women writers, [Manning's] career was interrupted by motherhood,' a challenge compounded by her emigration to the United States in 1935 (2010: 131). Those developments led to a hiatus in Manning's writing career – one that stretched well into the post-war years: 'it was not until the 1950s that she entered a new phase of creativity,' writes Leeney (ibid.). Manning produced a novel called *Lovely People* in 1950, and founded the Poets' Theatre in Cambridge, Massachusetts in the same period.

For that theatre, Manning adapted passages from Joyce's *Finnegans Wake* in a version called *The Voice of Shem*; it premiered in the United States in 1955, was staged in London in 1958, and made it to Dublin in 1961, where (Leeney writes) 'it was the hit of the Dublin Theatre Festival' (2010: 130). As we've seen, the Theatre Festival had been 'postponed' only three years earlier when Archbishop McQuaid objected to its inclusion of an adaptation of *Ulysses*. In such a context, the production of any adaptation of Joyce was far from being a neutral act: Manning was asserting the need for Joyce to be seen and heard in Dublin, but she was also asserting her own need and right to stage work in that city too. It was a brave thing to do.

That sense of determination is also evident in the script. While named for one of Joyce's male characters, Manning's play is keenly interested in the figure of Anna Livia Plurabelle, and it concludes with one of her long speeches. As Manning advised, the speech 'must not be acted; it must flow simply and inevitably as the river "old tird and wary" flows out to the sea' (1957: 71). We might see that instruction as evidence of fidelity to Joyce's original text, but the fact that Manning was giving such instruction was a demonstration of her own authorship as well.

*The Voice of Shem* cleared a path for other approaches to Joyce, many of them written, directed or produced by women. Phyllis Ryan's Gemini Productions brought Hugh Leonard's *Stephen D* (an adaptation of Joyce's *Portrait of the Artist*) to the 1962 DTF, giving Leonard one of his first major successes. Ryan, who had begun her career as an actor at the Abbey, had moved into producing in 1956. She overcame an early controversy over her staging of the Irish premiere of Tennessee Williams' *Cat on a Hot Tin Roof* in 1959 to become one of the major forces in Irish theatre, producing plays throughout the country right up to the early 2000s. Those included major premieres such as John B. Keane's *The Field* (1965) and, as we saw in Chapter 2, McCabe's *King of the Castle* and the English-language version of *An Triail*. But as she recounts in her memoir, *The Company I Kept*, it was the success of *Stephen D*, first in Dublin and then in the West End, that sent her company's reputation 'into orbit' (Ryan, 1996: 170) thanks to its daring theatricality and its willingness to frankly represent Joyce's negative views on Catholicism.

Nine years later, the Abbey staged the American writer Marjorie Barkentin's *Ulysses in Nighttown*, a production (directed by Tomás Mac Anna) that proved a hit for the theatre, being revived there once in 1971 and twice in 1974. Barkentin's version was also produced on Broadway in 1974, earning six Tony nominations. A free adaptation of the 'Circe' chapter of Joyce's novel, it explores how women are seen by men – not just in the sense that Barkentin literally gives flesh and blood to the many prostitutes that appear in that chapter (which is set in Dublin's red-light district), but also in her exploration of Bloom's androgyny (ATDA, 4629_PS_0001).

Other important examples would follow. As already mentioned, Siobhán McKenna made Anna Livia Plurabelle (ALP) her own when she put together *Here Are Ladies*: where Manning had taken ownership of ALP's words, McKenna was going one step further by embodying them too. And once Joyce's work was released from copyright in 2011, the number of adaptations of his work rapidly increased. These included versions by male authors such as Frank McGuinness (*The Dead*, 2012) and Dermot Bolger (*Ulysses*, 2012), but there were also a significant number by women. Annie Ryan and Michael West's *commedia* adaptation of *Dubliners* was a popular success when it played at the Gaiety Theatre at the 2012 DTF, for example; and on a much smaller stage Katie O'Kelly's *Dubliners Women* appeared at the sixty-six-seat New Theatre in Dublin in 2016.

A particularly important achievement in this series of new productions was *riverrun*, a sixty-minute performance written and performed by Olwen

Fouéré, which premiered in Galway in 2013 before touring internationally. During the performance, Fouéré stands in front of a microphone reciting – perhaps even incanting – the final section of *Finnegans Wake*. This means that, like McKenna, she is an example of a female Irish artist who was embodying and making her own the figure of ALP, and that, like Manning, she was demonstrating her skills as a writer in bringing Joyce's words to the stage. Particularly striking about the production was its treatment of the ALP character's status as an emblem, not just for Ireland but also for the night-time and the irrational (an emblematic status that is also held by Joyce's other great female character, Molly Bloom). As such scholars as States (1985), Carlson (2003) and Schneider (2011) have argued in different ways, we always bring to the theatre our memories of previous performances. When we watch an actor performing a role, our interpretation of that performance will be informed by memories of other actors in the same role, or the same actor in other roles, or other performances in the same space – and so on. The same is true for actors: when they take on new roles, they bring with them the knowledge they've gained from previous performances.

Just as Joyce's words in *Finnegans Wake* explode outwards to have multiple possible meanings and resonances, so Fouéré's body was at once ALP and simultaneously represented many other iconic female figures. Watching the performance in 2014, I found myself being reminded of Fouéré's other roles: Hester from *By the Bog of Cats*, Wilde's Salome, Medea, Antigone, Synge's Pegeen Mike and Widow Quinn, Queen Maeve in Fabulous Beast's *The Bull* (2005), Lady Macbeth, Cathleen ni Houlihan, and Mouth in Beckett's *Not I*. The way in which Fouéré evoked those memories put Joyce's creation of ALP in the context of other female characters created by men, showing how the stage history of the representations of women has so often been mediated by a male perspective. The fact of Fouéré both speaking and enacting this character was thus a powerful act of reclamation: a statement that this embodied female character exists not just as an object to be looked at, or as a metaphor for nation or something else, but also as the author of the production's meaning – the object had become the subject.

This brief discussion reveals the existence of one of the patterns of repetition that I began this chapter with – and here I am thinking about repetition in two senses. In adapting Joyce's works, these artists were restaging them, making them new – and this needs to be seen as a form of authorship that is different from composing original plays, but which should not be dismissed as inferior to that act. But also important is that we have identified a tradition, one that has not (to my knowledge) been acknowledged

**Figure 6** Olwen Fouéré in *riverrun*, produced by TheEmergencyRoom and Galway International Arts Festival in association with Cusack Projects, 2013. Photograph by Colm Hogan.

in detail before: that of female theatre-makers taking Joyce's women and making them their own, through playwriting or performance or both. We find in that tradition a model for how female artists could engage with other iconic figures (were theatres to give them opportunities to do so).

In order to explore that observation in more detail, I want now to consider the career of Garry Hynes, showing how her work as a director should in its own right be considered a form of authorship, an act of reappropriation and adaptation that is different from but analogous to the work of playwrights. By including in our understanding of authorship the work of directors, I would suggest that we can begin to form a more capacious understanding of the achievements of Irish theatre during the contemporary period.

## Making Synge new: Garry Hynes and Druid Theatre, 1975–2005

Garry Hynes has been centrally involved in the development of new Irish writing since the early 1980s, having directed the premieres of several major plays, including Tom Murphy's *Conversations on a Homecoming* and *Bailegangaire* (both 1985), Carr's *Portia Coughlan* (1996) and *On Raftery's Hill* (2000), and Martin McDonagh's *Leenane Trilogy* (1997). However, my suggestion is that her major accomplishment as a director has been to revive and reanimate the works of a significant number of Irish dramatists – not just canonical figures such as O'Casey and Beckett, but also relatively neglected or misunderstood writers such as M.J. Molloy, John B. Keane and Eugene McCabe. But chief among her accomplishments has been a transformation in the reputation of John Millington Synge, whose drama has allowed Hynes to develop three of her most important traits: a willingness to show that plays change their meanings as they move from place to place, a determination to treat playscripts as if they have been newly written every time she directs them, and a belief that the meaning of a production is co-created by the ensemble that performs it.

The history of Hynes' work on Synge dates to 1975, when she co-founded Druid Theatre with the actors Marie Mullen and Mick Lally. The trio were keen to produce professional theatre but also knew that they needed to attract an audience. So *The Playboy of the Western World* was chosen as their inaugural production – not because Druid particularly liked it, but because they assumed it would bring in a tourist audience, generating income that would allow the group to do other, more interesting things.

That attitude to Synge was entirely understandable. His reputation at that time had suffered from a style of production that mixed excessive piety with overfamiliarity – and it had also declined due to the perception that his plays had become outdated, that the language that Synge had intended to seem fresh and authentic had itself become clichéd, reinforcing stereotypes rather than revealing truths. The overall result was that his plays were gradually dropping out of the repertoire. *Playboy* had been produced almost constantly at the Abbey until the early 1950s but was falling out of fashion, disappearing altogether from the theatre between 1957 and 1968, and again between 1971 and 1988. And productions of his other plays became even scarcer. *The Well of the Saints* went entirely unproduced from 1945 to 1969, and from 1979 to 1994. Similarly, since 1950 *Deirdre of the Sorrows* has appeared twice at the theatre, and *The Tinker's Wedding* only three times. Even the perennial favourites *The Shadow of the Glen* and *Riders to the Sea* began to disappear, with fewer than ten productions of either play having appeared at the Abbey since 1950.

That gradual decline contrasted with Synge's positive reputation internationally. That status was underscored by the release of film adaptations of *Playboy* in 1963 and 1974, as well as the continued influence of Synge on international playwrights – something that had been evident in the 1930s in the work of Brecht and Lorca (whose *Señora Carrar's Rifles* and *Blood Wedding* respectively respond to *Riders to the Sea*). But perhaps that international reputation contributed to a sense in Ireland that Synge's plays were becoming museum pieces, of interest only to tourists and academics. Even Tom Murphy had explained that as a young playwright he had little interest in Synge, coming to his works only through Lorca; in his early years it seemed as though 'anything Irish [was] a pain in the arse', he told Michael Billington in a 2001 public interview (qtd by Grene, 2002: 94).

This context explains why Druid were surprised by the power of Synge's work when they first staged *Playboy* – and so they resolved to return to him at the earliest opportunity. That happened in 1976, when they presented *In the Glens of Rathvanna*, an adaptation of Synge's prose that included performances of *The Tinker's Wedding* and *The Shadow of the Glen*. In 1977, another production of *Playboy* was presented, this time in a Galway pub – the beginning of a pattern of presenting Synge in site-specific locations that would continue into the years ahead.

In those early Druid productions, both the company and their audiences were able to come to the plays free of the burden of theatrical history: there were no major traditions for Druid to draw from in their Galway home, no conventions to follow, no senior actors to reinforce a sense of how things 'must be done'. This allowed Hynes to read and cast the play as if it were a new work – which meant that, by 1982, she was jokingly referring to Synge as Druid's 'house playwright'. That was the year when Druid staged their definitive production of *Playboy*, a version that they took to Edinburgh, London, New York and Sydney. It also toured throughout Ireland, including a celebrated visit to each of the three Aran Islands, reconnecting Synge's play with the locations that had inspired it.

That pattern of going on what Druid jokingly dubbed URTs – unusual rural tours – would prove one of the defining features of their interpretation of Synge. As would also be true for Field Day and Charabanc a few years later, Druid saw the task of bringing theatre to audiences outside of the island's metropolitan centres as being important in its own right: they were staging professional theatre before audiences that had few opportunities to watch it otherwise. But touring was also a way of activating new meanings in the plays. The reconnection of Synge's theatre with the landscapes and communities that had inspired it broke down the distinction between the metropolis and the idealized west of Ireland that had informed the reception of *Playboy* in 1907. Where some of Synge's original audiences had rejected the play with cries of 'that's not the west', Hynes situated it actually *in* the west – and in demonstrating how accommodating the landscape, accents and communities of the west were for *Playboy*, she refuted the suggestion that Synge was an outsider, a disinterested ethnographer who took from the regions whatever he needed and then brought it back to the metropolis.

But those tours also had the impact of demonstrating how the meaning of Synge's plays was not always fixed – as would also be true for the other

**Figure 7** Druid co-founder Mick Lally bringing props for Druid's *The Playboy of the Western World* from a boat to the Aran Islands, 1982 (DTA, T2/729).

playwrights whose work Druid staged. I've written elsewhere of how, during the company's tours of Martin McDonagh's plays, jokes about the Irish language met with varying reactions in different parts of Galway – in some places touching off a nerve, and in others being greeted with warm laughter of recognition, depending on whether Irish was still spoken by the people in the audience (2012: 49–50). Of course, it's a truism to say that actors face different groups of people every night, that the theatre audience is like a river that cannot be stepped into twice. But by being performed not just before different audiences but in different locations, Druid's productions have always shown how the meaning of a play is a collaborative effort between author, director, actors, audiences – and places.

As a result of that approach, Hynes' 1982 *Playboy* was a revelation to audiences both in Ireland and abroad. Synge's play hinges on the contrast between the ideal and the real, between the 'gallous story' and the 'dirty deed' of Christy Mahon's 'murder' of his father. Hynes and her actors knew how to capture the beauty of the play: the poetry of the language, the wickedness of the humour, the depth of Pegeen's feelings. But they hadn't forgotten about the dirt. Where the play had fallen into a pattern of sentimental performances, Hynes presented her actors in ragged costumes, their faces and hands grimy, their poverty all too evident. So when, at the start of the action, Pegeen decides to buy a fine-tooth comb (as Synge's stage directions require her to do), Hynes' direction showed that this was because her scalp was infested with lice. By rooting Pegeen in that squalid context, Hynes created space for her actors to develop their characters, and thus made the transformation of both Pegeen and Christy seem all the more miraculous and life-affirming – intensifying the impact of the play's final moments (DTA, T2/84).

Also given new attention was Synge's understanding of the ugliness of violence, which was shown to arise not from heroism but from baser motivations: vanity, drunkenness, greed, feelings of inadequacy and, especially, loneliness. The resulting sense of danger allowed for the power and agency of the women in the play to be rediscovered and emphasized, particularly in the case of the Widow Quin. Synge had created that character as a proud, cynical and sexually assertive thirty-year-old woman, but during the decades that had passed since its premiere, she had often been played as a much older figure, a person whose pursuit of Christy was presented only in terms of economic self-interest, and who had therefore become more ridiculous than admirable. Under Hynes' direction it became possible to understand anew why *Playboy* riots had started when the audience encountered Christy's visualization of 'a drift of chosen females, standing in their shifts itself' (Synge, 1982: 167). The power of Synge's women was now undeniable.

Most of the playwrights whose work Hynes has directed are men – but we should also consider that Hynes' *oeuvre* needs to be seen as a form of authorship in its own right. Her directorial perspective on Synge placed new emphasis on the role of women, moving them to centre stage (literally), and giving them a form of agency and depth that was present in the original script but which had gradually disappeared from performance. She has adopted a similar approach to the works of John B. Keane which, for many years, were dismissed as old-fashioned melodramas but which under her direction were revealed to be incisive explorations of how male sexual dysfunction manifests itself through the imposition and maintenance of misogynistic social structures. And in 2015 her *DruidShakespeare* – a staging of the Henriad in a new adaptation by Mark O'Rowe – presented a version of Shakespeare that was both feminist and postcolonial in having two of Shakespeare's three English kings be played by women who spoke in their own Irish accents (Aisling O'Sullivan and Derbhle Crotty as Hal and Bolingbroke respectively). Hynes' career thus needs to be seen as a feminist reworking of the male-dominated Irish canon.

These characteristics extend into Druid's other major engagement with Synge, which is the *DruidSynge* project of 2004–6. After the success of the 1982 *Playboy*, Druid for the first time formed a relationship with a living writer: Tom Murphy. Hynes then left Druid for the Abbey in 1991, returning in 1995. One of her first productions upon her return was *The Beauty Queen of Leenane* by Martin McDonagh, whose plays she had discovered in the company's pile of unsolicited scripts. For her work on *The Beauty Queen*, Hynes won a Tony Award for directing in 1998, becoming the first woman to do so. Hynes and Druid toured McDonagh's plays internationally until 2001, preventing her from fulfilling her ambition of returning to Synge's work. But, in an example of how a new playwright can help to create space for the re-evaluation of an old one, Druid's work on the *Leenane* plays paved the way for *DruidSynge*, in at least two ways. The first is that the branding of McDonagh's three plays as *The Leenane Trilogy* provided a model for how Synge's work might be staged. McDonagh's plays are a trilogy only in the loosest possible sense: there is no progression of plot from one story to another, and while characters from one play are sometimes mentioned in another, those details are always incidental, and are sometimes cut when the plays are produced by themselves. Their grouping together thus functions theatrically rather than thematically: the primary link is that they were performed by a single company of actors and that it was possible to see all three in a single day. Part of the experience of *The Leenane Trilogy* was not just the enjoyment of McDonagh's writing, but the pleasure of seeing the ensemble at work: watching as Brian O'Byrne (for example) moved from playing Pato in *Beauty Queen*, to Tom in *A Skull in Connemara*, to Valene in *The Lonesome West*. When it works well, the sense of investment and commitment necessitated by this kind of 'event theatre' leads to a sense of shared purpose between the audience and the ensemble. *The Leenane Trilogy* thus demonstrated that audiences could take pleasure in completing a kind of theatrical marathon, an experience that was rewarding *because* it was physically and intellectually demanding, testing their endurance by asking them to spend eleven hours in a theatre in a single day.

That model allowed Druid to think about how they might persuade audiences to watch plays by Synge that would almost certainly have been ignored if staged individually. This led to the decision to present all of Synge's plays in a single day, encouraging audiences to commit to the 'event' of watching them all being performed consecutively in the order of their first production. Hence *DruidSynge* began at about 1 pm with *Riders to the Sea* and finished after 11 pm with *Deirdre of the Sorrows* – with *The Shadow of the Glen*, *Well of the Saints*, *The Tinker's Wedding* and *The Playboy of the Western World* appearing between the two (together with two intervals, mercifully).

*DruidSynge* was not just a performance of the plays, then, but an investigation of Synge's writing life, allowing audiences to witness chronologically the development of his drama from 1902 to his death in 1909. This brought new correspondences into view: we saw how his ideas about female sexuality were presented embryonically in *The Shadow of the Glen*, teased out in *The Tinker's Wedding* and *Well of the Saints*, and fully realized in *Playboy*. But so too did we understand how the development of his six plays can be seen as Synge's preparation for his own untimely death, with the focus on mortality in *Riders* and *Deirdre* bookending the production in a way that made the *joie de vivre* of the young female characters in *Tinker's Wedding*, *Well* and *Playboy* seem all the more poignant. What Hynes did, in other words, was infuse the individual plays with her knowledge of how they all speak to each other. This was not just an act of rewriting but of revelation.

A further pleasure for audiences lay in the sharing of the theatrical experience with the actors: to witness, for example, Marie Mullen playing Maurya in *Riders to the Sea*, followed by Mary Doul in *The Well of the Saints* and Mary Byrne in *The Tinker's Wedding*, then the Widow Quin in *Playboy* and Lavarcham in *Deirdre*. As I mentioned in the discussion of the work of Olwen Fouéré, we always watch actors in the context of our memories of their other roles. To watch Mullen move from one part to another in a single day was a distillation of that experience to a very intense degree. Hence, the maternal indifference of Mary in *Tinker's Wedding* was informed by the tragic sense of acceptance offered by the mother in *Riders to the Sea* – and both fed into the characterization of the childless Widow Quin in *Playboy*. To witness Mullen's technical mastery as she moved through these roles was a pleasure in itself, but what was being performed in *DruidSynge* was a sense of the diversity and individuality of Synge's characters – something that was made clearer in being enacted through one actor's physical presence.

Of special importance was a shifting in the sexual politics of *Playboy*. Mullen had played the Widow Quin in 1982 as Synge had intended: as a still young woman who had gained wisdom through practical experience. By having dispelled the cliché of Quin as an older woman who provoked ridicule rather than fear, Hynes was in a position to recast Mullen in that role in 2005 where – contrary to Synge's instructions – she was now played as being significantly older than Christy. That allowed for a new approach to the casting of Pegeen, played in *DruidSynge* by Catherine Walsh, who performed the role as if Pegeen was in her thirties (and thus much older than Christy). Those casting decisions shifted both the meaning of the play and the power relations between men and women, demonstrating how sexual agency and power is possessed by women of all ages, but also underlining that Pegeen's loss of Christy is not the agony of innocence being met with experience but rather the tragedy of potential that knows it will never be realized.

Other directors had also been working towards a re-evaluation of Synge during this period. Patrick Mason at the Abbey directed a justly celebrated *Well of the Saints* in 1995–6, one that capitalized on audiences' growing knowledge of Beckett to give them new ways to interpret Synge's presentation of two blind characters. And in 2001, Niall Henry of Blue Raincoat was hired by the Abbey to offer a new production of *Playboy* on its Peacock stage. Known for his indebtedness to European performance practices, Henry stripped back the play to its essence, performing it on an almost bare stage and casting radically against type, with Pegeen being played by Olwen Fouéré and Widow Quin by the younger actor Cathy Belton.

Nevertheless, it was Hynes' work on Synge in the 1980s that had made these approaches possible – and in a similar fashion *DruidSynge* created

**Figure 8** *DruidSynge*, 2005. Left to right: Catherine Walsh (Pegeen), Aaron Monaghan (Christy), Marie Mullen (Widow Quin) (DTA, T2/231). Photograph by Keith Pattison.

space for new innovations. Lynne Parker's *The Taming of the Shrew* in 2006 was directly inspired by *DruidSynge*, setting Shakespeare's play in rural Ireland and using Irish accents to demonstrate the links between Elizabethan speech and Hiberno-English, while also framing the plight of Katherine through audiences' memories of Pegeen Mike. Synge's indebtedness to Shakespeare came stunningly into view in Parker's production – which also showed that it was possible for Irish actors to make Shakespeare their own.

It was also significant that the growing multiculturalism of Irish society from the early 2000s would be signalled by two productions of *The Playboy of the Western World* – such that, as Charlotte McIvor suggests, productions of Synge's play became 'the paradigmatic example (or, for some, the climax) of an emergent intercultural Irish theatre' (2016: 72). The first, by Pan Pan in 2006, relocated the action from the Mayo shebeen to a contemporary Beijing 'whoredressers' – a hairdresser's that doubles as a brothel. In its Dublin production, all of the action was performed in Mandarin, with the company using surtitles that did not translate the script directly but which instead displayed Synge's original text – creating a contrast between the action on stage and audiences' knowledge of the canonical play, and thus performing explicitly the production's own act of rewriting and adaptation.

Similarly, in the following year, the Nigerian dramatist Bisi Adigun and Irish writer Roddy Doyle collaborated on a new version of *Playboy*, which opened at the Abbey during the 2007 Dublin Theatre Festival. Reset to contemporary Dublin, the production imagined the arrival of a Nigerian immigrant to a working-class pub, with Christy's outsider status being deployed in the most literal way possible, performing for audiences at the Abbey the status of African immigrants to the country.

Hence, by 2009, the centenary of Synge's death, his reputation was higher than it has been at almost any other stage during the previous hundred years. And rather than being based on a sense of fidelity, that reputation was strong precisely because directors such as Quinn and writers such as Adigun and Doyle felt that it was possible to say something new about Ireland by revisiting and revising Synge. But my suggestion is that this approach was made possible through the work over the previous four decades of Garry Hynes: she had succeeded in making Synge seem central again, and in demonstrating the power that could arise from rewriting or reimagining him she provided a model for Pan Pan and Adigun/Doyle to follow.

Hynes' act of reimagining was made possible because she was willing to embrace a status that might have been considered negative by other people: rather than seeing her company's Galway location as being in a peripheral relationship to Dublin, she instead saw that place as offering freedom – from tradition, expectation and the burden of history. In Northern Ireland at the same time, Christina Reid was doing something comparable – as I'll discuss in the next section.

## Inheritances: Christina Reid and the Troubles, 1983–9

Introducing Christina Reid's *Plays 1* in 1996, Maria Delgado called attention to the difficulty of categorizing Reid's work. The role of women has, Delgado wrote, 'often [been] overlooked in histories of Irish theatre, which tend to focus on a male literary canon' (Reid, 1997: vii). That focus undermines awareness of 'women's prominence as directors, designers and performers, both in the theatrical mainstream and in the alternative structures of music-hall, fringe, children's and community theatre, as well as theatre-in-education' (ibid.). In the case of Reid, that problem was exacerbated by her status as a writer from Northern Ireland. 'Critics have avoided classification based on the North–South divide because so many Northern Irish writers have stated that they perceive themselves to be Irish rather than British,' writes Delgado, pointing out that this has meant that 'classification has taken place largely according to genre and subject matter' (viii). While that approach was understandable, it meant that the distinctive characteristics of work from the north were ignored – at least until the appearance of important studies by Ophelia Byrne (1997), Tom Maguire (2006) and Bill McDonnell (2008).

Delgado's remarks were written many years ago, and things have changed since then – to an extent. Thanks to the work of Melissa Sihra (2007) and Cathy Leeney (2010) in particular, there is a better understanding of the importance of female theatre artists in the Irish tradition – though much work still has to be done. And important books by Imelda Foley (2003) and Fiona Coleman Coffey (2016) have given detailed attention to women in Northern Irish theatre, identifying the unique qualities of their work while also situating them centrally within Irish theatre history. Even so, it is important to be aware of the context in which Reid's plays were produced, one that required her to write from a sense of being marginalized at least three times over – first by her gender, then by her religious background, and finally by social class.

Reid was born in 1942 into a Protestant family in working-class Belfast, and began writing plays in the late 1970s. That was a period in which northern Protestantism was poorly understood in the rest of the UK and the Republic. As we'll see later, Frank McGuinness' *Observe the Sons of Ulster* (1985) was an exception in placing on stage people from northern Unionist communities, but its setting was in the past and all of its characters were men. In the case of Reid, that neglect was compounded by a hostility from both critics and scholars to working-class performance traditions which, in both Dublin and Belfast, have a long history. For Reid, those traditions have an integrity that needs to be respected: they offer shared experiences to families and communities alike, but also have artistic validity in their own right.

All of Reid's original plays are set in working-class Belfast, with the Troubles being presented from the perspectives of people whose stories have often been ignored in official histories of that conflict: women, people with disabilities, children and the elderly, among others. Those plays set out to demonstrate that the sectarian conflict in the north had masked other forms of discrimination, especially on the grounds of gender and social class. Reid was also one of the first Irish writers to tackle the issue of racism, in her neglected 1989 play *The Belle of the Belfast City*. By creating a lead character who embodies multiple identities – black, Irish, English, female – Reid relates the experience of women and immigrants in Northern Ireland to a broader international context that included the African-American Civil

Rights movement, decolonization and second wave feminism. Hence in *Belle*, as in all of her plays, Reid presents feminism as having the potential to transform the societies of Ireland and Britain in their entirety, offering liberation from patriarchy as well as sectarianism.

For those reasons, her plays reimagine elements of Irish performance history, and – as Manning and Fouéré did in rewriting Joyce – Reid was asserting her own authorship in appropriating work by male authors. For example, *Joyriders* (1986) is framed by allusions to Seán O'Casey's *The Shadow of a Gunman* (1923): its opening scene is set in a theatre where that play is being performed, and it ends with a death scene that consciously mirrors and contrasts with O'Casey's original. Reid uses O'Casey to propose a continuity between pre-Independence Dublin and Belfast in the 1980s, and she also asserts an affinity between her and O'Casey based on their shared working-class Protestant background – one that transcends history and gender. *Joyriders* also includes a number of songs written by teenagers living in Belfast's Divis Flats, showing that Reid's interest in politics was more than theoretical: she was quite literally giving voice to people.

Her other works also rewrote theatrical traditions. *Did You Hear the One About the Irishman?*, which was premiered in 1985 by the Royal Shakespeare Company, concerns a doomed relationship between a middle-class Protestant woman and a working-class Catholic male. Despite the differences in their backgrounds, Reid shows they have much in common, including the fact that both are related to political prisoners on opposing sides of the conflict. The man and woman are told by their communities that their relationship is inappropriate and must end; they refuse to be intimidated and are murdered.

That plot is self-evidently a response to Shakespeare in Reid's use of a Romeo and Juliet motif (a very common strategy in Troubles drama, perhaps best explored in Graham Reid's *Remembrance* from 1984) – so the play can be seen as an attempt by an Irish dramatist to write her way into the English dramatic tradition. Crucially, however, Reid combines that approach to literary culture with a critique of popular culture. This comes in the form of a series of interruptions to the action from an English stand-up comedian, who tells a series of offensive Irish jokes in a manner that at the time of the play's production remained common on British television. The juxtaposition of the lovers' tragedy with this style of humour challenges the unwillingness of the British public to engage seriously with the Troubles.

But the play that perhaps best exemplifies Reid's achievements is her first produced drama, *Tea in a China Cup*, which premiered at the Lyric in 1983.

*China Cup* focuses on three generations of Belfast women, with action taking place against the backdrop of two military conflicts: the outbreak of the Second World War in 1939, and the early period of the Troubles in 1972. Reid places those conflicts in comparison with each other, suggesting that, from the perspective of the young men who have to go and fight, the north is trapped in a cycle of Beckettian repetition. She underlines that allusion to her Irish predecessor by having each of her acts begin with the departure from Belfast of a soldier, called Samuel in the 1940s and Sammy in the 1970s, and played in both cases by the same actor. In Reid's analysis, this is a community that is failing to fail better.

While military conflicts tend to be dominated by men, Reid's interest is in how those events are experienced from the perspective of women, especially the semi-autobiographical character of Beth. The action begins with Beth arranging the funeral of her mother, Sarah – and the clash between loving and letting go is used by Reid as a way of thinking about the Troubles. As Beth analyses events from her past, she is reminded of the images that define Unionism: Orange marches, bonfires on the twelfth of July, and the memory of the sacrifices made by soldiers in the British Army. But she sees those images not as politicized abstractions but in personal terms: they are memories mediated by her love for her mother, grandparents and other family members. *Tea in a China Cup* thus gives a human perspective to one of the dilemmas at the heart of the Troubles: how can communities remain loyal to traditions that were handed down to them by parents who were loving and loved, while also changing those traditions sufficiently to allow for an accommodation to be reached with people on the other side?

For Beth, the answers to that question lie in confronting two forces: sectarianism and patriarchy – and in acknowledging how one feeds the other. The play opens with Beth attempting to find a suitable place to bury her mother; she is shocked when she's asked whether she wants a 'Protestant or a Catholic plot' in the graveyard, demonstrating how the segregation of Northern Ireland's community extends even into death (1997: 4). Also notable is how identity is presupposed to fall into one of two categories, a binary that denies space for other ways of being. As Beth thinks about her mother, she is aware of the need to maintain family traditions: 'You mind all the family stories, tell them to your children after I'm gone,' Sarah tells her (10). But Beth knows that she suffers from another form of inheritance: she has repeated her mother's mistakes, falling into a loveless marriage that closely mirrors her parents': 'I'm moving from my mother's house to Stephen's house… I've been my mother's daughter, and now I'm going to be Stephen's wife. I've never been just me' (50). Later in her life, she is shocked to discover that her husband has many of her father's failings; her marriage is thus presented as another form of recurrence: that of the child who repeats the mistakes of the parent. Her need to break free from a cycle of destructive relationships thus becomes a metaphor for the need for the north to break free from a cycle of violence.

The repetition of those cycles is attributed by Reid to a lack of education, especially of young women. The girls in the play, both Catholic and Protestant, are entirely ignorant of sexual matters: 'We knew nothing. We found it impossible to get an accurate answer to anything related to bodily functions. Babies were a gift from God to married women' (28). Little wonder, then, that their marriages are often unhappy. When Beth has her first period, she meets the following reaction: 'God help you child, this is the start of all your troubles' (30). That, of course, is a bitterly ironic statement, entwining the personal experience of bodily change with the Troubles writ large. But that ignorance extends to knowledge of themselves: Beth has never been 'just me' because she simply doesn't know who that 'me' might be.

That lack of education includes the way in which Catholics and Protestants fail to understand each other. One of the funniest jokes in the play is that both Catholics and Protestants claim to be able to recognize people of the other religion because they have 'close-set eyes'. But Reid is also careful to show that the experiences undergone by Beth in her youth are matched by those of a Catholic girl called Theresa. One of the outcomes of the sectarian conflict is to restrict both girls to very narrow roles, to remove the space that might allow them to grow, become themselves, realize their potential.

The china cup in the play's title thus acts as a metaphor for what we inherit from our families. It is an object infused with meaning by Beth's mother: a symbol of status, of respectability, a way of marking her family as different from the other side. But it is also a family heirloom, a much-loved object that contains traces of memories of family events both happy and sad. Beth is thus faced with the choice of what to do with that object. And like Teresa in *The Hostage* or Marian in *Pentecost*, her response is not to abandon the object but to give it new meaning. In the play's final stage directions, Reid writes as follows:

> She opens her handbag and takes out a small tissue-wrapped parcel. She removes the tissue paper, looks at the Belleek cup and saucer, and smiles. She sings quietly to herself 'On the hill there stands a lady, who

she is I do not know . . .' As she sings she wraps up the Belleek cup and saucer and carefully replaces it in her handbag. She walks off the stage, still singing

(83)

Beth's action locates her in the tradition of plays in which female characters walk off stage at the end: like Ibsen's Nora in *A Doll's House*, she is leaving behind a social environment that is restrictive and that has stopped her from understanding who she is. Her choice of song is important: a traditional folk melody called 'Oh No John'. Its first lines place the emphasis on the female figure who is free of identity – 'who she is I do not know'. Beth's departure thus signals a new period of self-invention, a new freedom. But that self-invention does not involve total abandonment of the past: she will not take her mother's entire tea set but one cup and saucer (rendering the set economically worthless). It will be used not as an implement for drinking from but as a memento, a reminder of her roots. Likewise, Reid is taking from her own cultural predecessors what she needs: a bit of Ibsen, a bit of folk music.

In their entirety, Reid's plays are about how we reimagine culture – whether that is a play by O'Casey, Shakespeare or Ibsen; a twelfth of July marching song; or a music-hall routine. In the context of Northern Ireland, the aim is to explore how identities are constructed through culture – to show that we form a sense of self from the way in which our identities are performed around us. Those performances affect our sense of gender, sexuality, nationality, ethnicity – but they also determine how we see others. By highlighting the way in which identity is performative, Reid's plays offer a way through the Troubles, showing that it is possible to retain fidelity with the past while changing into something new – a process that also involves an acknowledgement of what we share as well as how we differ.

## 'Let's trust the Bard': Marina Carr and the canon, 1989–2016

While Christina Reid's plays are very obviously concerned with politics, the assertion has been made that Irish dramatists usually avoid direct political engagement of the kind found in work by English dramatists such as Churchill, Hare, Arden or Brenton. By placing the work of Marina Carr in the context of the achievements of Hynes and Reid, we can see how such statements are incorrect: Carr's work *is* political because it has always directly addressed Irish society, highlighting its flaws, demanding that it change. The difference between Carr and someone like Hare, perhaps, is that audiences prefer to imagine that the worlds she creates on stage are not real, that her concerns are not serious, because the truths she unveils might be too uncomfortable.

Many discussions of Carr's career group her plays into three phases, a kind of 'before, during and after' sequence that places special emphasis on her most popular works, a violent and quasi-mythical quartet set in the Irish midlands that began with *The Mai* (1994) and continued with *Portia Coughlan* (1996), *By the Bog of Cats* (1998) and *On Raftery's Hill* (2000) – a list that is sometimes stretched to include *Ariel* (2002), a loose adaptation of *The Oresteia* that includes a Faustian narrative about an Irish politician who sells his soul (it is a script that even Carr herself has described as a 'monster' (2009: ix)).

These have been by far the most successful of her plays. *Portia Coughlan* transferred to the Royal Court in 1996 and also had the distinction of being revived for the Abbey's centenary season of 2004. *By the Bog of Cats* was one of the most popular plays of Patrick Mason's artistic directorship of the Abbey (1994–9); it has since been anthologized by John Harrington in *Modern and Contemporary Irish Drama* (2009) and was given a West End production that starred Holly Hunter in 2004. *On Raftery's Hill* toured to the United States after its premiere in Galway – albeit controversially, as Melissa Sihra has discussed (2004). It was revived at the Abbey in 2018, making Carr the first woman to have four original plays produced on the Abbey's main stage since Elizabeth Connor premiered *Mount Prospect, Swans and Geese, An Apple A Day* and *The Dark Road* there between 1940 and 1947. Indeed, if we count Carr's 2015 adaptation of *Anna Karenina*, then the only women writers to have appeared more often on the Abbey's main stage are Lady Gregory and Teresa Deevy.

In contrast, her first four works, produced between 1989 and 1991, have been neglected – and, to be fair, Carr has not discouraged this. The exception is *Low in the Dark* (1989), an absurdist treatment of gender and fertility that might be read as a commentary on Irish debates about reproductive rights. *The Deer's Surrender* appeared in 1990, and *This Love Thing* in 1991. *Ullaloo*, having been given a rehearsed reading in 1989, was produced at the Peacock in 1991 – and it met with exceptionally negative reviews, most of them sneeringly hostile. In the *Irish Press*, for example, Patsy McGarry called it 'pretentious gibberish', an unusually dismissive remark for any play, especially one by a young writer (ATDA, 0535_PC_0001: 10). Other reviewers were similarly ungenerous and wounding. The script of the play can be read in both the Abbey archive and the National Library (ATDA, 0535_PS_0001;

**Figure 9** Druid Theatre, *On Raftery's Hill* by Marina Carr, 2000. Photograph by Derek Speirs (DTA, T2 807 4).

NLI, MS 36,099/3/8); while it is clearly the work of an inexperienced playwright, its blend of surrealism and absurdism would more fairly be described as experimental than pretentious. It is also notably frank in its exploration of sex – one of Carr's most common themes.

After *Ariel* met with a negative reaction in 2002, most of Carr's plays premiered outside Ireland. They have seen her take on iconic female figures such as Cordelia, Phaedra, Hecuba and Anna Karenina – not to mention Chekhov, as we saw in the last chapter. Reactions have been mixed. *The Cordelia Dream* (2008) received mostly negative responses: in *The Guardian*, for example, Michael Billington called it an example of the Royal Shakespeare Company's tendency to commission 'duff stuff from good dramatists' – another surprisingly dismissive remark (18 December 2008). *Marble* (2009) and *Sixteen Possible Glimpses* (2011) were also received negatively upon their premiere at the Abbey. However, her 2015 *Hecuba* for the Royal Shakespeare Company was well received, as was her *Phaedra Backwards* – perhaps because both characters occupied the kind of mythical realm that Carr has so successfully explored in her midlands plays.

This division of Carr's career into three phases can be useful, if only in demonstrating that her work has been better received when it has been less experimental, something that might tell us more about critics than it does about Carr herself. But this approach risks obscuring two important features: the coherence and consistency of her exploration of major themes, and the extent to which her plays can be seen as a commentary on the development of the status of women in Ireland since the 1980s.

That is a period in Irish life that has seen important milestones on the way to gender equality – such as, to give just three examples, the legalization of the sale of contraceptives in 1979 and 1985, the election of Mary Robinson as the first female president of Ireland in 1990, and the passing of a series of laws prohibiting discrimination on the grounds of gender from the 1970s to the 1990s. But many examples of the persistence of problems can be cited too. Were it to be staged today, Carr's first play, *Low in the Dark*, might seem like a Beckettian comedy about gender and parenthood, and as being wholly devoid of any immediate social relevance. But its first audiences would most likely have seen its treatment of pregnancy in the context of then-recent events that had demonstrated the persistence of conservative attitudes to extra-marital sex, contraception and abortion. Those events included the 1984–5 Kerry Babies Case, in which an infant was discovered on a beach in south-west Ireland, dead from multiple stab wounds; the Irish police falsely accused a woman who lived eighty kilometres away of being both the mother and the killer of the child – a deliberation that they seem to have reached partly because she had previously had a child with a man who was married to someone else (see Inglis, 2002).

Similarly, in Longford in 1986 a fifteen-year-old girl called Ann Lovett was found dead in a grotto for the Virgin Mary, where she had given birth to a baby boy. Her family had not known she was pregnant, and she and her child died alone. And lest we imagine that such events are from an earlier era of Irish history, we must note that in 2012 Savita Halappanavar died in hospital in Galway during a septic miscarriage. She had been denied the abortion that would have saved her life and which would have terminated a pregnancy that was going to end anyway. Her doctors said they were simply following Irish law at that time, which imposed a custodial sentence on anyone who carries out an abortion. So to summarize: Carr's treatment of motherhood and gender can often seem absurd and fantastical, but that is only because it reflects the values of her society.

Carr has also written regularly about the difficulties of combining writing with motherhood. She has explained, for example, that she was obliged to write *The Cordelia Dream* in less than a week: 'I had five days before my husband arrived with our son, five days with no one screaming for marshmallows,' she writes, joking but (as any parent can attest) also not joking (2009: x). The same concern is evident in her obvious sympathy for the perpetually pregnant Dolly in her adaptation of *Anna Karenina* – which is shown by her inclusion in the list of characters the need for 'loads of babies' on stage (2016: 10). She's also considerably more critical than Tolstoy was of Levin's attitude to women, especially insofar as sex and parenthood are concerned – though, like Tolstoy, she is contemptuous of the double standards that cause Anna to be banished from her society while Vronsky is readily readmitted to it. All of those examples demonstrate her concern to highlight the continuing inequality in the distribution of caring responsibilities (and work) between women and men.

That political element extends into her approach to form and content – particularly insofar as she positions herself in relation to what I'm going to loosely describe as the canon. The role of feminism in reimagining the canon has of course been the subject of a very extensive literature, but here I'm referring simply to the way in which particular plays are considered great or important, and how that determination is reflected in such measures as the frequency of their revival, their production by prestigious companies (especially national theatres or festivals), their publication either alone or in anthologies, and the critical writing that has been published about them. I'm also thinking of how ideas about the canon form expectations about what writers can and can't do: that it determines (to return to the example from the last chapter) how critics and audiences responded when Carr wrote *Sixteen Possible Glimpses*, but also determined the response when Friel and Kilroy adapted Chekhov.

But I'm also interested in how the canon shapes a writer's sense of a career: who are the influences to acknowledge, repudiate, disguise and celebrate? Carr has always been explicit about the writers she admires: Beckett, Tennessee Williams, Shakespeare, Chekhov and others. So my argument is that Carr's *oeuvre* should be seen as an extended investigation of the canon, and in particular of how women are imagined by men in canonical plays – but also the question of how a female author should engage with her predecessors. Through rewriting those representations, Carr shows how writers can occupy (and change) that canon: they can engage with the writers they love, but they can also be seen and respected for who they are.

That theme is present from her earliest plays. *Low in the Dark* is in dialogue with Beckett, for example, while *This Love Thing* reimagines three iconic women: Eve, Mary Magdalene and Mona Lisa. Her midlands plays also explore such characters. Hester in *By the Bog of Cats* is modelled on Medea, but she also calls to mind Hester Prynne from *The Scarlett Letter*, Miss Havisham from *Great Expectations*, and Lady Macbeth. Portia Coughlan is named for Shakespeare's heroine from *The Merchant of Venice*, but because she commits suicide she also can be seen as a response to the protagonists of such plays as *Hedda Gabler* and *Miss Julie* – and, indeed, to Anna Karenina. And as already mentioned, Carr's later plays give us new versions of Hecuba and Phaedra, while *The Cordelia Dream* sees, in the relationship between Lear and his daughter, a model for how any female playwright might think about her indebtedness to Shakespeare.

In order to bring this discussion into closer focus, I want to explore one play, *Woman and Scarecrow*. Like her other works, it's received a variety of responses, positive and negative. Its premiere at the Royal Court in 2006 was praised because of the performance of Fiona Shaw in the lead role – though in my own viewing, I felt that it suffered from a style of direction by Ramin Gray that was excessively literal. He presented the action as if it was happening to real people in a version of the real world, and this had the effect of making the language seem artificial, the relationships contrived and the situation implausible.

The following year, it was given a new production in the Peacock by Selina Cartmell, where it seemed like a wholly different play. The casting of Olwen Fouéré as Woman may have helped: she had already played the lead in *Ullaloo* as well as the Mai and Hester Swane, so she was very familiar with the demands of Carr's work. But also important was the style of direction, which both embraced and amplified the strangeness of the script, using lighting, projections and design to give a skewed representation of the world of the play – tipping it into a Gothic style without becoming melodramatic or wholly fantastical. Of all of Carr's directors, Cartmell has most consistently shown that these plays need to be presented in a slightly heightened, exaggerated fashion so that audiences can then bring them back down to earth again.

But it's also possible that the Peacock production succeeded because its Irish contexts – both literary and political – were more legible in the setting of the Irish national theatre. *Woman and Scarecrow* should be seen as a feminist reappraisal of the Irish dramatic tradition, but it is also engaged with the visual arts, music, fiction and many other forms of representation, including myth. And if it's ambitious in range, it is also hugely ambitious in its approach to theme, exploring nothing less than the meaning – or meaninglessness – of life.

It presents a fundamentally Beckettian situation: two figures, waiting for something to happen – but in this case that 'something' is the death of Woman, who is bedridden and in a mercilessly straight-talking dialogue with Scarecrow, a kind of Mephistophelean anti-self whose commitment to truth-telling helps Woman to prepare for her end. As in *Godot*, other people come and go. Woman's husband is tellingly called not 'he' but 'him', a personal pronoun that puts him in the role of object rather than subject and thus subtly undermines his status (and which might be a nod on Carr's part towards Beckett's use of pronouns in *Not I*). Also present is Auntie Ah, a vindictive and self-absorbed surrogate mother-figure whose presence emphasizes how Woman has sought but been denied suitable role models.

To anyone familiar with Irish drama, the relationship between Woman and Scarecrow will seem immediately familiar – albeit that we've only ever seen it in relationships between men. The Irish male double act is a trope that stretches from Yeats' Fool and Blind Man in *On Baile's Strand*, to O'Casey's Joxer and Captain Boyle in *Juno and the Paycock*, to Didi and Gogo in Beckett's *Godot* – and the joke in those plays is always that it takes two Irish men to carry out the actions of one fully functional human being. Carr extends that joke into a comparison with Friel's *Philadelphia, Here I Come!*, with Woman and Scarecrow acting as revisions of Gar's Public and Private selves – except that in her play the duo work together to imagine a departure that is not from Ireland but from the world of the living. She even includes a scene that directly alludes to the moment in *Philadelphia* when Gar wonders if his father shares a memory about a blue boat from a day they spent fishing. In Carr's play Woman imagines being given a red coat by her mother, hoping that this moment of affection between herself and a parent who died when she was very young is not an invention, is not wish fulfilment: 'for one brief moment, a mirror glance, I was the thing she had yearned for and found,' she says (Carr, 2009: 185). This passage presents beautiful writing in its own right, and is very effective on stage – but it also alludes to Gar's description of his time with his father in Friel's play: 'between us at that moment there was this great happiness, this great joy . . . and young as I was I felt, I knew, that this was precious' (Friel, 1996: 64). Both passages are deployed as examples of how we form our sense of self based on memories, giving rise to the question of how the unreliability of memory might impact upon our sense of who we are. Carr's appropriation of Friel's play is itself a way to remember something from the past: the transition from blue boat to red coat is like the development of a family memory that has been embellished in the retelling.

But she is not just in dialogue with Friel. In naming her character Woman (with a capital W), Carr is presenting her protagonist not so much as a psychologically realistic human being (though she can be performed as one) but as a playful representation of the iconic female figure who dominates Irish drama – mostly in plays written by men, of course. Her loquacity and freedom of speech contrast with her restriction of movement: she is trapped in a bed that she will never leave, but her conversation ranges across space and time. Visually, she will therefore remind audiences of comparable figures: Winnie in Beckett's *Happy Days* (1961), Mommo in *Bailegangaire*, McDonagh's Mag from *Beauty Queen of Leenane* (1996), Daughter in Enda Walsh's *bedbound* (2000), and many others who are physically restricted but verbally unfettered. Carr's repetition of this image places Woman in a long line, but what is important is that she fully possesses this figure – but then kills her off. She displays mastery over the trope but also says that it's time for it to be dispensed with.

That appropriation of male versions of women extends to other figures. Woman compares herself at various times to Ophelia ('now she had a good death' (Carr, 2009: 160)), Mary Magdalene (163), Cleopatra (181) and Anna Karenina (183). Carr also broadens her analysis beyond literature, to contemplate visual art in her discussion of Caravaggio's *Death of the Virgin* – a painting that includes both the Virgin Mary and Mary Magdalene, but which, Woman points out, shows them not in an idealized form but rather with a brutally carnal realism: 'Her feet were blue. Her dress was red . . . Yes, blue is too kind. Her feet were more a putrid greeny black. Bad circulation maybe, varicose veins, or maybe [Caravaggio] was just faithfully recording the rot . . . She's just another of those invisible women past their prime' (193). Carr also includes Dvořák's 'Ode to the Moon' from *Rusalka* – an opera that is about a woman who becomes a spirit of death (like Scarecrow); again we find a strong image of woman being rewritten by Carr.

In the play's last scene, Woman writes her will. She does not care about her possessions and their redistribution but rather about how she will be seen by others in death: she gives very strict instructions about her hair, her hands and the placement of religious artefacts on her body (Carr, 2009: 206). In presenting her character in this way, Carr is giving us Woman as emblem – but she is an emblem who *knows* that she is an emblem and is determined to assert her own authorship of how she is seen and understood. This is why the play's last minutes involve Scarecrow writing an account of Woman's life, but using Woman's own blood for ink. The act of writing is inherently violent, Carr demonstrates: it kills the living, ever-changing person in order to fix the icon on a page for eternity.

*Woman and Scarecrow* thus clears a space for new ways of writing, new ways of representing, new ways of thinking – including in Carr's own subsequent work. *By the Bog of Cats* and *Ariel* didn't openly declare their indebtedness to *Medea* and *The Oresteia* respectively, but after *Woman and Scarecrow* Carr would explicitly name her *Hecuba*, *Phaedra* and *Anna Karenina* as new versions of old stories. And in deconstructing the representation of women by male authors she also freed herself to begin exploring her own representation of men: Shakespeare, Chekhov, Lear. *Woman and Scarecrow* thus bridges the different stages of Carr's career but also shows how she has been working on core themes consistently since the beginning.

The achievement of Carr's work in its entirety, then, is to repurpose the canon, to ensure that we can't see it as we used to do: that *Woman and Scarecrow* will change how we see *Godot* or *Philadelphia, Here I Come!*; that *Bog of Cats* will change how we see *Medea*; that *The Cordelia Dream* will change how we see Lear; and that Carr herself might change how we think of Chekhov.

## Dirty deeds: Martin McDonagh, 1996–2015

The artists discussed in this chapter thus far have sought to rewrite Irish drama from perspectives that were viewed (or dismissed) as peripheral or marginal – because of gender identity, social class, geography, religion and so on. In their different ways, Hynes, Reid and Carr have used feminist strategies to transform Irish theatre, making space for the expression of new and neglected forms of identity.

Other forms of rewriting were also carried out during this period, including by male writers who acted with a variety of motivations. As I discussed in Chapter 1, Tom Murphy began his career by expressing exasperation with plays set in Irish country kitchens; in 1985 he put *Bailegangaire* in exactly that setting. And in the case of Beckett, I've suggested that the duo of Didi and Gogo in *Godot* can be seen as new versions of characters originally created by Yeats, Synge and O'Casey. So by way of concluding this chapter, I want now to explore the work of Martin McDonagh, showing how the feminist innovations of Garry Hynes cleared space for the production and reception of his work. His success in turn demonstrates how the feminist strategy of rewriting can be appropriated and redeployed in other contexts. He is one of the world's most successful playwrights, has produced regularly in the West End and on Broadway, has translated into dozens of languages, and (thanks in part to his successful movie career) is probably the most famous Irish playwright since Beckett. Yet his work remains divisive: his 2017 movie *Three Billboards Outside Ebbing, Missouri* drew accusations of insensitivity for its portrayal of racism, just as, two decades earlier, he had been accused of peddling anti-Irish stereotypes when his first plays were produced. The hostility generated by McDonagh tends to be related to his critics' views on his revision of images and ideas – which comes down to whether one thinks he is repeating racist or anti-Irish sentiments, or exposing them so that they can be rejected.

His plays and films are often described as exercises in pastiche, the argument (or, sometimes, the accusation) being that they ought to be seen as a collage of images from old Irish plays and gangster movies and pop culture (for a comprehensive overview of these debates, see Wallace, 2005). Whether positively or negatively inclined, those interpretations usually describe McDonagh's approach as an example of postmodern playfulness: he is reusing ideas simply for the fun of it, and it is foolish to seek meaning below the surface. Viewed in the context laid out in this chapter, however, it becomes possible to locate McDonagh within a broader pattern in Irish theatre: to argue that, like Hynes, Reid and Carr, he is rewriting earlier cultural forms in order to force his audiences to see old things in new ways.

As I've discussed earlier, one of the most admirable skills of Garry Hynes is her ability to allow Irish plays to be seen in the context of other works, to place playwrights in conversation with each other, and to bring to light correspondences that might never have been seen otherwise. While it is possible that McDonagh would have achieved success without Hynes' work on his early Druid productions (after all, the Royal National Theatre had *The Cripple of Inishmaan* under commission in 1996, when *Beauty Queen* premiered), Hynes' direction framed his work and thus determined how it would be received from the outset.

In the case of *The Beauty Queen of Leenane*, Hynes ensured that the production would be seen in the context of its multiple Irish precursors, many of which McDonagh himself was unaware of when he wrote the play. In dramatizing the feeling of entrapment that a middle-aged woman experiences as a result of having to care for her elderly mother, Hynes was encouraging audiences to remember the relationship between Mary and her grandmother Mommo in *Bailegangaire* – a link that she underscored by having Marie Mullen (who had played Mary in Murphy's play) take the role of Maureen in McDonagh's. That correspondence was evident too in the design for these plays, both of which were set in rural kitchens and deployed similar iconography. Murphy's play takes place in 'a room, a country kitchen. There are some modern conveniences: a cooker, a radio, electric light – a single pendant. Framed photographs on the walls, brown photographs of uncles, one of a christening party' (1993: 91). McDonagh's has a similar blend of the modern and the traditional:

The living room/kitchen of a rural cottage in the west of Ireland . . . On the kitchen side of the set is a door in the back wall leading off to an unseen hallway, and a newer oven, a sink . . . a small TV down left, an electric kettle and a radio on one of the kitchen cupboards, a crucifix and a framed picture of John and Robert Kennedy on the wall above the range

(1997: 3)

*Bailegangaire* begins with a forty-one-year-old woman working in the kitchen while her grandmother eats and drinks something from a mug; *Beauty Queen* begins with a forty-year-old woman preparing a similar kind of drink (Complan) for her elderly mother. Murphy's play is about a story told endlessly, night after night. In its earliest moments, McDonagh's play itself seems a repetition of Murphy's story.

The correspondences continue. With its use of melodramatic conventions – letters that are destroyed, love thwarted through outside interference – *Beauty Queen* speaks directly to Keane's *Sive* (1959). And in telling a story about a woman who finds hope in the unexpected arrival of a man who has come from afar, McDonagh's play re-presents Pegeen Mike's loss of the 'only Playboy of the Western World'. There are also Beckettian echoes, in, for example, the characterization of Pato and his brother Ray, another male double act that descends from *Godot*'s Vladimir and Estragon – a resemblance that Hynes emphasized in a 2016 revival of *Beauty Queen* in which Pato and Ray were played by Marty Rea and Aaron Monaghan respectively, actors who had just performed Vladimir and Estragon in a Druid production of *Godot*.

In interviews at the start of his career, McDonagh rejected suggestions that he had been influenced by those Irish predecessors, citing his indebtedness to Borges, Nabokov, Pinter and other non-Irish writers (see O'Toole, 2006). He also pointed out that he hadn't known Synge's work when he drafted his first plays – though of course he'd read *Playboy* by the time they were produced, as evident in his use of a phrase from Synge's play, 'the lonesome west', as the title of the trilogy's third part. But – again showing how Hynes' direction shifts our attention from authorial intention to audience interpretation – what was important was not that McDonagh was deliberately alluding to those writers (often, he wasn't) but that audiences saw his plays in the context of their knowledge of that prior work anyway.

The impact of Hynes' direction was to show what McDonagh had in common with his predecessors – but this also rendered all the more shocking his differences from them. In those earlier Irish plays, the female characters are forced to react to what has been done to them by men: Pegeen laments the loss of Christy because he has a freedom to leave that is denied to her, while in *Sive* the title character dies the night before her forced marriage to a much older farmer. In *Beauty Queen* Maureen is forced to stay in a hated environment that Pato escapes from – but unlike Sive she carries out an act of violence rather than being a victim of it, murdering her mother and then taking steps to evade conviction by the police. Maureen may be trapped, but she is certainly not a passive bystander in her own life. By building up audiences' expectations about what McDonagh's characters should do, Hynes showed that it was possible for exhausted tropes to be reinvigorated.

But if her direction sought to translate those tropes, McDonagh's other Irish plays likewise reinterpreted the Irish tradition. That was evident in *The Cripple of Inishmaan*, a play that ruthlessly sends up Ireland's willingness to celebrate how it is seen internationally – even though those representations usually fail to correspond with the realities of Irish life. In that play, McDonagh's characters constantly remark that Ireland 'mustn't be such a bad place' – but they draw, as evidence of that claim, from examples of international endorsement: if 'Yanks come to Ireland to do their filming' or if 'French fellas' or 'coloured fellas' or 'German folk' want to live there.

*Cripple* thus shows how Ireland's love of international performances of itself represents a kind of Faustian pact, delivering much-desired attention but at the price of misrepresentation. That approach is evident in one of the play's cruellest jokes, in which the audience forms the false impression that the eponymous protagonist has died alone in Hollywood when, in the play's seventh scene, they find him giving a moving monologue on the death of his parents:

> Can't I hear the wail of the banshees for me, as far as I am from me barren island home? A home barren, aye, but proud and generous with it, yet turned me back on ye I did, to end up alone and dying in a one-dollar rooming-house, without a mother to wipe the cold sweat off me, nor a father to curse death o'er the death of me, nor a colleen fair to weep tears o'er the still body of me.

> (1996: 52–3)

And with those words, Billy seems to die. We learn, however, that what we had taken to be a real moment in the plot of the play was actually a performance of a scripted scene from a film. And indeed, it wasn't even a real performance taking place in a film studio but Billy's rehearsal for a screen test, for a part that he didn't even get: the movie's producer determined that it would be 'better to get a normal fella that can act crippled than a crippled fella who can't fecking act at all' (66). McDonagh's joke is that only a fool would believe that these kinds of recycled images of Ireland represent the real world, and if we fall for the trick we may need to consider our willingness to believe such nonsense. The impact of Hynes' and McDonagh's approaches, then, is to remind audiences of the necessity that they bring their own interpretative faculties to bear on what they are seeing: our role is not to accept what we see passively but to evaluate the action carefully, making the story our own.

After *The Lieutenant of Inishmore* premiered in 2001, McDonagh began to move away from Irish stories. His short film *Six Shooter* was set in that country (there's even a character called Pato Dooley in it – the name of the male protagonist of *Beauty Queen*), and the 2008 movie *In Bruges* features two Irish hitmen. But his subsequent films *Seven Psychopaths* (2012) and *Three Billboards* are set in the United States, as is the play *A Behanding in Spokane* (2010). Similarly, *The Pillowman* (2003) and *A Very Very Very Dark Matter* (2018) draw on European fairy-tale traditions rather than Irish precursors.

Nevertheless, McDonagh continues to display Irish influences, notably in *Hangmen*, which premiered at the Royal Court in 2015. That play is set in Oldham in the 1960s, and its main character, Harry, is a man whose place in his society has been redefined against his will: he is a hangman whose job has been rendered obsolete by the 1965 abolition of the death penalty. One consequence of his enforced redundancy is that Harry will never be able to surpass the achievements of his rival hangman Pierrepoint; Harry will always be known as England's *second* most famous hangman. In this set-up we have a play that derives much of its dramatic momentum from Harry's refusal to accept that the story is over – he will instead seek to repeat his past in order to revise others' conception of who he is and what he's worth.

This plot is put into the service of exploring the ethics of state violence. From its opening, *Hangmen* probes the motivations and morality of the public executioner. What inspires an individual – and, by extension, a nation – to take the life of another person in the name of justice? Is this act grounded in a dutiful sense of upholding the law, whatever the cost? Is it a form of revenge? Or does it arise because the differences between the murderer and the hangman are less straightforward than we might think? Such questions haunt the play, shifting us from thinking about why Harry does what he does to analysing our own motivations and responsibilities.

With its 1960s setting and its coiled, intimidating dialogue, *Hangmen* will evoke memories of the early plays of Harold Pinter. Like that writer, McDonagh creates characters whose use of language (and silence) to coerce, threaten and overpower others is deeply unsettling. Yet *Hangmen* also recalls *The Playboy of the Western World*; indeed, despite (or, knowing McDonagh, probably because of) its English setting, it is his most obviously Syngean play. As in Synge's *Playboy*, McDonagh brings us to a pub in the middle of nowhere, a place whose owner spends his days spinning yarns before a small group of hangers-on and drunken flunkeys, while his lonely daughter dreams of better things. That scene is interrupted by the arrival of an eloquent stranger who first delights and then enrages the locals by confronting them with the truth about their attitudes to violence. As in Synge's play, the final scene will see the locals turning on the outsider, stringing him up in an act of impromptu justice. It's no surprise that although the play is set in England, and although the character comes from London, McDonagh has given his outsider an Irish surname: Mooney.

Synge's play set out to show that although we might enjoy telling stories about violent acts, actually taking another person's life is, in reality, messy, sordid and anything but heroic. *Hangmen* too seeks to chart the gap between gallous stories (like Harry's boastful newspaper interviews) and the reality of what it means to string someone up until he is dead. Far from being an act of postmodern playfulness, McDonagh's use of Synge is both serious and socially engaged. *Playboy* appeared at a time when Irish culture was dominated by images of masculine heroism and self-sacrifice; Synge's portrayal of Christy aimed to show what happens when violent wish fulfilment is made real. McDonagh deploys the same strategy to demonstrate how members of a society collude in and make possible state violence against its citizens.

The play is therefore an attack on the death penalty – which, though banned in the UK and Ireland, remains legal in more than fifty countries. But like McDonagh's other plays, it is a 'a violent play that is wholeheartedly anti-violence' and is thus written from what McDonagh has called a position of 'pacifist rage' (qtd in O'Hagan, 2001: 32). This places *Hangmen* firmly into a contemporary context, a period in which governments are increasingly willing to set aside human rights in their attempts to combat the appalling violence of religious extremists. By reusing Synge, McDonagh is able to extend Synge's implicit critique of militant nationalism into the present, shifting it from an Irish to a global context.

How, then, are we to characterize McDonagh's work? While it is clearly inappropriate to describe McDonagh as marginalized, given his dominance in the world of both film and theatre, I would nevertheless assert that he writes from a position that is considered marginal within the Irish theatre – that of the second-generation Irishman, a status that gives him a sense of belonging that is matched also by feelings of distance if not rejection. One useful way of thinking about that position is by alluding to McDonagh's characterization of Pato in *Beauty Queen*, a man who has mixed feelings about Ireland and England: 'when it's there I am, it's here I wish I was, of course. Who wouldn't? But when it's here I am . . . it isn't *there* I want to be, of course not. But I know it isn't here I want to be either' (1997: 26). That status – of not fully belonging to either place – means that McDonagh experiences distance from the Irish tradition: a distance that has allowed him the freedom to write plays set in England, central Europe and the United States. But he also has a sufficient sense of belonging to make Irish stories his own and deploy them in new contexts.

But again we must acknowledge the importance of what has come before: at the start of his career, McDonagh did not set out to rewrite Synge, but through working with Garry Hynes he gained the capacity to do so. That has allowed him to think about how Irishness is performed on world stages: to be sympathetic to the need in a small country for outside validation, while being satirical about the distorting impact of that need.

# CHAPTER 5
# ENCOUNTERING DIFFERENCE

## Introduction: *Translations*, 1980

Brian Friel's *Translations* is one of the most famous Irish plays of the modern period, often revived and the subject of extensive discussion by scholars, journalists and practitioners. Despite that status, it has also been one of his most misunderstood works. Upon its premiere, a 'number of critics gave every appearance of having taken the play's version of history disturbingly literally,' writes Marilyn Richtarik (2001: 56) – a tendency that has also been evident in some of the later scholarship, which presented the views put forward by his characters as if they accurately represented historical facts or Friel's own outlook.

Those misreadings are regrettable but understandable: as I argue below, they arise from one of the most important features of *Translations*, which is its prioritization of ambiguity in meaning over precision in how Friel (and his characters) communicate. I want to discuss how that prioritization is evident not only in his script but also in the play's production history, and to show that Friel's aim is to use ambiguity to create spaces that can allow for differences to meaningfully coexist and interact. Those differences can relate to identity and language (Irish/English), but also to space (the formal theatre building as opposed to improvised or informal performance spaces), time (the past and the present), modes of writing (history and literature), geography (Ireland/Britain/Northern Ireland/the UK) and so on.

Certainly we can situate that aim in a political context: the play shows apparently exclusive interpretations of the world coexisting quite peacefully, and it is not too great a leap from there to suggest that this demonstrates that one solution to conflict in Northern Ireland is not for one 'way of seeing' to triumph over the other, but for both to coexist. But as this chapter develops, it will become possible to see how Friel's approach to difference has been used in other contexts, allowing Irish theatre-makers to find new ways to think about sectarianism, sexuality, migration, gender and other themes. I therefore want to use *Translations* as a way of anchoring a discussion of three other playwrights: Marie Jones, Frank McGuinness and Enda Walsh.

By doing so, I want to draw attention to how those different writers use similar strategies but with very different ambitions and outcomes.

The premiere of *Translations* took place in Derry on 23 September 1980, and is now regarded as one of the iconic events in the history of Irish drama, taking its place alongside the premieres of *The Playboy of the Western World* and *The Plough and the Stars* – while contrasting with those events for offering a glimpse of the possibility of peace, where Synge and O'Casey's plays had exposed divisions in the society. That premiere was itself an act of reconciling differences, as evidenced by the choice of venue: Derry's Guildhall, a space where the city council meets and thus a site for the setting of laws that were enforced under the auspices of the British government, which was regarded by many of Derry's citizens as an occupying force. Because of the gerrymandering of constituency boundaries, the Guildhall was also perceived as a symbol of Unionist domination – something Friel had explored in *The Freedom of the City*, and which also explains the bombing of the building by the IRA in 1972 and 1978. By staging a play there, Friel was showing how it could be hospitable to other activities, to other interpretations, to other ways of thinking about nation and identity – and he was showing too that a Nationalist appropriation of the Guildhall could be carried out without violence. That symbolic power arose because of the way in which differences were put into dialogue with each other: the political space was in dialogue with the performance space, in a play by a writer from a Nationalist background that was being staged in a building associated with Unionism.

That transformation of space needs to be seen in the context of the ideas of the 'fifth province' that have often been associated with Field Day. That concept was put forward not by Friel or his company (as is sometimes asserted) but by Richard Kearney and Mark Patrick Hederman, in the first edition of the journal *The Crane Bag*, in 1977. They saw their publication as an attempt to create an imaginative space that might be free of the constraints of politics, geography and history – and which might therefore inspire new ways of imagining Ireland and Irishness. They called this place a 'fifth province' of the mind, an imaginative space that would exist apart from (but in relationship to) the four geographical provinces of Ireland. 'This province, this place, this centre, is not a political position. In, fact, if it is a position at all, it would be marked by the absence of any particular political and geographical delineation, something more like a dis-position,' they wrote, adding that the fifth province would allow for the 'excavation of unactualized spaces within the reader', thus allowing a 'new understanding' to emerge (Hederman and Kearney, 1977: 4).

The need for such an approach arose due to the emergence of the Troubles in Northern Ireland from the late 1960s, a conflict that became increasingly violent from Bloody Sunday onwards, with bomb attacks being carried out in Northern Ireland, Britain and the Republic of Ireland by the various paramilitary and terrorist organizations on each side, alongside ambushes, assassinations and other acts of destruction. Those clashes were often expressed (sometimes simplistically) as arising from issues of identity: an apparent incompatibility between a Catholic/Nationalist community that wanted a united Ireland on one side, and a Protestant/Unionist community that wanted Northern Ireland to remain part of the United Kingdom on the other. As a result, the conflict was enacted not just through violence but through culture: through the displaying of flags or other emblems, the refusal to change traditions relating to marching and parades, the use of Irish or English place names, and so on. Such debates invariably had an impact on the theatre, even when companies sought, as far as possible, to be neutral. In 1968 and 1969, for example, the Lyric only barely survived a public clash among its directors about whether the (British) national anthem should be played at the end of its performances – a debate that led to the temporary resignation of its co-founders Mary and Pearse O'Malley (LTA, T4/816).

So the ideas of the fifth province put forward by Kearney and Hederman were an attempt to address the cultural issues of the conflict and to use culture to offer new possibilities. In the *Crane Bag* introduction, they were thinking mainly of the act of criticism (rather than creativity per se), but the fifth province idea would prove readily applicable to the arts – and especially to theatre, a form that is dedicated to multiplying the potential meanings of a single space. With Field Day, a place such as the Guildhall could become a performance space, neutralized of any 'political or geographical delineation' but also existing in contrast to the political and geographical contexts that surrounded it. By showing that the signified object (the Guildhall) could be separated from its symbolic significance (as an emblem of Unionist domination), Field Day created the possibility that other symbols could be reconstituted: symbols of identity such as flags; symbols of nation such as territory, language or indeed theatre itself; and symbols of power and control such as maps and uniforms. If the Guildhall could change but stay true to its past, then so too could Nationalism and Unionism. The point was not to change the meaning of the Guildhall from one fixed point to another, but to suggest that perhaps the meanings of the Guildhall were multiple and need not be fixed at all.

But allowing for a multiplicity of meanings will inevitably mean that some interpretations will be inaccurate. It also means that there has been surprisingly little consensus about the meaning of *Translations* itself. Friel, perhaps at pains to reject the accusations of historical inaccuracy that greeted its premiere, said that it 'has to do with language and only language' (1999: 75). Nicholas Grene states that the 'main theme' of *Translations* is not so much language as 'interpretation' (1999: 184), while Richard Pine declares that it is a play 'about time' (1999: 180). For Mary Trotter, it is a 'drama about language, history, colonization and partition' (2008: 157), while Anthony Roche identifies 'the possibility of a gay sub-text' in recent productions (2011: 147). Aidan O'Malley sees the task of *Translations* as the 'shifting [of] apparently fixed *topoi* through the motions of metaphor and translation' (2011: 13) in order to overcome the 'deterministic conceptions of geography and demography' that sustained the Troubles. When asked if the play has a political message, Friel replied, 'Well, if it has, I don't know what it is!' (qtd by Richtarik, 2001: 49) – yet Colm Tóibín once described Field Day as the 'literary wing of the IRA' (1995). We can probably disagree with some of those statements, but it's much more difficult to argue that any one of them is the single correct approach to the meaning of the text or its performance.

That uncertainty is exactly what the play aims to evoke, however – as is clear from its first moments. We begin with Manus and Sarah, and we are told in the stage directions that the latter could be any age from seventeen to thirty-five – a range that many actors can be situated in happily enough, but one that makes our interpretation of Sarah's feelings very difficult. There is no doubt during the play that she is motivated by feelings of love for Manus, but the love of a 17-year-old will be very different from the love of a 35-year-old. Manus is teaching Sarah to speak, telling her how he'll at last be able to uncover 'all the secrets that have been in that head of yours all these years' (Friel, 1996: 251). Friel is showing how language is used not only to explain the world but also to control it, and it is important for the overall shape of the play that Sarah remains almost entirely inscrutable for its duration – like a terrain refusing to be mapped.

That imprecision of meaning runs through the play. A child is born but we never learn who its father is; the English soldier Yolland disappears but we're never sure what has happened to him; a young woman called Maire dreams of leaving Ireland for America but, as with Gar in *Philadelphia*, we'll never know for sure if she gets there. And the imprecision is present also in the stage directions, as for example when Friel's script calls for the staging of a 'vaguely "outside" area' (1996: 291) for the love scene between Yolland and Maire. His refusal to define specifically for the director or designer how the space should function stands in contrast to the efforts made by the map-makers in the play to capture as much as they can.

Famously, the imprecision extends to the use of language in *Translations*, to the fact that the audience is listening to actors speaking English but must imagine that (most of the time) they are hearing characters speaking in Irish. This act of linguistic bait-and-switch is nothing new in the world of theatre, of course: when we watch Shakespeare's *Julius Caesar* we imagine that the English we hear is Latin; we know that a real Danish prince would not have spoken as Hamlet does, and that Romeo really wooed Juliet in Italian. But we pretend, or more precisely we suspend our disbelief. Similarly with *Translations* we find that, just as the Guildhall is pretending to be a hedge school, and the year 1980 is pretending to be the year 1833, the English language is pretending to be Irish. And that act of pretence is analogous to the process of translation: it is the substitution of one sign for another.

That suspension of disbelief has the impact of undercutting and ironizing most of the play's political statements, particularly those given by the drunken schoolmaster, Hugh. 'I explained that a few of us did, on occasion [speak English] – outside the parish of course – and then usually for the purposes of commerce, a use to which his tongue seemed particularly suited,' he says (Friel, 1996: 269) – an assertion that English is not a language appropriate to the expression of ideas that are beautiful or intangible or that exist apart from the economic. Hugh's words are incorrect, of course, and we know this because Friel's play is written in English and expresses more than the merely commercial or everyday. Also important is Hugh's profession of ignorance of the existence of Wordsworth – 'did he speak of me to you?' he asks, probably disingenuously. Hugh goes on to speak dismissively of English literature, praising Greek and Roman poetry instead. But given that we know how beautifully Wordsworth used English – and given too that Friel's text is directly mirroring the map scene from Shakespeare's first part of *Henry IV* – it is evident that Hugh's views do not accord with Friel's. 'English', Hugh says, 'couldn't really express [Irish people]' (269). But Friel's point is that Hugh's statement, delivered in English (albeit English pretending to be Irish), has indeed just expressed something about Ireland and the Irish: in the act of delivery on stage, Hugh's sentence negates its own validity. Friel makes the same point more humorously in calling one of his characters Doalty, a name that in English reveals the character's personality (he is indeed quite doltish), even though as an Irish speaker he would most likely have been unaware of the interlinguistic pun – it is English, not Irish, that 'expresses' Doalty's true character.

By putting into Hugh's mouth many of the 'diamond absolutes' (to use a phrase from Friel's friend Seamus Heaney, in the poem 'Exposure') of Irish Nationalism, Friel shows that excessive fidelity to markers of identity, whether geographical or linguistic, can lead to stasis or, to use the play's word, 'fossilization'. Hugh comes to recognize this by the end of the play, when he expresses a willingness to begin teaching his students English. Change may be painful but it is necessary, he acknowledges – soberly (in every sense of that word), for once. But it also becomes possible to map the play's aesthetics onto the Troubles: if it is possible to change apparently essential characteristics in a theatre, perhaps those markers of identity could also change in Ireland generally.

That treatment of language shows how difference can function both socially and dramatically. The differences between the Englishman Yolland and the Irishwoman Maire become a source of romantic and sexual attraction between them; they also allow Friel to appropriate a plot from the melodramas of Boucicault, whose *The Shaughraun* deals with a similar romance between an Irish woman and an English soldier (Behan stole this plot for *An Giall* and *The Hostage* too). We also find other clashes being either resolved, transcended or placed into creative tension: clashes between imperialism and literature, the Irish and English languages, male and female, the rural and the metropolitan, aggression and persuasion, coercion and collaboration, silence and revelation, inside and outside, and so on. Friel's argument is that those collisions do give rise to conflict and can result in terrible losses – but they might also produce something new, something of value, a way to move forward. And even if they don't, we may have no choice but to change anyway.

The multiplicity of meaning that is a feature of both the play's form and content is also evident in its production history, which shows audiences responding to it in ways that were heavily dependent upon local contexts. Richtarik places the critical response to the play into three broad categories by distinguishing between the responses of audiences in Northern Ireland, the Republic of Ireland, and England:

> The interpretations given in the different regions were so divergent as
> to suggest that audiences were watching, in effect, different plays. In

the North, the ritual aspect of theatre was uppermost, with the act of performing and attending the play on a level with the dramatist's words themselves. In the Republic, the play was applauded in large part for what was seen as its nationalist political and social message. Finally, in London, it was the entertainment value of *Translations* that assured its success

(2001: 51)

O'Malley remarks that Richtarik's analysis is overdependent on press response (2011: 22), and while it is indeed important not to conflate media reaction with audience interpretation, her research nevertheless provides evidence of a diversity of responses based on where the play was performed. That diversity was evident in critics' views about what happens to the English soldier in the play. At its midway point, Yolland recounts how Doalty 'cut a pathway round my tent and from my tent down to the road', an act that he interprets as a kindness intended 'so that my feet won't get wet with the dew' (282). But perhaps Doalty was instead marking the landscape, providing a pathway that would allow the Donnelly twins to abduct Yolland, making Doalty complicit in his probable murder. As Richtarik explains, 'We are left to guess the lieutenant's fate. While Irish critics had hardly hesitated to assume the worst, the English continued to hope for the best' (63). Such responses directly contradict each other, but the value of *Translations* is that it functions like a theatrical Schrödinger's cat, allowing two contrasting ideas to be correct at the same time, suspending a final determination of 'the truth' indefinitely.

This multiplication of the potential interpretations of the play demonstrates the power of touring theatre to activate new forms of imaginative engagement in audiences. As I've discussed, Field Day's tours coincided with the evolution of Druid's 'Unusual Rural Tours' in parish halls and community centres throughout Ireland from the late 1970s, and Charabanc began touring in 1983 also. It is often forgotten that many of the important Irish plays of the 1980s were written to be toured: most of the works of Charabanc as well as Friel's *Translations* and *Making History* (1988), Murphy's *Conversations on a Homecoming* and *Bailegangaire* (1985), and Kilroy's *Double Cross* (1986), among others. The extent to which those tours influenced the composition and reception of those plays has yet to be fully explored. For Field Day's co-founder Stephen Rea, 'the freedom of movement between traditional theatres and the more unpredictable community centres should be a liberating experience for the company and therefore for the audiences' (qtd by O'Malley, 2011: 5). In an interview with Martine Pelletier, Rea also spoke of the importance of touring:

> We went to a lot of one-horse towns but you were really talking to the people of that place. They weren't coming into a theatre where they felt intimidated, or that they had to have some kind of theatrical understanding that would make things easy for them. They really had an experience. When we did *Making History* [Brian Friel's 1988 play for Field Day] in Dungannon, which is where Hugh O'Neill had his seat of power, it was very different from doing it anywhere else. When we talked about the Devlins and the Quinns having a feud they roared laughing in Dungannon because presumably they're still having that feud. It was an intense experience, talking about the conquest of Ireland and the demise of Hugh O'Neill meant something in Dungannon that it couldn't mean anywhere else.
>
> (2000: 60–1)

I argued in Chapter 4 that Garry Hynes' artistic direction of Druid worked towards the dismantling of theatrical hierarchies, and we can see something similar happening in Field Day's work, which disrupts the idea that a play has one meaning that must be articulated in one space. The meaning of *Translations* needed to be in a state of dynamic flux, and this could only happen through keeping the production in motion. For once, the words of Hugh seem apt: it is 'not the literal past that shapes us, but images of the past embodied in language', he says, offering a good description of what the play itself is doing (Friel, 1996: 306). 'We must never cease renewing those images; because once we do, we fossilize,' he concludes.

The importance of *Translations* from a political point of view has been analysed in detail, but here I would draw the conclusion that we also need to understand that its importance lay in Friel's willingness to show how different meanings can coexist – between an English soldier and an Irish woman; between an audience in Dungannon and an audience in London; between one language and another; between a building used for legislation and a building used for art. Those differences were activated through the process of touring, but were present in the script anyway. As we'll see in the rest of this chapter, other forms of difference would also be activated in the Irish theatre from the 1980s onwards, using similar strategies but for different aims. To advance that discussion I want now to turn to another company from Northern Ireland that toured during the 1980s but which differs from Field Day in many ways.

## Sectarianism and difference: Charabanc and Marie Jones

The question has often been asked as to why Field Day has received so much more attention than Charabanc. Friel and Rea's company has been the subject of at least three standalone books – by Richtarik (2001), O'Malley (2011) and Carmen Szabo (2007) – as well as numerous articles. In contrast, Charabanc only began to receive academic sustained attention in the early 2000s, first in Foley's *Girls in the Big Picture* (2003) and then in Claudia Harris' critical edition of four of their plays (2006). Subsequent studies by Trotter (2008), Coffey (2016) and Parr (2017) have begun to redress that omission, though we still await a full-length study of the company and its legacies.

Such a study is rendered difficult (but by no means impossible) for a variety of reasons. Field Day produced eleven plays between 1980 and 1995; all were published upon their premiere and all have received detailed critical attention as well as careful archival preservation. During the same period Charabanc produced twenty-two plays, of which only six remain in print; most were published only after the demise of the company, and while there are papers about Charabanc in the Linen Hall Library, the archive is not comprehensive. Field Day was established by people who were part of the theatrical and academic establishment; Charabanc was a collective response to omission from that establishment: it was set up in 1983 by Marie Jones, Maureen McAuley, Eleanor Methven, Carol Moore and Brenda Winter in response to their shared conviction that there was a lack of good roles for Irish women – a problem that they set about redressing by creating plays themselves.

It's not the fault of Field Day that Charabanc was neglected, though we can and should note that none of its eleven original plays was written by a woman – and that those plays provided fifty-eight roles for men but only thirty-two for women, with only Parker's *Pentecost* having more female than male roles.[1] But for Victoria White and others, the neglect of Charabanc is wholly about gender: 'The press have tried to marginalize them by concentrating on their being women, and they have been referred to as catering for a minority audience … Charabanc were referred to as "the best all-women theatre company in Ireland" ' (1989: 34). Given that the company was Ireland's only 'all-women theatre company' at that time – and given too that the 'minority' they represented made up more than half of the population (and a considerably greater proportion of theatregoers) – such statements demonstrated a dismissive attitude on the part of critics.

An additional explanation for this neglect was that the company's collaborative ways of working subverted the traditional power structures of the Irish theatre, sharing authorship rather than asserting the primacy of a single authorial perspective. Its first play, *Lay Up Your Ends* (1983), was devised with Martin Lynch – and although that approach produced a play that is dynamic and multifaceted, it also meant that the script could not be included in Claudia Harris' collection due to a disagreement about how much credit Lynch should receive (a disagreement that was later resolved, allowing the play to appear in 2008). That problem exemplifies how many of the legal structures surrounding theatre – particularly relating to copyright (and hence to royalties) – tend to privilege the work of the lone author over the collaboratively devised text.

But the difficulty in labelling Charabanc arose due to a deliberate decision on the part of the company, and bears comparison with Friel's embracing of ambiguity in *Translations*. Eleanor Methven told Victoria White that they were reluctant to embrace the label of feminist theatre for fear of alienating their audiences – but there was no doubt that their work was feminist. As White explains, 'They are concerned to show reality through womens' [*sic*] eyes . . . and they would not be happy with a situation where there were more men than women in their plays' (1989: 35). Connal Parr points out that this reluctance to be pinned down also characterizes the later work of Marie Jones, which, he writes, was based on a 'fear of labels estranging, and thus diminishing, the audience'. He quotes from an interview in which Jones expresses this thought directly: 'Once you label you alienate. Plays speak for themselves' (Parr, 2017: 243).

That avoidance of labels also relates to the company's determination to avoid falling into the trap of alignment with one side or the other in the Troubles – and there too there is a distinction from Field Day, which was strongly informed by a Nationalist outlook, even as its board of directors comprised men from Catholic and Protestant backgrounds. As Coffey explains, the Charabanc actors also came from both religious traditions, but they embraced any potential differences: 'Deriving strength from [their] identity as theatre practitioners meant that the women of Charabanc put their professional identities before their religious or ethnic identities. Their status as an integrated group allowed them the legitimacy and access to perform in both Catholic and Protestant neighborhoods and to include stories from both communities in their repertoires' (2016: 85).

Jones left Charabanc in 1990, but those early experiences informed the subsequent development of her work – and the relative critical neglect of Charabanc has been matched by indifference, if not hostility, to Jones' *oeuvre* too. The links between Jones' days with Charabanc and her solo career are made evident by Tom Maguire and Eugene McNulty: they praise her for an 'openness to collaboration with others . . . engagement with popular culture . . . and an unerring sense of what works on stage' (McNulty and Maguire, 2015: 5) – all of which can be said of Charabanc's work too. But in the discussion that follows, I want to go further, by suggesting that, for Jones, engaging with difference is the primary driver of her artistic sensibility. While she has written or co-written more than forty plays, many of them have in common a single theme: how the encounter with otherness can be used to develop a better understanding of the self.

That theme is explored in detail in her most popular play *Stones in His Pockets* (1999), in which a Hollywood film crew tell a story about Ireland – but make clear that they are not trying to film the real country, but rather to match American audiences' preconceptions about it. Jones adopts a more complex approach to the same theme in another popular hit, *Women on the Verge of HRT* (1996), in which two middle-aged Belfast women travel to the Donegal hotel of Irish entertainer Daniel O'Donnell. In the naturalistic first half, the women discuss their unsatisfying relationships with men, but in the expressionistic second half, they sit on a cliffside and summon various people in their lives to account for themselves. The play concludes with a call for a reappraisal of Irish gender roles, challenging the notion that equality for Irish women has been achieved. For Shonagh Hill, *Women on the Verge* offers a radical form of resistance to what she describes as neo-liberal attempts to govern public expressions of female aging (2015). It achieves that objective as a result of Jones' interest in border-crossing, I would suggest: literally in the sense that her characters leave Northern Ireland for the Republic, but formally in her blend of popular and literary forms. After all, no one else in the Irish theatre can so convincingly create a work that requires an awareness not only of the country and western songs of Daniel O'Donnell but also the dream plays of Strindberg.

Jones is particularly effective in using such approaches to think about sectarianism, and in this context I want to dedicate some attention to a pair of plays that explore one 'side' in the north from the perspective of the other: *A Night in November* (1994) and *The Blind Fiddler* (2003). The first of those plays falls into a tradition of Irish dramas about football that were inspired by the successes of the Irish soccer team at the European Championships of

1988 and the World Cup finals of 1990 and 1994. The titular night in November happened in 1993, when the Republic of Ireland played Northern Ireland at Windsor Park in Belfast, with the former knowing that they would only have to avoid losing to the latter in order to secure qualification for the following year's World Cup. The match was bad-tempered, concluding in a 1–1 draw, but the event is remembered mainly for the behaviour of the crowd, which chanted sectarian slogans while also targeting the Republic's black players for racist abuse. Most notoriously, they also chanted the words 'trick or treat' – a phrase that had been used in an attack two weeks earlier, during Halloween, on a pub frequented mainly by Catholics. That massacre had left eight people dead (six of them Catholic), and was itself a retaliation for the bombing by the IRA of a fish and chip shop on the Shankill Road, which had killed nine people as well as the IRA bomber himself. This cycle of indiscriminate killing of civilians based solely on their religious background seemed particularly intractable at that time – which is an important context for our understanding of the play.

*A Night in November* is a one-man show, which in its original production was performed by Dan Gordon, a prominent Belfast actor and frequent collaborator with Jones. His character is Kenneth, a northern Protestant who is so repulsed by the behaviour of his side's supporters that he decides to follow the Republic's team to the World Cup. The theatrical techniques used by Jones operate as a metaphor for social transformation: just as Gordon can shift between gender, age, nationality and religion in performing all of the play's characters, so should we see that apparently inherent markers of identity can be changed quite easily. Kenneth rejects sectarianism while maintaining his core identity: his background need not be defined in opposition to the 'other side' but can embrace it, rejecting the binary for a 'both/and' mode of being. That transformation is mirrored in the style of performance, with the actor's movement from one role to another enacting the notion that identities need not be fixed, that we can choose what to take with us and what to leave behind. *A Night in November* has sometimes been criticized as Nationalist wish fulfilment, but it might be fairer to argue that Jones is attempting to show that one way to break the cycle of murder in the north is to find common ground between Catholic and Protestant, Unionist and Nationalist, north and south – with the playing fields of an international football tournament operating as a kind of depoliticized space that allowed for new ways of being Irish to be imagined.

*The Blind Fiddler* is a different kind of play, not least in the fact that it was produced after the achievement of the Good Friday Agreement of 1998 had brought peace (or relative peace) to the north. It had originally appeared in a Charabanc one-act in 1990 but was revised and expanded by Jones for a 2003 production at the Lyric. But where in *A Night in November* Kenneth willingly decides to engage with a positive manifestation of Irishness, here we find a Catholic family that is driven apart by the desire to escape its roots – both in terms of religion and social class. So it dramatizes a similar kind of journey, though here the transformation is seen as negative rather than positive, largely because (unlike Kenneth) Jones' characters reject their roots.

The play begins on Lough Derg, a place that has inspired many great works of Irish writing, Heaney's poem cycle *Station Island* (1995) being the most relevant – since, like Heaney, Jones wants to use the metaphor of the religious ritual as a way of thinking about the cyclical nature of violence in the north. Like Heaney, Jones uses the island's three-day Catholic pilgrimage to frame an attempt to come to terms with the past. In her case, the pilgrim is Kathleen (played in the 2003 production by her former Charabanc colleague Carol Moore), who has come to Lough Derg in the footsteps of Pat, her recently dead father, who had visited the island for each of the previous thirty years (or so she believes – she learns at the end of the play that he had secretly been performing in an annual festival of traditional music).

As a child, Kathleen had been inspired by her father's story of the Blind Fiddler, whose music had so delighted people that they forget their hunger. It's a romantic tale, but one that Mary, Kathleen's mother, believes is inappropriate to the life of a poor Catholic family in 1960s Belfast, causing her to insist that Kathleen and her brother reject their father's romanticism for an upbringing that gives them financial security and social acceptance – at the cost of estrangement from their parents. In adulthood, Kathleen is resentful and confused about this, particularly at her father's compliance with her mother's insistence on her upward mobility. Her visit to Lough Derg is therefore an attempt to come to terms with her past, which she reconstructs in a series of vignettes set mainly in her father's pub. Those scenes are populated by a multitude of characters – and in typical Jones fashion, they are played by only four actors. Each scene is accompanied by a traditional score that was performed live, blurring the boundaries between the stage play and the traditional Irish session, and again demonstrating Jones' commitment to collaborative approaches to performance.

At the play's heart is the Catholic notion of sacrifice. The people who walk barefoot through Lough Derg do so to better enjoy the lives they'll resume after their pilgrimage. This ritual is poignantly contrasted with the sacrifices made by Pat and Mary for the sake of their children – which are well motivated but result in unhappiness. This consideration of sacrifice allows Jones to think about the impact of sectarianism, which is shown not just to cause discrimination by one side against the other, but which also, more perniciously, causes people to change themselves. Although ostensibly acting in her children's interests, Mary is motivated by shame about her own status, insisting that her children speak in accents different from her own and that her husband cease playing the fiddle, and refusing to allow a traditional wake to be held in their pub lest her family's Catholic background become too obvious to their Protestant neighbours. This shame involves Mary alienating herself from her own family, who see her desire to be different in terms of religion rather than social class: 'she'll clean herself into a Protestant' suggests her sister Bridie, wryly, demonstrating the way in which an association of Catholicism with poverty and ignorance motivates Mary's actions (Jones, 2008: 7). She is unapologetic about this: 'We can't sit by and watch the children try and grow up surrounded by drink and foul language and no-hopers. We are Catholics . . . They have to do well . . . They are going to get no favours in [Belfast] if they don't' (11).

Tragically, these sacrifices prove justified (at least on financial grounds): Mary's children acquire stability and status, whereas their father's clientele are forced to emigrate because of Belfast businesses' refusal to employ Catholics. But the parents lose as much as they gain: Pat's pub is bombed during the Troubles and their children have been educated to such an extent that the parents have lost the ability to relate to them, and vice versa.

That exploration of the guilt experienced by people who leave working-class communities is an important theme in British drama (one thinks of Willy Russell's 1983 musical *Blood Brothers* as a work that Jones appears to be in dialogue with). But in Ireland the subject of class has often been set aside in favour of explorations of the 'national question' – though here, as in so many other things, Tom Murphy is an exception, exploring the guilt caused by the upward mobility of his characters in *A Whistle in the Dark* (1961), *The Wake* (1997) and *The House* (2000), among other plays. It tells us much about Jones' openness to a multiplicity of influences that she finds in British performance a way of thinking about the interplay between social class and sectarianism in the north.

She is able to address those links particularly effectively because of her decision to present the action *around* the Troubles, in the early 1960s and in the post-Good Friday Agreement era of the early 2000s. Doing so allows her to show how social class and sectarianism are closely related – an idea that's relevant to the Troubles, while also resonating with other aspects of British and Irish life. She is therefore attempting to reclaim Irish traditions from the political: she shows that traditional Irish music has been undervalued and devalued; and her inclusion of music in the play, as well as the musicians' movement from the stage's wings to its centre during the 2003 production, are examples of how the use of stage space can combat the marginalization of people, ideas and ways of making art. Jones also shows that the problems faced by people in relation to social class are shared by communities across Britain and Ireland – that tensions relating to nation and religion have the impact of driving people apart who might otherwise share the same struggle.

The transformation of Kenneth in *A Night in November* proceeds from feelings of shame, and involves a deliberate decision to embrace an identity that is pluralist, celebratory and (like all national identities) a useful and temporary fiction. *The Blind Fiddler* presents a much more nuanced approach, showing how Kathleen's family similarly embraced a new form of identity as a response to feelings of shame – but where Kenneth found that transformation a liberation, she and her brother experience it as a loss. Jones has multiple aims here, one being to show the way in which prejudicial values can be so embedded in a society as to cause communities to inflict damage upon themselves. But she also calls for balance: Kenneth embraces difference in order to get back in touch with himself, and *The Blind Fiddler* concludes with Kathleen and her brother embracing their father's love of traditional music – something they have become alienated from – as a way of understanding themselves.

That approach is also present in her use of theatrical form. Jones is unapologetic in her use of popular culture, whether that is the songs of Daniel O'Donnell, the traditional Irish music of *The Blind Fiddler*, or the expressions of Irishness that were built up around football in the early 1990s. But she also demonstrates a desire to place those popular forms in dialogue with more 'literary' forms: *The Blind Fiddler* may have reminded audiences of *Riverdance* when it premiered, but it was also drawing on the work of Heaney, Synge and Friel, as well as Boucicault. And we must also take account of how she herself is reaching out to 'the other', writing about the life of a Catholic family whose early years coincided with her own upbringing in East Belfast.

To return to the question explored at the beginning of this section, it might be argued that Jones and Charabanc have been neglected not because of any deficiency in their work, but rather because both the company and the author draw so expansively upon new ways of making work that they cannot be categorized and theorized as readily as companies such as Field Day. This should be seen as representing a fault not with Jones (nor with Field Day) but with the methods that have been used to understand such work. As Irish Theatre Studies have moved from focusing primarily on printed playscripts to performance histories, the work of Jones has gained a little more attention – but we must be alert to the way in which her neglect demonstrates how gender determines not just who is written about but how they are written about. As we move now to a discussion of the plays of Frank McGuinness, we'll see how gender and sexuality interplay in similar ways.

## Sexuality and difference: Frank McGuinness

In 2014, shortly before Ireland became the first country in the world to vote for the introduction of same-sex marriage in a referendum, the performance artist and activist Panti Bliss (Rory O'Neill) took to the stage of the Abbey to deliver a 'Noble Call'. Her speech was part of a series of codas to the performance of a play by James Plunkett called *The Risen People* (1958) that had been revived by the Abbey to commemorate the 1913 Dublin 'Lockout', a notorious clash between workers and employers that had left thousands of striking Dubliners on the brink of starvation. For the Abbey production, artists, politicians, scholars and other public figures had been invited to provide a reflection on the play's themes after the curtain call, with a different guest appearing each night.

Panti's 'Noble Call' happened towards the end of the production's run. Those involved had not imagined that it would reach any audience greater than the one in the theatre that night, but Panti had been accompanied by the documentary-maker Colm Horgan (who would later release a film about her called *Queen of Ireland*); he videoed the speech and it was then uploaded to YouTube.[2] The events that followed were wholly unexpected: the ten-minute clip was viewed more than 200,000 times in its first two days online and, by the end of 2017, had been seen more than 800,000 times. It was the subject of immediate global attention, attracting praise from celebrities such as Madonna, while also galvanizing support for the same-sex marriage campaign within Ireland (for Panti's own account, see O'Neill, 2015).

The speech was passionate in its exploration and excoriation of how the individual experiences homophobia – and of how the society at large allows such prejudice to happen. It was also a magnificent act of public performance, made deeply moving by Panti's ability to hold in careful tension her feelings of rage and vulnerability. It was a moment when someone who had been marginalized took centre stage, and even if her speech was impactful because it had been posted on social media, its symbolic power lay in its delivery at the national theatre. By inviting Panti to give the Noble Call, the Abbey was making clear that the national space needed to include voices like hers – something that was all the more brave for happening in a context in which the state broadcaster RTÉ had been threatened with legal action for a TV interview in which Panti had described two prominent journalists as homophobic (for an in-depth analysis of the event and its consequences, see Emer O'Toole, 2017). This was a moment when the Abbey's importance for its society was newly underlined – not just because of the delivery of the speech in its auditorium, but also because the use of the national space for that speech was a clear assertion of the rights and equality of gay men and women. That event provided a decisive boost to the campaign towards equal marriage in Ireland, and is a fine example of the capacity of theatre to influence and even redirect the course of a national debate.

While the appearance of Panti at the Abbey surprised many international commentators, it can be seen as the culmination of a long period within the Irish theatre of activism and engagement in relation to gay rights. As I've written elsewhere, the artistic directorship of Patrick Mason at the Abbey was very important for its promotion of sexual equality – not just by staging plays about gay men such as Kushner's *Angels in America* (performed in 1995), but also in using the symbolic power of the Abbey to protest against the exclusion of gay rights groups from St Patrick's Day parades in the United States (see Lonergan, 2009: 145–52). And in such actions Mason was building on earlier work by Irish dramatists, who had sought to create space for the expression of gay identities on the Irish stage – as seen in plays such as Kilroy's *The Death and Resurrection of Mr Roche* (1968), Friel's *The Gentle Island* (1971) and Mac Liammóir's *Prelude in Kazbek Street* (1973), each of which in different ways asserted the need for Irish society to be more tolerant.

The experiences of gay women in Ireland would be even more marginalized, going largely unexplored until the production in Dublin of *I Know My Own Heart* by Emma Donoghue (1993) – though later works such as Deirdre Kinahan's *Passage* (2001) (among others) would begin to put that omission to rights. The appearance of Fintan Walsh's anthology *Queer Notions* in 2010 was an important moment in giving visibility to the work of LGBT artists in Ireland – as was the directorship of Mac Conghail at the

Abbey, not just in his willingness to host people like Panti but also in his production of Wayne Jordan's queer reimagining of *Twelfth Night* (2014) and his co-production of *Alice in Funderland* (2012) with THISISPOPBABY, a company that aims to 'rip up the space between popular culture, counter culture, queer culture and high art' (as described on thisispopbaby.com).

But the most important figure in these developments has been Frank McGuinness, probably the leading Irish dramatist of the generation that followed the 'second renaissance' period of the 1960s. He has had an unusually varied career. *Someone Who'll Watch Over Me*, his dramatization of the fate of the Irish hostage Brian Keenan in Lebanon, was a success on Broadway in 1992–3 – yet only ten years later McGuinness struggled to have his plays produced in Ireland, meaning that important works such as *There Came a Gypsy Riding* (2007) premiered in England instead. His subject matter is similarly varied. Like Friel, he wrote a response to Bloody Sunday, in the 1988 play *Carthaginians*, but he has also written about figures as diverse as Caravaggio (in *Innocence*, 1986), Marx and Engels (in *Mary and Lizzie*, 1989), Shakespeare and Spenser (in *Mutabilitie*, 1997), Edwards and Mac Liammóir (in *Gates of Gold*, 2002), King James I (in *Speaking Like Magpies*, 2005) and Greta Garbo (in *Greta Garbo Came to Donegal*, 2010). As already discussed, he has also adapted many plays – work that has fed into the composition of his own drama, as seen in his borrowing of elements from Greek tragedy in *The Match Box* (2012) and *The Hanging Gardens* (2013), or his allusions to Ibsen in *Dolly West's Kitchen* (1999). And like Marie Jones he has demonstrated an ability to draw on popular forms, as seen in his country and western musical *Donegal* (2016) or his adaptation of *Dracula* for Druid in 1986 (DTA, T2/132–3).

Yet despite that variety, there are common strands. More than any other male Irish dramatist, he has created a diverse range of strong female characters. One of his earliest successes was *The Factory Girls*, a 1982 play about five women who stage a sit-in at a Donegal shirt factory when they are threatened with unemployment. *Dolly West's Kitchen* is an intensely moving play about war, sexuality and family that features an unforgettably strong female figure in the family matriarch, Rima West. And in *Greta Garbo Came to Donegal* he explores the tensions between the real woman and the iconic figure named in the title. He has also presented new versions of many of the great female characters of world drama: Electra, Hecuba, Phèdre, Miss Julie, Nora Helmer, Hedda Gabler, Yerma and Chekhov's three sisters, among others.

His work is also marked by a determination to reveal truths that mainstream audiences find unpalatable, such as the epidemic levels of youth suicide in

Ireland (movingly explored in *There Came a Gypsy Riding*), the ethics of Irish neutrality in the Second World War (in *Dolly West*), the way in which the relationship between Ireland and England has informed subsequent colonial and neo-imperialist conflicts (as shown in *Mary and Lizzie* and *Someone Who'll Watch Over Me*), and so on. But perhaps his most common theme is the capacity of an outsider figure to transform a repressive social environment. Those outsiders take many forms: sometimes they are women who refuse to accept patriarchal expectations about how they should behave; sometimes they are gay men who choose to define how they can and should be seen by others; sometimes they are Irish people in England (and sometimes they are English people in Ireland). And sometimes the outsider figure is McGuinness himself, who has spoken about how his own identities situate him unusually in relation to the theatres that have commissioned his work: as an Irish artist working with Britain's national theatre and Royal Shakespeare Company, as a gay man writing for the Abbey during a period when homosexuality was illegal in the Republic, and as a writer from Ulster operating in a theatrical tradition that has (with some exceptions) tended to be dominated by Dublin. The argument of his plays has always been that difference, far from being a threat to social stability, is necessary for the growth of any community. In using difference as a dramatic device, he has also sought to change the way that Irish society imagines what is normal, natural or necessary. That trait features strongly in his 1985 *Observe the Sons of Ulster Marching Towards the Somme*, and is evident in many different ways.

The first is its treatment of Irish history. At the time of its premiere, the reality of Irish participation in the First World War was something of a taboo subject in the Republic: the fact that hundreds of thousands of Irishmen had fought in that war as part of the British Army disrupted the simplistic narrative about the achievement of independence from Britain from 1916 to 1921 – and so its memory was suppressed or forgotten (see Pine, 2010: 127– 51). McGuinness was one of a small number of Irish playwrights who sought to reveal that history in its complexity, being joined by Sebastian Barry, whose play *The Steward of Christendom* (1995) and novel *A Long, Long Way* (2005) dramatized the impact of the war on a middle-class Catholic family in Dublin. Both writers were following the example of Jennifer Johnston, whose 1974 novel *How Many Miles to Babylon* showed how the First World War was experienced by different sections of Irish society. And of course O'Casey's *The Silver Tassie* (1928) was an important influence.

The desire to expand the understanding of history demonstrates McGuinness' awareness of his intended audience. Although it was originally submitted to Field Day (which rejected it), *Observe the Sons of Ulster* premiered on the Peacock stage at the Abbey – and while it would later be produced in Belfast, it's essential to understand how the original production of the play sought to revise McGuinness' audience's understanding of what the national stage could and should express. He wasn't simply trying to show his Dublin audience an important element of the island's history; he was also revealing in their variety and complexity the cultures of Ulster Protestantism – a group that was often misunderstood or wrongly considered unworthy of the effort of being understood, in the south. Where the tendency in the Republic had been to see the Troubles as involving a clash between Catholic and Protestant – as if those two communities could only be understood in monolithic terms – McGuinness instead presented a community that was diverse but, perhaps paradoxically, therefore more easily recognizable. Though they nominally share one religion, what makes his characters notable are their distinctions from each other, in terms of age, social class, education, religious experience and sense of home – and of course their sexuality too. Those differences sometimes cause conflict between them: 'I was only sticking up for my place', explains one, showing how his first loyalty is to his locality rather than any shared sense of religion (McGuinness, 1996: 113). But what brings them together is the trauma of war: they are unified in their shared blood sacrifice on behalf of (what would become) Northern Ireland. For McGuinness, one of the tragedies of that Great War was that it caused a community to harden its sense of identity to such an extent that change would feel like a betrayal.

In making that argument, McGuinness was measuring himself against – and mirroring – W.B. Yeats. If the 1916 Battle of the Somme was a key moment in the formation of Unionism, the Easter Rising of the same year likewise had hardened into a creation myth for Irish Nationalism. Yeats is often misunderstood as having written in a celebratory fashion about that rebellion, but he knew all too well what its likely outcome would be: 'too long a sacrifice can make a stone of the heart', he wrote in 'Easter 1916', expressing the fear that any form of Nationalist blood sacrifice would cause his society to calcify around a set of values that would ultimately imprison it.

The same analysis haunts *Observe the Sons of Ulster*, with McGuinness drawing on Yeats' imagery by having his primary protagonist, Kenneth Pyper, be a sculptor – a character who (by his own description) 'turn[s] people into stone' (McGuinness, 1996: 150). McGuinness understands that art, politics and culture – and the interplay of the three – can cause identities to harden, can fix things into place eternally. A major question for him is how his play can both capture an identity faithfully yet imagine the possibility of that identity changing for the better – something that he dramatizes in his characterization of the elder Pyper. At the beginning and end of the play, Pyper is presented in old age, existing in 'the present' of the audience. Blind and (in many of the Abbey's productions) also bedridden, he seems trapped in a tradition of similar stage figures from Oedipus to Lear to Beckett's Hamm – men whose failure to recognize truths has caused them to lose everything. But so too is he trapped in a tradition of political recalcitrance: 'There would be, and there will be, no surrender', he states (98), repeating a slogan from the Rev. Ian Paisley and thereby showing how much he differs from his younger self, a man who was an original thinker with a distrust of authority. A major theme of the play, then, is about how the fear of change can be matched against the need to move on from destructive traditions – and what the role of the artist might be in preventing or enabling such transformations.

The fact that change is frightening but inevitable is made clear from the start of the play, when Pyper's colleague and eventual lover David Craig describes a conflict with his father, a blacksmith: 'It's a dying skill. I've been at him to get into the motor business ... That's where the future lies. But you know what it's like working for your own people. Once they get to a certain age it's all clinging on to whatever's there in their time' (McGuinness, 1996: 116). This father–son dispute is likely to be familiar to any member of the audience who has ever been part of a family business, and has the effect of situating loyalty to tradition (often seen as a unique dysfunction of Ulster Unionism) in a broader human context. But McGuinness' point is plain: much as we can empathize with David's love for his father, we must also acknowledge that he was right: the motorcar replaced the horse, and the future David imagined indeed came to pass.

For much of the play, then, we watch as the characters attempt to resist or effect change in their lives – something that is rendered metaphorically in a variety of ways such as the traversal of a bridge, the celebration of a July holiday at the 'wrong' time of year, the recalibration of religious faiths, or the transformation of a friendship into a loving sexual relationship (McGuinness, 1996: 138–69). In all of those examples, McGuinness shows that change first involves acknowledging a personal truth. He also makes clear that art and culture can facilitate such acts of transformation – though not always with positive outcomes. We see this in the staging of a play-within-the-play in the final scene, when the soldiers work together to perform the Battle of Scarva, which is itself a re-enactment of the Battle of the Boyne, the 1690 defeat of

King James II by William of Orange that established the supremacy of Protestantism in Ireland and Britain. In re-enacting that battle, the soldiers are reperforming a tradition, setting themselves into the pattern of re-enactments that are celebrated every year on 12 July, and which are seen both as a celebration of the Protestant tradition in the north, and (by many Catholic communities) as a deliberate act of triumphalism, intimidation and provocation. In the Battle of Scarva, King William must be victorious – but in *Observe the Sons of Ulster* he is defeated when Pyper (accidentally?) stumbles in his role as the king's horse, knocking the soldier playing the king to the ground (181–2). That fall is seen as both a betrayal of the past and an omen about the likely fate of the soldiers as they prepare to leave their trenches. Here we begin to understand how performance can reveal truths that we might not wish to openly acknowledge.

Moments later, however, the soldiers engage in another re-enactment of tradition, which is the wearing of the orange sash – an emblem intended to celebrate the victory of King William. But the sash is reimagined as a gift by each man to one of his fellows. Pyper, who had initially expressed reluctance to wear it (putting it on only after being threatened), willingly takes it from Roulston, the character with whom he had most frequently disagreed prior to that moment. While there is no doubt that the exchanging of the sash becomes a way of binding the men into one unit, it also acts as a gift, one that allows Pyper to acknowledge that the unity of the soldiers lies not in a shared memory of violence but in a love felt in the present: 'I love their lives. I love my own life. I love my home' (McGuinness, 1996: 196). McGuinness appears to be ambivalent about this reimagining of the sash – the exchanging of which turns the group from a collection of individuals into a single body of men willing to fight and die for Ulster. But as an act of transformation this scene merits comparison with Teresa's reinvention of the miraculous medal in Behan's *The Hostage*, showing how apparently fixed symbols of faith and identity can be seen in new ways.

Pyper's openness about love also relates to McGuinness' frankness about homosexuality, and here too we must see the play's relationship to its first intended audience in Dublin. *Observe* begins with Pyper and Craig arguing over an apple, an Edenic symbol that suggests that, in coming together, Pyper and Craig can, like Adam and Eve, rename the things before them, can define for themselves how to be and who to be. 'I wanted a fight', explains Craig. 'I felt that because I wanted to save somebody else in the war but the somebody else was myself. I wanted to change what I am. Instead I saved you, because of what I am. I want you to live' (McGuinness, 1996: 164). Craig is showing that freedom lies not in fighting to be someone else, but in accepting oneself, in accepting his own sexuality and his love for Pyper, and what both mean for his place in his society. Here the Peacock stage was being used to show the truth and dignity of this man's acceptance of his own sexuality – setting the national theatre in opposition to the national legislature, which still deemed homosexuality illegal at that time.

The overall impact of the play, then, is to demonstrate how difference can be liberating for all of Ireland's communities. To an audience watching the play in Dublin, there is the obligation to recognize that they identify with and share much with the men on stage: to acknowledge the dignity and reality of Ulster, Protestant and gay identities, but also to acknowledge the dignity and reality of a shared humanity that transcends such boundaries. But McGuinness is also speaking to communities in the north, using the Edenic motif to point to a prelapsarian version of life there, one in which people felt free to be loyal to traditions but also to invent new versions of themselves. His play offers hope that such a vision of the past could offer a way forward.

*Observe* has encountered a variety of interpretations as it has been revived. Its productions at the Abbey from 1994 to 1996 addressed both the decriminalization of homosexuality in 1993 and the emergence of the Northern Irish Peace Process – which meant that a play that in 1985 had seemed aspirational was now celebrating the first signs that transformation was really happening. It also found new forms of resonance after the invasion of Iraq in 2003, when British and American productions were staged in order to argue that the pointless destruction of young life dramatized by McGuinness could offer a way of thinking about those countries' latest military misadventure. And at the Abbey in 2016, the play took on a new symbolic power – showing that the national theatre was willing to commemorate the centenary of not only the Easter Rising but also the Battle of the Somme, and thus demonstrating that a hundred years later it might be possible for the national imagination to make space for both Nationalist and Unionist identities.

As was also true for *Translations*, the play's openness to interpretation was both a strength and a weakness, in that it exposed it to misreading. Notoriously, the premiere was lambasted by the *Irish Times* critic David Nowlan, who referred to it as 'one of the most comprehensive attacks ever made on Ulster Protestantism' (19 February 1985). That statement led Jennifer Johnston and Kevin Barry to write to the *Times* in defence of McGuinness, but it says much about Irish culture at that time that Nowlan could have so badly missed the play's point (ATDA, 2874_PC_0001: 12). In subsequent years in Ireland there has been a tendency to see *Observe* as a history play, revealing truths about the country's past rather than questioning its present – and in that respect too it shares a problem faced by *Translations*, which is that its speedy admission to the national canon has tended to limit the sense that it might have something to say about current dilemmas.

There's also been a tendency for directors to play down its treatment of homosexuality, especially in its third part when Pyper and Craig openly acknowledge their feelings for each other. While McGuinness' stage directions avoid making the point explicitly, it is apparent that the pair declare love for each other and then express those feelings sexually – with the lights tactfully dimming when Pyper responds to Craig's use of the word 'stone' with 'flesh'. In its productions by Patrick Mason at the Abbey, in 1985 and from 1994 to 1996, the two actors embraced at that point of the scene – doing so with an intimacy and sexual hunger that could not have been misunderstood. Yet when the play was revived at the Abbey as part of its centenary celebrations in 2004 (demonstrating the fact that by then it had obtained the status of being a 'classic'), the embrace of the two actors was more chaste and comradely. When next performed at the Abbey in 2016, the interaction of the men was clearly sexual, showing how much Ireland had changed over thirty years – though as noted in the introduction to this book, the production was included in a season that disproportionately featured plays written and directed by men, showing that in other areas the need for change remained acute.

It is notable that a play which in 1985 was seen as celebrating people on the margins was by 2016 seen as exemplifying a problem of the dominance of Irish theatre by men. Taken with Panti's Noble Call, we might form from such evidence an inaccurate understanding of how much Irish theatre has really changed, however. While the Abbey has been relatively hospitable to work about the experiences of gay Irish men, plays that address lesbian or transgender perspectives remain comparatively rare. And although *Observe* has become one of the most frequently revived Abbey plays, the theatre has shown markedly less interest in dramatizing the experiences of the Ulster Protestant community. Graham Reid and Stewart Parker were produced at the theatre occasionally (especially in the 1970s and 1980s), and Owen McCafferty's *Quietly* (2012) and *Fire Below* (2017) consider the ongoing legacies of sectarianism – but otherwise there have been few positive representations of the community (indeed, David Ireland's *Cyprus Avenue* in

2016 retrogressively presented the politics of Ulster Unionism as arising from toxic masculinity rather than social forces such as social class, colonialism or British nationalism). And, despite being one of Ireland's most successful contemporary playwrights, Marie Jones has only had one play – Charabanc's touring production of *Somewhere Over the Balcony* (1987) – produced at the Irish national theatre. Finally, as mentioned earlier, there has also been a reluctance to engage with McGuinness' later plays, demonstrating how there has been only a partial willingness to accept the truths he wishes to bring to light.

The plays discussed in the chapter thus far have been heavily informed by the conflict in Northern Ireland. As I bring the argument towards a conclusion I want to consider how the strategy of engaging with difference continued into the post-Ceasefire period, and to show its use in other contexts. For that reason, I want to move to a discussion of the work of Enda Walsh.

## Migration and difference: Enda Walsh's *The Walworth Farce* and *Once*

In Enda Walsh's 2006 play *The Walworth Farce*, there is a moment of unusual beauty, when a young man called Sean recalls a game that his brother Blake used to play. 'Blake's full of talk about being an astronaut. He's read a book on it and knows some big words to do with space,' says Sean. 'He says he'd feel safe up there. He said if he got nervous he'd hide the Earth behind his thumb' (Walsh, 2006: 74) These words encapsulate the value and importance of Walsh's theatre. His characters exist on the edges of society, and often on the edges of sanity. When faced with the vastness of the world – with the multitude of responsibilities and choices that everyone encounters – they often react with fear, and become isolated. And so they choose to hide Earth behind their thumbs, using tiny spaces such as bedrooms, warehouses, drained-out swimming pools and prison cells as performance spaces in which they create new worlds for themselves.

Where the plays of McGuinness are marked by their variety in terms of form, setting, characterization and theme, Walsh's are defined by an exceptionally high degree of uniformity – such that it could be argued (though not unkindly or dismissively) that he has been writing different versions of the same play since his first major success, *Disco Pigs*, premiered in 1996. Almost all of Walsh's protagonists live in spaces that are confined and restrictive – and usually they have a very vivid imaginative life, albeit that their imaginations are used to reconstruct obsessively a traumatic event from their past. His plays thus establish a tension between a confined stage space and the large imaginative world that is created by his characters. There are the rural and provincial spaces imagined in *bedbound* (2000), *The New Electric Ballroom* (2008), *Misterman* (1999, revised in 2012) and *Ballyturk* (2014); the virtual and online spaces of *Chatroom* (2006); and the mythic or fantastical spaces of *The Small Things* (2005), *Penelope* (2010) and *Arlington* (2016). And in all of those plays Walsh shows how the imagination can act like Sean's thumb, covering up things that are too vast or frightening to be fully accepted – but he also shows that the imagination can trap people in patterns of repetition that must eventually be broken. In this sense Walsh is the most direct inheritor of Beckett's interest in repetition – as something to be escaped but which also, perhaps paradoxically, must be returned to as the subject of new artistic investigations.

As we've seen already, a confrontation with difference was proposed by Friel, Jones and McGuinness as something that could offer people the chance to escape restricted environments and to break patterns of repetition. It is significant in this context that *The Walworth Farce* (2006) and *Once – The Musical* (2012) are among the very few of Walsh's works that allow their characters some measure of escape – in both cases through an interaction with an outsider figure. Here I want to consider how two of Walsh's dramas address the impact of immigration into Ireland by showing how his imprisoned characters – and his restrictive environments – can be reimagined through the presence of an outsider figure, and how that outsider can allow for the cycle of repetition to be broken.

The theme of migration dominates modern Irish theatre, being addressed in works such as M.J. Molloy's *The Wood of the Whispering* (1953) and Murphy's *A Whistle in the Dark*, both of which were a response to the very high rates of emigration from Ireland in the 1950s. Where Molloy was preoccupied with the damage emigration was doing to rural Irish communities, Murphy showed how Irish emigrants often brought their problems with them. Set in Coventry, his play concerns a West of Ireland family called the Carneys who have fled a society deeply divided by social class, but who find themselves in a country where all Irish people are seen as the same: 'We're all Paddies, and the British boys know it,' says one of them (Murphy, 2006: 54). In such a context, Irishness becomes a badge of shame, but it is also defensively asserted: through racism against non-white immigrants, a refusal to integrate and the use of violence to perform the value of the Irish identity.

Murphy would return to that theme when the next major wave of Irish emigration happened in the 1980s, addressing it in *Conversations on a Homecoming*. Its two central characters, Michael and Tom, are often referred to in their community as 'the twins' – and in yet another example of the Irish stage double act they are described as making up 'one decent man' between them. Michael has escaped Ireland for a career as an actor in New York; Tom has given up dreams of writing literature and instead teaches teenage students in his local school. Michael seems to retain a sense of idealism: he is the only character in the play who uses such words as 'beauty' and 'love' with sincerity; Tom in contrast is overwhelmingly negative, furious with his 'ridiculous country' and his 'ridiculous race' but unwilling to leave Ireland or contribute to its improvement. Yet we gradually see that both suffer from the same problem, which is that their society has restricted their ability to express themselves fully – something that has trapped Michael as much as Tom, even though the former did leave Ireland. For Murphy, emigration was undoubtedly a tragedy – but the deeper tragedy was how Ireland's problems were inescapable even abroad.

Friel too would address emigration – in *Philadelphia, Here I Come!* and *The Loves of Cass Maguire* directly, but also in *Dancing at Lughnasa*, in which two of the five sisters flee Donegal for London, dying there, homeless and impoverished. And from the 1980s, such dramatists as Dermot Bolger, Peter Sheridan, Paul Mercier and Declan Hughes explored the experience of Irish people who had been forced to leave their country too – often drawing on tropes and ideas from Murphy and Friel to do so. Marie Jones and Charabanc also took on the topic from the point of view of Northern Ireland in *Gold in the Streets* (1985–6), which shows women from three different eras being forced to emigrate to England.

By the time Walsh came to stage *The Walworth Farce* in 2006, however, Irish theatre had begun to address the topic of inward migration – as was demonstrated that same year in Pan Pan's Chinese adaptation of *The Playboy of the Western World* (discussed in Chapter 4). From the 1990s, Ireland had become increasingly multicultural due to the arrival of large numbers of emigrants, especially from the UK and the United States, but also from Africa, Brazil, China and Central and Eastern Europe. The theatre quickly moved to reflect those changes, first in plays written by Irish dramatists, such as Donal O'Kelly's *Asylum! Asylum!* in 1994 or Charlie O'Neill's *Hurl* in 2003. But soon many new Irish citizens themselves began to write plays, often directly addressing Irish themes and tropes from new perspectives – as Bisi Adigun had done in his co-written 2007 adaptation of *Playboy*. Those new plays included autobiographical or semi-autobiographical works such as

George Seremba's *Come Good Rain* (2005) and Mirjana Rendulic's *Broken Promise Land* (2013), but also important was the establishment of theatre companies such as Adigun's Arambe Productions, and Kasia Lech, Helen McNulty and Anna Wolf's Polish Theatre Ireland. The publication in 2014 of Charlotte McIvor and Matthew Spangler's *Staging Intercultural Ireland* was a major development, providing the first anthology of Irish plays that were written by authors from multiple national and cultural origins. Its appearance coincided with the onset of yet another major wave of Irish emigration, as thousands of young people were forced to leave the country after the financial crash of 2008: the experiences of Nigerian, Polish and Croatian dramatists who had been writing about coming to Ireland in the early 2000s was now available as a model for how young Irish people might think of their own flight to Canada, Australia, Dubai or elsewhere. Ireland is therefore unusual in having a theatre that is concerned with the impact of both outward and inward migration, though more could be done to allow the two strands to speak to each other. Accordingly, the significance of both *The Walworth Farce* and *Once* for the present discussion is that they provide a bridge between the two strands, drawing on the tradition of plays that consider what happens when Irish people are forced abroad, but also demonstrating the benefits to Irish culture and society of inward migration.

*The Walworth Farce* is about emigration, but it also explores the not unrelated theme of how trauma is passed on to the next generation through storytelling. In it, a Corkman called Dinny murders his brother Paddy in a row about an inheritance. He flees Cork for London, staying in Paddy's bedsit on the Walworth Road, where he is eventually joined by his sons, Blake and Sean. For the next quarter of a century the trio spend each day acting out a reimagined version of Dinny's departure, told as a farce – but one that Dinny insists is an accurate reflection of reality. Dinny expresses himself, and exercises control over his sons, by creating a strong contrast between an idealized version of Cork and a dystopic representation of London – an attempt on Walsh's part to show how the emigrant always takes a version of home away with him or her, but also imagines the place that they have gone to.

In the plot of the farce that Dinny creates, Paddy is a returned emigrant, whose life in London contrasts sharply with the apparent prosperity Dinny has achieved in Cork. 'London's a tough old nut,' Paddy says. 'For a while I was working the sites but London's all grown up now and not much building for fellas like me' (Walsh, 2006: 9). Paddy seems immediately like a stock figure from many Irish plays: the returned emigrant who no longer feels at home in his native place, rather like Pato in McDonagh's *Beauty Queen*.

Contrastingly, Dinny claims to be a brain surgeon, and pretends to own a mansion overlooking Cork – though in fact he is a painter-decorator and the mansion belongs to one of his clients. This characterization is a satirical response to the behaviour of people during the Celtic Tiger period: Dinny's desire to pretend to be wealthy is enacted through the ownership of property, and Walsh shows how foolish such performances were.

But in Dinny's characterization we see another exploration of the important Irish theme of how home is used to perform a sense of self. In the farce, Paddy is asked to describe the area he lives in, to 'paint . . . a picture of' the Walworth Road. 'On my palate is only grey', replies Paddy. 'Grey and muck. For these are the two primary colours that make up much of the Elephant. . . . To sum it up in pure Cork parlance . . . the place is a hole' (Walsh, 2006: 15–16) – though what is important here is that these words are not really Paddy's but are instead authored for his character by Dinny.

Dinny then describes life in his home town: 'I liken Cork to a large jewel . . . A jewel with the majestic River Lee ambling through it, chopping the diamond in two before making its way to murkier climes . . . towards the poisonous Irish sea for example. Ah yes, Cork City. You could call it Ireland's jewel but you'd be a FUCKING IDIOT, BOY, FOR IT IS REALLY AND TRULY IRELAND'S TRUE CAPITAL CITY' (Walsh, 2006: 16).

**Figure 10**  Druid Theatre, *The Walworth Farce* by Enda Walsh, 2006. Photograph by Keith Pattison (DTA, 1.34).

The representations of London and Cork are both false: they have been created by Dinny as part of the farce he has written, and they function dramatically rather than representing the real world. The representation of Cork is intended to make Dinny's departure from the city seem more tragic; the representation of London is intended to make Paddy's murder seem less regrettable: the dual spaces of home and away are used to convey Dinny's aesthetic sensibility but they also betray his ethical outlook.

Another function of these representations is to control Sean and Blake. Blake has never left the flat, and is terrified of doing so. Both sons have learned Dinny's story of his departure from Cork by heart: it is a narrative which is separate from the farce but which comes from a similar sense of guilt and self-deception. Dinny begins the story of his arrival in London before insisting that Blake continue telling it: 'And then there's the people. They come out of their houses and shops and they're after you. Their skin, it falls to the ground and them bodies running you down and wanting to tear you to shreds … And they're all snapping teeth and grabbing hands they have' (Walsh, 2006: 31–2). Then Sean is forced to take up the story:

At the window and you're looking out past the end of Walworth Road, past where London stretches into the green countryside, past the green and over the sea to Ireland and to Cork and past the River Lee and high up into the estate and our little terraced house … And there's Mammy standing by the sink washing the dishes in the kitchen.

(Walsh, 2006: 32)

These descriptions have some basis in reality. But this landscape is much more an expression of Dinny's state of mind – his sense of remorse for having murdered his brother, his fear of being held to account. The London he imagines is not a real place but a metaphor for the guilt he has brought with him from Ireland.

The London Dinny acts out – and forces his sons to co-create – is also used to control them. Blake's belief in this London makes him feel that he would rather die than leave the flat. And although Sean leaves the flat every day to buy groceries – or, more correctly, props – in the local Tesco, he also will be too frightened to leave the flat at the play's conclusion.

The farce breaks down, however, because the real London interposes itself in the form of Hayley, a young English woman who visits when Sean accidentally takes the wrong bag of shopping from Tesco. Her speech is full of references to real places such as Brighton, to real TV programmes such as

*Ready, Steady, Cook* and so on. She is so 'normal' as to heighten our awareness of the terrifying absurdity of Dinny's actions. Yet she also shows that the experiences of Dinny and his sons can be mapped onto everyday life. 'Sorry I'm talking so much', she says. 'My mum reckons it's from working at Tesco. You talk all day to the customers, get home and I can't stop talking. It's not intentional! You get stuck in a pattern' (Walsh, 2006: 45). This description of someone who is compelled to keep talking, and who finds herself trapped in a pattern of repetition, makes Hayley sound like – well, like a character in an Enda Walsh play. Walsh is demonstrating that Dinny's farce is merely an extreme example of behaviour that many people – perhaps all people – indulge in.

Dinny soon attempts to integrate Hayley into the story but is unable to do so effectively, first because of her nationality (she is English) and then because of her ethnicity (she is black). Her characterization thus operates as a metaphor for the transformation of Ireland, showing how difference allows for the breaking of the cycle of the old narratives about Irish exceptionalism and oppression. But Dinny's adherence to those stories demonstrates how Irish people continue to perpetuate myths about their country, both at home and abroad. And it shows too how racism is often a manifestation of a deep insecurity on the part of the bigot about the security of his own sense of self. A further consideration, however, is what Walsh's play says about the relationship between theatre and real life. A characteristic of *The Walworth Farce* is how closely the play that represents the 'real world' of the action is mirrored by the farce: both involve a tragic act of fratricide, both turn dramatically on the unexpected arrival of someone to a home, and both are occasioned by the characters' attempts to pretend to be someone they are not.

Ostensibly, Walsh's adaptation of John Carney's movie *Once* (2007) is very different from *The Walworth Farce*, providing a romance between two musicians, one Irish and one Czech, in a musical that is set in a recognizable version of the real world and which avoids Walsh's usual linguistic density and intricacy. But upon closer inspection there are many resemblances. For example, *Once* makes use of space in much the same way that his other dramas do. 'As the audience takes its seat and waits in the auditorium', state the stage directions, 'there's a session on stage with musicians and singers belting out songs to one another. It's raw, chaotic and hugely positive. Suddenly it's dark and silent. A light fades up on the GUY singing' (Walsh, 2012: 4). And from there, the play begins, with the lives of the characters and all of the settings being enacted in the setting of the pub. So just as in *The*

*Walworth Farce* the flat becomes a performance space that recreates Cork City, in *Once* a pub becomes a performance space that allows for the recreation of Dublin.

In the original production as directed by John Tiffany, audience members were encouraged to go on stage, both before the play began and at the intervals, in order to have a drink – which was served by real bar staff from authentic kegs and bottles. Furthermore, the set as designed by Bob Crowley positioned a series of mirrors of varying shapes and sizes along the walls of the pub, allowing the audience to see a reflection of themselves staring back out from the stage. The impact of both decisions was to blur the boundaries between the stage and auditorium, to show the audience that this play is – to a greater degree than would normally be the case – about an entity that we should consider to be 'us'.

So even before *Once* formally begins, the audience has been told that the performance space on the stage is a small world that is going to be used to construct a much bigger one. This is the case in two senses. The production uses the pub to reconstruct the city of Dublin, but it also constructs a much bigger imaginative and emotional world that the audience is intended to consider itself part of.

But that Dublin had changed in the years between the release of the movie and the creation of the stage version. In the movie, the Celtic Tiger period was still underway: the Czechs who come to Dublin do so as economic migrants – and while the characters in the film don't participate in that orgy of vulgarity and materialism, the presence of the Celtic Tiger is still felt. By the time Walsh came to adapt the movie, however, Ireland had suffered the 2008 economic crash – so the presentation of Dublin is now more negative but, curiously, more affectionate. For instance, when Guy and Girl meet each other at the start of his script, they have a discussion about suicide which concludes with Girl saying that 'Life is good . . . even in Dublin' (Walsh, 2012: 8). Things may be bad for Ireland, she concedes. But perhaps they are not quite so bad as we might think.

Similar sentiments are expressed towards the end of the performance, when two other Czech characters watch the sun coming up over Dublin. 'Look at it lying there, waking up', says Svec. 'A little flat city and a new day . . . Dublin's really lovely'. His friend Andrej replies, 'A million times heartbroken and Dublin keeps on going. You've got to love Dublin for dreaming' (Walsh, 2012: 59). This may seem sentimental, but these lines bring to fruition a theme that runs through the entire production, which is the way in which foreign cities become spaces that allow us to play out – or dream – our own sense of self. The theme of dreaming runs through the play. Girl's mother Baruska encapsulates it when she tells a story about a man to whom nothing happened, but who decides one day to go and face the world, having 'imagined great adventures':

> But then . . . as he faced his front door to the world outside he closed his eyes and that same mind began to imagine the most terrible things . . . The world outside was there to torture and crush him! Love was there to tease and break him . . . He . . . returned to his bed and promised never to dream of anything ever again. He remained in that bed for eternity, emaciated and rotting, lying in his own shit . . .
>
> (Walsh, 2012: 32)

This operates as a metaphor for the state that Guy finds himself in during the performance – but it also sounds very like a plot for some other, as-yet-unwritten Enda Walsh play.

The story shows that for the emigrant cities are not just places that we live in, but also spaces that we dream about and imagine: they stand symbolically for our hopes and fears. So it is notable that it is the Czech characters who are most positive about Dublin, even though, as Girl says, 'it never became what I wanted it to be' (Walsh, 2012: 48). In Walsh's book, the plight and the responsibility of the immigrant is to dream, not only about the place left behind but also about the place now inhabited. Music offers one way of imagining both spaces, and the production shows how one performance space – the pub – can be used to recreate a living city. This puts *Once* in the tradition of such Irish plays as Murphy's *Conversations on a Homecoming*, but it also shows that the musical is doing with the pub what Walsh had done with bedrooms and warehouses in his earlier plays.

The action concludes with the Irishman leaving Dublin for New York – bringing to an end his budding romance with Girl but also allowing him to break free from an Ireland that was holding him back. Walsh's point is clear: the interaction with the girl from the Czech Republic gave the Irishman a sense of (to borrow the phrase from Friel) 'necessary perspective', which then allowed him to rediscover a sense of artistic purpose. We never find out how he fares in New York, but what matters is that through meeting the Czech girl, he gains the confidence to leave.

I'd suggest, therefore, that Walsh's cities are like his characters. The characters are located in a world that we might recognize as our own, even as their actions strike us as fantastical or indeed farcical. In a similar fashion, his cities correspond to the real places, even when imagined through nostalgia or sentimentality (as Cork is in *The Walworth Farce* and Dublin is in *Once*) or as a dystopic underworld, as happens with London in *Farce*.

But what is most palpable is the relationship between self and place: Walsh shows that cities make us what we are, but he also shows that we help to construct cities. Cities in Enda Walsh's plays are built not just from concrete and steel but also from emotions: guilt, fear, despair certainly – but also, sometimes, hope and even love. His plays therefore can be mapped onto everyday Irish realities, showing his awareness that the particular Irish neurosis is the way in which patterns are repeated, even when they have been shown to be destructive – but showing too his belief that opening Ireland out to new influences can bring new forms of escape, creativity and imagining.

## Conclusions

The purpose of this chapter has been to demonstrate the effectiveness of a strategy of engaging with difference, as it has been used in a variety of different contexts since 1980. My aim in doing so is not to conflate important developments, many of which have been the subject of book-length studies in their own right, such as Charlotte McIvor's *Migration and Performance in Contemporary Ireland* (2016) and Fintan Walsh's *Queer Performance and Contemporary Ireland* (2014). Nor do I want to blur distinctions between the theatre in Northern Ireland and the Republic. But I do want to show that the Irish theatre has been at its strongest when difference has been seen as something to be welcomed rather than feared.

We've seen this conviction in other contexts elsewhere in this book: in the willingness of Irish directors to stage work by non-Irish writers; in the revision of a male-dominated canon by female writers and directors; and in the way in which secularism and Catholicism have interacted on the stage, allowing for new understandings of power, faith and society to emerge. I want now to conclude the book by considering the impact of economic success on the country and to show how this has been felt in our theatre.

# CHAPTER 6
## AFTER THE FALL: IRISH DRAMA SINCE 2000

### The crash

In a press interview in 2008, Conor McPherson anticipated the imminent collapse of Ireland's economy. 'We're not comfortable with success in this country,' he told *The Sunday Business Post.* 'It's post-traumatic stress from our colonial past or whatever. As Irish people, we're not able to celebrate what's good about Ireland. Ireland is going to get back to what it knows now – hardship. That's where we're more comfortable. We can't wait for it to start' (27 April 2008).

In those comments, McPherson was referring to the Celtic Tiger period, a decade-long economic boom that was driven by foreign direct investment and a property bubble – and which transformed Ireland into one of the world's richest countries. Beginning in the mid-1990s, the Celtic Tiger era was marked by new investments in infrastructure, education and the arts; by the growth of multiculturalism; and by the end of mass emigration – but it also produced an enormous expansion of the inequality between rich and poor, led to the passing of a divisive citizenship referendum in 2005, and resulted in the development of a national culture that wavered precariously between confidence and complacency (for a full discussion see Lonergan, 2009).

The economic boom in the Republic was matched (and undoubtedly influenced) by a new prosperity in Northern Ireland, following the Good Friday Agreement of 1998. That deal set out new arrangements for the government of the north, allowed for the decommissioning of paramilitary weapons, and attempted to move away from the binary opposition between Nationalist and Unionist identities by suggesting that a citizen of Northern Ireland could be both British and Irish. It is not quite accurate to state that the Good Friday Agreement brought peace to Northern Ireland: less than six months after it was signed a group styling itself the 'Real IRA' bombed Omagh, murdering twenty-nine people in what was the single worst atrocity of the Troubles. There have been intermittent acts of violence since that time, and occasional disputes about such matters as the flying of flags or the status of the Irish language demonstrate the persistence of sectarian tensions. Nevertheless, life in Northern Ireland since 1998 is considerably different from what came before, and that has been reflected in its theatre.

What I'm describing, then, is an Ireland that as the century began was ostensibly doing well – a booming economy, a conflict resolved – but which in reality was grappling with problems both old and new, many of them only barely acknowledged. This explains McPherson's comment a few years later, which – though undeniably expressed with a little flippancy – was an attempt to expose a persistent insecurity and uncertainty in the culture.

And his prediction was proven correct. In September 2008, the government was forced to guarantee the assets and deposits of all six Irish banks, exposing the Irish state to liabilities of up to €500 billion. Rather than bringing stability, that guarantee caused a collapse in confidence in the economy, and within two years Ireland had been forced to apply for a bail-out from the International Monetary Fund (IMF), the European Central Bank and the European Commission. As noted in Chapter 2, those events coincided with the revelations of decades of abuse in the Ryan Report, which meant that the country was facing not just a future of financial hardship but also had to come to terms with guilt about its history. In the year 2000 Ireland was experiencing a newfound cultural confidence, but it entered the second decade of the century in a state of profound moral, economic and political crisis.

As had been the case since the early 1960s, it was Tom Murphy who stepped forward with the play that most directly – and most unforgivingly – spoke to the nation's dilemmas. He did so with *The Last Days of a Reluctant Tyrant*, an adaptation of the 1880 novel *The Golovyov Family* by Mikhail Saltykov-Shchedrin. In Murphy's version, the story concerns a powerful woman called Arina (played in the 2009 premiere by Marie Mullen). Her tragedy is that (as her son Peter claims) she cared only about 'Property, land, money. That's all she ever thought of. She sold her soul' (Murphy, 2009: 41). Arina operated as a way for Murphy to characterize the Celtic Tiger era as involving a kind of Faustian pact – with Ireland finally having to pay its dues.

But, being Murphy, he didn't stop there. At a time when many in Ireland were seeking to blame others – the Church, bankers, politicians, the EU – for the country's unhappy state, he suggested that the ferocity of his audience's anger might arise from a desire to avoid facing their own culpability. Hence, in *Last Days*, the clergy are not figures of authority who can be blamed for the society's ills; indeed, the only member of the Church with any power is a bishop, whose role was cut entirely from the play when it was performed at the Abbey in Conall Morrison's production. Instead, the clergy are weak figures, who are manipulated by the wealthy. The dynamics of that relationship are revealed when Arina's son, Peter, gets his maid, Vera, pregnant, and places their child in an institution run by the Church rather than causing scandal by raising it as his own. Murphy's audience knows that an unhappy future awaits the child, but *Last Days* forces them to focus on the family members – indeed, the whole community – that sent it away in the first place. For Murphy, we can only move forward by acknowledging the truth about our own responsibilities.

My aim in this final chapter is to show how Irish dramatists such as Murphy have, since the turn of the century, engaged with the society as it lurched from the illusion of wealth to the reality of hardship. In doing so, I want to show how Irish drama has devised new strategies to come to terms with austerity, but has also demonstrated a determination to face truths that, both before and after the crash, the society at large seemed determined to ignore.

## McPherson: selling our souls

Tom Murphy was not the only Irish dramatist to suggest that the Celtic Tiger represented a Faustian pact: this was also a theme of Conor McPherson's play *The Seafarer*, which opened in London in 2006 before appearing at the Abbey in 2008 and 2009, in productions that happened before and after the banking guarantee. A combination of the Dublin folk tale about the Hellfire Club with elements of the Faust story, it involves a group of washed-out Dubliners who come together on Christmas Eve to play cards. They're joined by a mysterious stranger called Lockhart – who is actually Satan, newly arrived in Dublin to win the soul of the play's protagonist, Sharky.

Sharky, we learn, had bartered his soul in a game of cards twenty-five years previously (sometime in the early 1980s), when he was arrested after a drunken brawl that caused the death of a homeless man. Because he won that game, Sharky was never charged with his crime, but Lockhart demanded the right to play him again. This set-up recalls Christopher Marlowe's Doctor Faustus, a character who sold his soul in exchange for twenty-four years on Earth with Mephistopheles as his servant, at the end of which time Lucifer returns to bring him to hell. Sharky has spent a quarter-century trying to forget what he did: he drinks heavily, has separated from his family, has lost one job after another, and his only hope of an improvement in his circumstances is a fake compensation claim. Like Marlowe's hero, Sharky's deal with the devil has led him to spend twenty-five years trying to forget who he really is. As Faustus must ask, 'Where are thou, Faustus? Wretch, what hast thou done?' (5.1.51), so must Sharky finally confront the truth about himself, and accept his culpability.

In Chapter 2, I proposed that Irish artists had set about 'translating' features of Catholicism into secular contexts. McPherson builds on that strategy by using his story about souls, devils and hell as a way of thinking about the economy – and for that reason he tends to use the language of money and finance rather than religion to convey the Satanic elements of his plot. For instance, if Sharky loses his game of cards, Lockhart promises to take him to hell through what he calls 'the hole in the wall' (McPherson, 2006: 76, 96) – a rather sinister-sounding phrase that is also a colloquialism for a cash machine. And when he is asked to describe what it is like to fall from heaven into hell, Lockhart replies as follows:

> Well you know, Sharky, when you're walking round the city and the street lights are all come on and it's cold.... And you see all these people who seem to live in another world all snuggled up together in the warmth of a tavern or a cosy little house, and you just walk and walk and walk and you're on your own and nobody knows who you are ... Well, that's a fraction of the self-loathing you feel in Hell, except it's worse.

> (2006: 77)

The use of the damned or redeemed individual as an emblem for nation displays McPherson's links to Murphy in one other way, which is that *The Seafarer* is in conversation with the latter's 1983 *The Gigli Concert*. That work is, as Fintan O'Toole remarks, 'almost certainly' indebted to Jung's insight that 'Faust and Mephistopheles are different sides of the one being' (1994: 168). That dual identity is represented through the figures of J.P.W. King, an Englishman who earns his living as a quack psychotherapist, and a character known only as 'the Irishman'. Insofar as redemption is available to either – and Murphy shows some ambivalence about that possibility – it can be found through the merging of apparently opposite traits: speech and song, melodrama and tragedy and, most significantly, Irishness and Englishness. So again, one individual's Faustian experience operates as a metaphor for nation – and in that context, it is interesting to observe that *The Gigli Concert* enjoyed three different productions in Ireland during the period from the height of the Celtic Tiger to the crash, in the process becoming the only contemporary play to be staged by all three of Ireland's major companies: the Abbey (2001, 2004), Druid (2009) and the Gate (2015).

McPherson also draws from *The Gigli Concert* in his 2004 play *Shining City*, which reproduces the set-up of a therapist who is, in a manner of speaking, 'healed' by his patient – and which, like *Gigli*, concludes with a moment of miraculous theatricality. In Murphy's play, the action concludes with J.P.W. singing like Gigli; in McPherson's, the therapist sees the apparition of his patient's dead wife. In both plays, the writer is inviting his audience to believe the impossible, Murphy doing so to present a moment of transcendence, and McPherson to demonstrate how we can continue to be (literally and metaphorically) haunted by unresolved grief. The purpose of both *Gigli* and *Shining City*, despite their many differences, is to show that outward signs of economic success and self-satisfaction can often hide personal histories of violence or self-hatred. Sooner or later, a reckoning has to happen.

Indeed, it is a feature of McPherson's plays that the metaphor of the ghostly is often used to dramatize the distinctions between how things appear to be on the surface of a society, and what is really the case. In perhaps his most popular play, *The Weir* (1997), that link is present in the contrast between the four rural men in whose local pub the play is set, and a visiting Dubliner called Valerie. The play initially sets up a series of binaries that audiences will recognize from other Irish plays: between the active male storytellers and the passively listening female; between the colourful rural setting and the mundane urban capital from which the woman has fled; between a past that draws on legend, folktales and distinctive traditions, and a present that makes Ireland seem like just another Western country. But those apparent binaries are soon subverted.

The play involves the telling of five stories, all but the last of which have a supernatural element. Drawing on Murphy's *Conversations on a Homecoming*, the action is set in a pub in which the time experienced by the characters is different from the time experienced by the audience (the play usually runs to about 100 minutes in performance but we should imagine that the characters are in the pub for at least twice as long as that). The first story is told by Jack and seems to be drawn from a very old-fashioned version of Ireland involving fairies knocking at doors and (in a call back to *The Righteous Are Bold*) an exorcism being performed by a local priest; notably, it is the only story that recounts events that were not experienced directly by the teller. But as the action continues, the combination of alcohol and the novelty of the presence of Valerie (who is a classic example of the use of a 'stranger in the house' motif) causes the characters to open up about themselves, first in a story by Finbar about how he quit smoking, and then in a story by Jim about an encounter with the ghost of a paedophile. Again, the tales draw on familiar Irish images: with its combination of gravedigging and alcohol, Jim's story immediately calls to mind McDonagh's *A Skull in Connemara* (which opened a month before *The Weir*), while Finbar's story evokes images of a community that is tightly bound but isolated and somewhat innocent.

The accumulation of those stories encourages Valerie to tell her own tale, one that (unlike the men's) is set in contemporary Dublin and draws not on the familiar Irish images of the hearth and the whiskey glass and the country road, but on everyday technologies such as phones and cars. Her story, that is, exists in the present tense of the audience. It also contains echoes of what has come before. It concerns the death of her daughter, whose name – Niamh – is shared by the girl in Finbar's tale. As in Jack's story, Niamh is haunted by an inexplicable knocking and, as in Jim's, Niamh is threatened by a man whose intentions towards her are never stated directly but are all the more disturbing for that. All of those traces show how the details of the men's stories have been carried forward, the binaries of rural/urban, male/female, present/past thereby being set aside. McPherson's suggestion appears to be that contemporary Ireland may seem prosperous, civilized, technologically advanced – but that there are unresolved problems lurking under the surface. It would be an oversimplification to suggest that *The Weir* is 'about' the legacies of child abuse in Ireland in any kind of literal sense, and I agree with Helen Lojek's assessment that it would be wrong to see the play as being 'about' the Celtic Tiger (2011). Nevertheless, McPherson's portrayal of a community haunted by its inability to protect vulnerable young people was directly relevant to Ireland in the late 1990s. But as *The Seafarer* would later show, the metaphor of haunting can have many meanings in a troubled society.

The relationship between ghosts and memory persists into McPherson's other works. *The Veil* (2011) is a history play that seems to be in dialogue with Friel's *Translations*: set in 1822, it follows Friel in presenting action that is set on the eve of the Great Famine, but which audiences must interpret on the basis of their knowledge of that impending catastrophe. Similarly, his 2009 movie *The Eclipse* uses the metaphor of haunting as a way to provide an intimate investigation of a widower's sense of guilt about his desire to establish a new relationship after the death of his wife.

But even those of his plays that are not supernatural can be seen as being haunting – in the sense of dramatizing the lives of people who are preoccupied by an uncertainty or a memory that they cannot shake off. His 2013 *Night Alive* explores how a lonely man sees in the figure of a young woman a manifestation of his own sense of loss and thwarted desire – so that when she appears to him in the play's final scene, it is uncertain whether she is really there or not. And his 2017 musical *The Girl from the North Country* shows how past experiences shape the present – portraying action that is set in depression-era America but which in its Old Vic premiere seemed more directly to speak to the racial divisions and financial insecurity of post-Brexit England. Of particular impact is how McPherson as both writer and director uses the songs of Bob Dylan: rather than being a jukebox musical that replays the greatest hits, *The Girl from the North Country* rearranges the songs (under the musical direction of Simon Hale), blending them together, placing them in new contexts and allowing the audience to discover them rather than recognizing them. Hence, one of Dylan's more obscure songs, 'Tight Connection to My Heart', appears not as the breezy mid-1980s pop song he originally recorded, but as a moving ballad that was performed in McPherson's original production by Sheila Atim. Even allowing for how newspaper reviews draw on a limited vocabulary of clichéd adjectives, it's surely no coincidence that so many critics called her performance 'haunting'.

Many audiences enjoy McPherson's plays as good old-fashioned ghost stories: they respond to *The Weir* or *The Seafarer* as providing the kind of sensational thrill that made *The Righteous Are Bold* so popular half a century earlier. But of considerably greater importance is his ability to use the supernatural as a metaphor for contemporary Ireland. The supernatural, by definition, is something that we witness but cannot explain using the powers of reason: a sensation that is not unlike that of living in a society that is in the grip of an economic bubble – or one that has experienced a crash.

## The spirit of the staircase: Mark O'Rowe's monologue plays

One of the other major trends of the Celtic Tiger period was the appearance of a large number of monologue plays – stories that are directly recounted to the audience by a small group of characters (often just one, rarely more than three). I want to explore this phenomenon by discussing two plays by Mark O'Rowe, focusing especially on their treatment of gender, to demonstrate that the monologue form, like McPherson's supernatural dramas, is used to expose a disjunction in the society between appearance and reality.

Monologue plays, like ghosts, operate as metaphors for memory: characters in monologues aren't telling us a story because they think we want to hear it; they're talking because they can't stop talking. The storytelling thus operates as a compulsion, and the act of retelling can render metaphorically a character's sense of being tortured by memory: it is a verbal manifestation of the French phrase *l'esprit d'escalier* – the sensation of finally working out how best to respond to something only when it's too late to actually change a course of events. The way in which the monologue becomes a symbol for a guilty conscience is perhaps best realized in Beckett's *Play* (1963), with the characters' testimonies being summoned aggressively by a spotlight, showing how Beckett used the machinery of the theatre to render metaphorically the interior life of his characters.

*Play* also shows that the world of the Irish monologue is often a kind of purgatorial space, a place that is 'after life' but which shows the characters still trapped in a relationship with the living. This is true, for example, of Friel's *Faith Healer*, a drama of four interlinking monologues that inspired many similar works – and in which at least one of the characters is narrating the story of how he died. That play had a disastrous premiere in America in 1979 but appeared in Dublin in 1980, where it was directed by Joe Dowling and starred Donal McCann. It was not uniformly well received at that time – 'quite frankly, I don't know what to make of this play and I suspect Mr Friel doesn't either,' wrote one critic (ATDA, 0790_PC_0001: 10). But over time McCann's performance grew to be seen as one of the greatest feats of Irish acting of that period (comparable to McKenna's work in *Bailegangaire* five years later), and his involvement in successive revivals in the 1990s must explain why so many imitators of *Faith Healer* appeared in that decade.

If monologues are often delivered by the dead, does that mean that the characters are haunting the theatre – and hence the audience? Perhaps, but the audience is also in a privileged position: our task is not just to listen to the stories but to interpret them, to judge whether characters might be deceiving us, or themselves, or each other – and to piece together the full story. Quite often, each speaker believes firmly in the importance and integrity of his or her own story, but the audience always knows more than the characters do. That allows us to reconsider the relationship between subjectivity and objectivity – between the perspective of a lone individual telling a story and the audience that collectively listens to and analyses that story. The monologue thus shows us how truth is revealed not through a process of passive listening but rather though an active evaluation of evidence.

Mark O'Rowe has written plays in a variety of forms: of his naturalistic *Made in China* (2002), for example, he jokingly said that it was a 'proper play' because it features 'characters who actually talk to each other' (2011: ix), and in his later works such as *Our Few and Evil Days* (2014) and *The Approach* (2018) he shows an intense interest in how everyday speech disguises truths rather than expressing them (demonstrating his indebtedness to Pinter). But he has also written sophisticated and intricate monologues that are noted for their linguistic inventiveness as well as their uncompromisingly bleak subject matter.

His discovery of monologue was inspired, he writes, by coming across two texts. The first was McPherson's *This Lime Tree Bower* (1995): O'Rowe was shocked to realize that 'you can just have an actor tell a story directly to the audience' (2011: viii). The second was Beckett's novel *Molloy* (1955), in which, as O'Rowe writes, 'you can have two lead characters who never meet and a plot which doesn't even tie itself up at the end' (2011: viii). Like *Molloy*, *Howie the Rookie* (1999) would have two lead characters, and while they do meet – and while the plot does, more or less, tie itself up at the end – the two characters' stories are made fully meaningful only to the audience, since we can hear both of them.

*Howie the Rookie* is set in a Dublin that corresponds recognizably to the real place, but which also differs from anything seen in any other Irish play. Its named locations can be identified on a real map of the city; the number of the bus that the characters take matches a real route that was in service in the late 1990s; the names of shops and pubs have real-world equivalents. But that's where the similarities end. Howie describes how 'the new shops' in his area were 'built in a circle, with their backs face out to keep the bandits at bay', evoking images of wagons being circled in a western; he later finds himself thinking of John Wayne when faced with a difficult situation. The language used by the characters reproduces some of the speech patterns, rhythms and slang of Dublin speech, but it also draws on American gangster television: when they want to leave, they say 'vamanos'; and instead of goodbye they say 'adios'. Howie's biggest influence appears to be kung fu movies: his surname Lee is fairly common in Ireland, but he chooses to identify himself and his 'namesake in Lee-ness' (the Rookie) with 'the Bruce' – the martial artist and film star Bruce Lee (O'Rowe, 2011: 88).

We see in such examples evidence of how the men draw their sense of how to behave from role models that are taken from popular (non-Irish) cultural forms. Those models trap the characters into what they think of as a code of honour but which in reality is a morally chaotic system that prizes retribution over forgiveness. That code has a particularly strong determining influence on Howie's actions: it causes him to attack the Rookie but then, in the second half of the play, to defend him. Similarly, the reason that the Rookie is in trouble is that he's accidentally killed some fishes belonging to the play's antagonist, Ladyboy. For these men, moral decisions are made on the spur of the moment, and are reactive rather than reflective.

A consequence of this way of living is the imposition of very rigid gender roles upon the men, determining not just how they see themselves but also how they define and identify with women. For example, Howie considers babysitting to be a woman's job, and thus hires Skip Susan to take care of his brother, Mousey, rather than looking after him himself – a decision that leads indirectly to Mousey's death. And Howie's own demise is caused when his friend Peaches learns that Howie has slept with his sister, a transgression he considers unforgiveable: 'How dare he presume to fuck The Peaches' sister? How dare he fuck her an' dump her like a dirty toerag? Behind the Peaches' back? Makin' her think someone loved her when she was unlovable? Givin' her hope?' (O'Rowe, 2011: 220).

Perhaps surprisingly, sexual prowess does not itself function as a sign of masculinity. The Rookie is a self-described 'handsome bastard. Bit attractive to the dollies, they're into me. Find them easy to pick up, easy to get. Break hearts an' hymens, I do' (O'Rowe, 2011: 202). Yet he is often told that he's not a real man. For instance, when he tries to borrow money from a former lover called Bernie, the exchange goes as follows:

> You know nothing of manly things, she says, you know nothin' 'cos you
>     run away from people in pubs.
> Sore point, me lack of manliness, so it slips out.
> Cunt

(2011: 208)

So apart from an anxiety about being mistaken for being gay, both male characters express their masculinity through violence rather than sexual performance. Rookie's choice of a sexualized epithet for Susan also tells us much about him.

By far the most frightening character in the play is a man called Ladyboy. His name combines a grand word for a woman with a slightly derogatory word for a grown man, and it's that combination that seems to frighten people. The Rookie describes him in monstrous terms. When he was born, the legend goes, his mother threw away the body and raised the afterbirth; some say he has an 'ingrown flute' and that he has 'three sets of teeth instead of one – Like a shark' (O'Rowe, 2011: 204). In an environment in which categories are very rigid, Ladyboy doesn't fit in: he may have an 'ingrown flute', as the Rookie says, but you don't need to be a Freudian to see how the story about his shark-life mouth – used for biting off fingers – can be seen as evoking fears of castration. Howie also tells a story about how the Ladyboy was told that the correct English phrase for 'where's the toilet' was 'kick me in the nuts', a joke that combines the sexual with the scatological in a way that is shared by one other character in the play: Howie's sometime girlfriend, the Avalanche. She too is seen as monstrous because her 'sexual technique' is measured in 'poundage . . . or stoneage . . . or fuckin' tonnage', says Howie. We learn much about her 'grotesque' arse, her monstrous belching and farting – and about Howie's shame in being seen with her (O'Rowe, 2011: 186).

So there's a conflict in Howie's mind between how he appears to himself and how he is perceived by others. The play is therefore dramatizing a pressure to perform: not to be manly but to be *seen* to be manly. And by definition, the monstrous is anything that fails to meet the rigid classification of gender and social roles, showing how this is a society that defines difference as a form of almost unforgivable transgression.

Given that the play is about performance, it's unsurprising that it's seen as providing actors with an opportunity to showcase their skills (something else that *Howie* shares with *Faith Healer*). The original production featured Aidan Kelly and Karl Shiels, and did much to launch their careers. They played their characters as if they were in their late teens or early twenties, which gave the performance the poignancy that comes with stories about young people dying before their time. Those actors were cast again in the first Abbey production of the play, directed by Jimmy Fay and staged in 2006. The actors had (of course) aged but they played their characters as older too: Howie now is in his late twenties, still living with his parents, and the Rookie likewise seems more directionless and feckless for no longer having the excuse of being very young. Hence, even with the same actors, the two versions of *Howie* evoked slightly different responses in the audience.

The play engendered still other meanings during its next revival, a 2013 production for Landmark that was directed by O'Rowe himself, in which both roles were played by one actor, Tom Vaughan-Lawlor, who at that time was in his mid-thirties. At a post-show interview during its Galway run, I asked Vaughan-Lawlor if he'd had to do anything during the interval to prepare himself mentally or physically for the transition from playing Howie to playing the Rookie. He chuckled: 'I just change my tee-shirt,' he said. Where Kelly and Shiels had seen their characters as contrasting and complementary (in keeping with the Irish tradition of the male double act), Vaughan-Lawlor imagined them as different manifestations of one person, and thus played both roles with the same accent, voice, body language and movement. This is not to say that he intended the audience literally to see them as the same person, but instead to point out the validity of his choice as an actor not to differentiate the two characters from each other.

However we interpret them, the most important split is not between Howie and the Rookie but between the public and the private versions of each. O'Rowe in *Howie* is back to the problem faced by Friel in *Philadelphia, Here I Come!*: how do you put someone on stage whose environment is so restrictive that his private self is like a wholly different character from his public version? For O'Rowe, monologue is literally the only way that these characters can be expressed – and that acts as an implicit criticism of the society that stops them from revealing who they really are.

A similar approach is evident in *Crestfall* (2003), a play set in a fictionalized version of Dublin that features three female characters and which again explores what happens when people are trapped in rigid gender-based roles. Each of the three women exists in a role that both expresses and subverts a stereotype: Olive is a 'fallen woman', Alison is an idealized mother-figure, and Tilly is the prostitute with the heart of gold, who will ultimately synthesize elements of the other two characters. When viewed in the context of all of his works, it seems apparent that O'Rowe is trying to show that the literal violence experienced by women in *Crestfall* is matched by a kind of metaphorical violence imposed upon them by men's unwillingness to see them in any but the most limited roles. Indeed, when it was revived for Druid in 2017, its director, Annabelle Comyn, argued that 'It's a complex and explorative representations of women . . . who are both victims of violence as well as perpetrators of violence, both physical and emotional.' Siobhán Cullen, one of the performers in that production, added that 'In its very nature it's feminist ... It's three women on stage talking about their experiences. And while they're talking about violent things happening to them, they're also talking about their own survival' (*Irish Independent*, 9 July 2017).

However, at its 2003 premiere, the play was widely perceived as being misogynistic: in particular, there was a tendency to imagine that O'Rowe himself perceived the world as his characters do. Writing in *The Guardian* about the fact that the production was directed by Garry Hynes, Karen Fricker wondered how 'a woman as smart as [her] got within a million miles of this empty material' (24 May 2003). Those responses (and Fricker's was by no means the most harsh) may have been influenced by the venue for the production: it was staged at the Gate, a theatre that under Michael Colgan's direction over the previous twenty years had become famous for its Beckett and Pinter seasons, as well as sumptuous revivals of Wilde and adaptations of Victorian novels. Perhaps paradoxically, the production of *Crestfall* at the Gate did not make the theatre seem more daring (which is what Colgan intended), but rather made O'Rowe's work seem more conservative, such that the negative views of women presented in it were taken literally by critics and audience alike.

O'Rowe would try to make his intentions clearer by rewriting *Crestfall* when it was published in 2011: the original script in the Gate archive is less rhythmic and more violent, featuring one particularly gratuitous scene in which one of the characters recounts being forced to perform oral sex upon a dog (GTDA, 1236_PS_0001). That scene is cut from the published edition (and indeed, at the 2014 post-show talk mentioned above, O'Rowe told me that he had also rewritten portions of *Howie* in order to make clear that he does not personally share his characters' views of women). So he has clearly tried to sharpen audiences' understanding of what he intends, and the fact that the Druid revival of *Crestfall* was mostly well received suggests that his play is better understood now than it was in 2003.

Nevertheless, *Crestfall* is a difficult play, full of troubling images, starting with an apparently idyllic opening in which a boy dunks a girl who's swimming. She 'goes down thrashing' we're told, and while we might assume that the act is a bit of fun, it's evocative of the violence against women that's going to follow (GTDA, 1236_PS_0001: 1). There are also images of dying animals from the outset. Olive sets the tone early on when she speaks of being dragged

> through the wasteland
> behind the old slaughterhouse, the Boneland
> where bits of cow lie scattered

> (O'Rowe, 2011: 321)

Later we hear about a horse being beaten to death by a mob, whose actions are mirrored by a pack of hounds roaming the streets and led by a dog whose three eyes will remind audiences of the three-headed Cerberus, who guarded the underworld. The boundaries between animal and human, and between hell and our own reality, are very porous.

There's also a sense in which the boundaries between right and wrong seem unclear. Olive speaks of how she 'became a righteous sexual fiend, and wallowed in my many filthy rendezvous' (2011: 321): so she can be righteous *and* a fiend; she can wallow in something filthy. Similarly, sex, which should be pleasurable, is instead very closely related to violence – early in the play, for instance, the word 'pump' is used to refer to Iron Bru having sex with Olive, but less than five minutes later is also used to refer to Kit Rankin's sawn-off shotgun.

O'Rowe makes clear the damage caused by imposing narrow roles on women; despite being performed by three female actors, the plot largely centres around the insecurities of men. Olive has set out to corrupt her husband, Jungle, because, despite his name, he's too good for the world that he lives in:

**Olive**   he doesn't belong, you see
He's wrong
For this wicked place.
An anomaly

(2011: 322)

Jungle's discovery that he's not the natural father of his child, Poppin' Eye, brings about a massacre at the play's conclusion. O'Rowe shows that although he acts on his own volition, these events were caused by two women. First, by Olive herself, who seems to welcome his ensuing revenge, so that when he beats her she says that:

This is the man I longed for him to become
So why am I sorry now? So dumb . . . I lean forward into the punches he throws
and accept them, thinking, Fine, then. . . . In order to assist in your evolution, your gaining of strength, or resolution, of the will to be vile and, in being so, to belong, to fit

(2011: 335)

It's also brought about by Tilly, who tells Jungle the truth about his son's paternity, partly out of revenge against Olive, and partly from despair about her own life.

Early in the play, Olive refers to sex as 'the oldest sin', and this is a play that is full of sin – but there's no evidence at all of forgiveness. The only kind of redemption that seems possible is through an idealization of the mother role, especially in the characterization of Alison, who tries to protect her autistic son from becoming part of the mob that wants him to kill a horse. We see that idealization in the play's finale too, in which Tilly becomes a mother of sorts to Poppin' Eye. Upon the premiere, this finale was viewed as a reinforcement of conservative values, as if suggesting that O'Rowe was seeking to limit women to the role of mother or wife. But, on the contrary, he is putting on stage a society that can only see women in those narrow ways – and using the private testimony of his characters via the monologue form to call attention to the ways in which these women refuse to fill the roles that have been created for them. The women are speaking in monologue because their society has literally given them no other way of expressing themselves: the form expresses their imprisonment as eloquently as the content.

Here again it's worth seeing the direction of Garry Hynes as exerting a feminist interpretation upon the meaning of the performance in 2003. She cast three of Ireland's leading actors – Aisling O'Sullivan, Marie Mullen and Eileen Walsh – in the three roles. As the image in Figure 11 demonstrates, all wore black dresses of slightly different styles, rather than costumes that would have accurately recreated their roles in the real world of the play. And they delivered their lines on a set that, in Francis O'Connor's design, placed tilted mirrors across the back of the stage, shifting the lighting around in ways that disorientated the audience. This, Hynes was making clear, was an act of theatre and not of social realism; hence, our responsibility was to understand the artifice instead of passively accepting the play as 'real'. The use of mirrors emphasized this obligation: to watch it in the Gate auditorium involved seeing a hazy vision of ourselves on stage. It was not possible to see ourselves in anything but vague outline, but the impact was to show that, rather than the characters haunting us, we were in a sense haunting them.

As O'Rowe has moved into writing in a style of intricate naturalism, his work has become less controversial because the horrendous truths his characters recount in his monologue plays are implied in such plays as *The Approach* (2018), which is haunting because it is ambiguous where *Crestfall* is disturbingly explicit. To make this distinction is not to impose a judgement on the value of one form of writing over another but rather to point out that monologue serves the purpose of telling a story that cannot otherwise be known – which must force us to think about the social structures that

**Figure 11** *Crestfall* by Mark O'Rowe at the Gate Theatre. Left to right: O'Sullivan, Mullen and Walsh. Photograph by Tom Lawlor (GTDA, 1236_PH_0002.pdf | Ref. 8659).

prevent such truths from being revealed according to the conventions of realistic theatre.

## Fishamble and Deirdre Kinahan: rethinking relevance

On Sunday 28 September 2008, the Dublin Theatre Festival was just getting underway, and many of the seasoned theatregoers were saying that the year's best show had already appeared. That production was *Gatz* by the American company Elevator Repair Service; on that Sunday it was staging the last of its four Dublin performances.

The central idea of the production was disarmingly simple. A man arrives at his office to discover that his computer has broken down. Looking for something to do, he searches through his desk, where he finds a copy of F. Scott Fitzgerald's *The Great Gatsby*. He begins to read it aloud and, as he does so, events in his workplace gradually begin to follow those in the novel itself, as he and his fellow colleagues begin unconsciously to act out its plot until both settings merge into one. The entire play lasts eight hours, and by the end of it, the audience will have heard every word of Fitzgerald's text (and nothing but that text) – but despite its length, Dublin audiences seemed to agree that the experience was genuinely invigorating. Tickets for that final performance were scarce.

What no one realized as they filed out of that Dublin theatre where *Gatz* had been playing was that they were about to live through the last day of the Celtic Tiger era. On the next day, a Monday, the chief executives of two of Ireland's leading banks called the Department of Finance demanding a meeting with the minister, Brian Lenihan. They claimed that they were facing serious problems with liquidity and that when the markets opened the next day, there was a serious prospect of an Irish bank collapsing. Details on what exactly happened next are unclear, but we know that during that night a plan was implemented to provide an unlimited guarantee of the deposits and liabilities of all of Ireland's banks.

The subsequent transformation of Ireland was rapid. The country went from being a 'Celtic Tiger' economy into one of a group of nations known as the 'PIIGS', an unapologetically racist term coined by London bankers to describe Portugal, Italy, Ireland, Greece and Spain – the European economies that were considered most likely to default after the global credit crunch began in 2008. The scale of Ireland's transformation – its journey from tiger to pig, if you like – was shocking. In 2001, Irish unemployment was at 3 per cent, close to full employment. By 2012, it had reached 14.7 per cent. That latter figure would certainly have been higher if not for the impact of emigration: in 2001 there was net migration of 60,000 into Ireland; by 2012 almost as many people were leaving the country as were entering it. And perhaps the most severe transformation was in Ireland's national debt. In 2008, the Irish national debt stood at €50.7 billion; by the time the government fell in 2010 it had almost doubled to €93.4 billion.

So to look back to that performance of *Gatz*, on the second-last day of the Celtic Tiger period, is to see how that American production was founded upon values that would have greater importance in Ireland during the subsequent months. It was a celebration of the resilience of the written word over the impermanence of text on a computer screen, suggesting that the book will be there waiting for us when we need it – that we can, in all sorts of ways, go back and confront our roots. It was a reminder that play can be more productive than work, that the office can be a site for many different kinds of performance. Like Fitzgerald's original, *Gatz* attacks 'careless people ... who smashed up things and creatures and then retreated back into their money or their vast carelessness, or whatever it was that kept them together, and let other people clean up the mess they had made' (Fitzgerald, 1998: 142). Those words could have been an epitaph for the Celtic Tiger, just as they had been for the Jazz Age. So one of the most important things about *Gatz* – and indeed about *The Great Gatsby* – is that both reveal the capacity of art to be relevant in ways that can't be planned or predicted: like much great art, they reveal truths to us that we didn't know we already knew.

The issue of *relevance* – of the relationship between the artwork and the society that receives it – is important in many contexts. But as the Celtic Tiger collapsed it would take on new significance in Ireland, as critics and journalists would demand that theatre artists reflect upon the new situation that the country faced. The fact that those demands coincided with the collapse in funding for Irish theatre companies – just as audiences' disposable income was falling, reducing their capacity to buy theatre tickets – made things all the more challenging. But a company that responded almost immediately was Fishamble – and, in doing so, it revealed many of its most admirable traits.

Founded by Jim Culleton in 1988, Fishamble (originally Pigsback) dubs itself the 'new play company', and it has an impressive track record of identifying new writers and staging their works. Among the dramatists whose earliest plays it staged are Marina Carr, Mark O'Rowe, Stella Feehily and Joseph O'Connor. One of its most likeable features is its core belief in the idea of the 'undiscovered playwright': repeatedly during its history, Fishamble has presented open calls for members of the public to submit plays to them, and has frequently staged several of the submissions. Following the IMF bail-out in 2010, for example, they produced *Tiny Plays for Ireland* (2011), a compendium of three-minute plays that was the result of a public call-out that attracted 1,700 submissions. Many of those produced were by established writers such as Maeve Binchy, Colum McCann, Rosaleen McDonagh and Ardal O'Hanlon – but there were also several by people who had never before had their work staged. The title of the series is revealing: Fishamble showed that at a moment of crisis, the thing we might most need (like the office worker who finds a copy of *The Great Gatsby* in his desk) is a work of art: these were plays 'for' Ireland, but also plays of Ireland. This production was not the result of a hierarchical approach to commissioning work from established writers, but instead involved a democratic belief in the existence of writers across the island.

One of those tiny plays – *Guaranteed Irish* – was a brief account of the night of the banking guarantee, written by the journalist and theatre critic Colin Murphy. That work was extended into a full-length documentary drama which Fishamble produced as a 'script-in-hand' production in 2013, combining the play with a series of public debates that gave Irish audiences the opportunity to discuss what had been done to them and in their name. Watching one of those performances in Wicklow during the summer of that year, I was struck by the intensity of the audience's attention, and by their gratitude for Fishamble's attempt to place recent events into perspective. It was a rare moment of communal optimism, made all the more powerful by the fact that the company didn't let a lack of funding to pay for rehearsal time or a full production stop them from bringing the play to audiences.

Another important way in which Fishamble responded to the crash was to work with the Irish Theatre Institute and Dublin Fringe on a project called Show in a Bag from 2010 onwards, the aim of which was to help actors (many of whom, understandably, were struggling to find work) to develop new plays that they could write, perform in and take on tour. While there was already an established tradition of Irish actors writing plays for Rough Magic, the success of Show in a Bag has been transformational, bringing to the stage new voices such as Sonya Kelly, Aonghus Óg McAnally, Emmet Kirwan, Noni Stapleton and Niamh Shaw. A related project has been a long-standing collaboration with the actor Pat Kinevane, five of whose plays have been produced by Fishamble. The significance of such work is not just that it fulfilled the important task of enabling Irish actors to keep making a living during the most severe recession in eighty years – and not just that it led to the production of many new plays – but also that it has led to the creation of new drama by people who have an intimate professional understanding of how the actor performs before audiences. This collection of plays is irreducible to a single set of characteristics, but they share a belief in theatricality, in the connection of the performer to an audience, and the ability of both to come together to create a communal experience that brings meaning to shared lives.

A play that demonstrates the company's commitment to producing work that engages directly with the society is the 2014 Dublin Theatre Festival production of *Spinning* by Deirdre Kinahan. She had emerged in the early years of the 2000s as a strong example of a new generation of theatre artists who, rather than waiting for the major companies to 'discover' them, had simply set about putting on her own work – something that she mostly did with her company Tall Tales. Her early plays ranged across a variety of topics: *Knocknashee* (2002) is one of the first Irish works to engage respectfully with issues of disability, but it also demonstrates her long-term interest in characters who have been marginalized by their societies, through drug addiction, prostitution and mental illness, for example – but also through old age, something she would explore in *Halcyon Days* (2012). And, like many Irish dramatists, she's also very interested in family dynamics, showing how families often have to learn to create a repertoire of interactions that allow them to cope with their problems, ranging from severe trauma to the more mundane emotions of regret, jealousy and frustration.

The story of *Spinning* exemplifies Kinahan's willingness to take on difficult subjects, and to find the humanity that lies behind stories that are often presented sensationally in print and broadcast media. Her primary male character is called Conor, a man who – estranged from his wife and in danger of losing access to his daughter – decides spontaneously to drive his car into a lake, killing a young girl called Annie who had befriended him. Conor survives and is forced to live with the guilt of what he's done – and with the fact that his actions have brought about the thing he most feared: the complete loss of contact with his family.

Kinahan is dramatizing the growth of murder-suicides in Ireland, of which there had been at least one case every year since 2000 at the time of *Spinning*'s premiere. Almost without exception, those crimes were committed by troubled men, such as Arthur McElhill, who killed himself, his partner and their five children in a house fire in Tyrone in 2007; or a case in Cork in 2010, when John Butler murdered his daughters, Ella and Zoe, before killing himself. Kinahan does not want to excuse the actions of such men, but she does try to understand them, so she is careful to show how Conor's mental state had gradually deteriorated – starting with attempts to control his wife, Jen, developing into manipulative behaviour towards Annie, and concluding with an act of violence that was unplanned but which also seems inevitable.

*Spinning* makes clear that Conor's actions arise from what might glibly be termed a crisis in masculinity: he is attempting to fill a role of husband/ father that no longer corresponds to the realities of his society and relationships. But Kinahan's aim is not journalistic but artistic: she also wants to allow for the possibility that someone like Conor might be forgiven. She explores this theme by putting on stage the figure of Annie's mother, Susan, who wavers during the action between needing to hear Conor's version of events and not wanting anything to do with him (and thus acts as a kind of surrogate for the audience, who will be similarly ambivalent about Kinahan's male protagonist). At the play's conclusion she manages to dissuade Conor from committing suicide, partly out of compassion (including for Conor's wife and daughter) but also because she knows that justice demands that he live with what he's done.

In the Fishamble production as directed by Culleton, the style of performance sought to disrupt distinctions between past and present, between the living and the dead. Annie appears on stage, but it's never possible to say that we are seeing her in a flashback or as a kind of ghost: this is because Kinahan does not want to write a memory play but to show how memories can persist into the present with such force as to seem like they have a kind of life of their own. It would of course be incorrect to suggest that *Spinning* is literally about the post-Celtic Tiger era, but – as with *Gatz* – it shows how the work of art is *relevant* not because it addresses matters of topical concern but rather because it allows us to think about our current needs. At the heart of *Spinning* is the question of how we go on after the unthinkable has happened – and Kinahan makes clear that we must go on living, forgive those who have wronged us if we can, and, as Susan says in her final lines, 'start something . . . start something . . . somewhere else' (Kinahan, 2014: 82). For an Ireland that had been radically transformed, in which lives had been destroyed, homes lost and relationships severed, her play was providing answers to the questions that most needed to be explored.

## New directions

As the beginning of an economic recovery started to be felt in 2015, the Irish theatre found itself transformed in many ways. In a good example of how challenging times can sometimes bring out the best in people, one of the major developments of the period was that austerity encouraged the emergence of the so-called 'theatre-maker'. This process had been beginning before the crash but greatly intensified thereafter, and involved a situation whereby people who might in the past have written a play and sent it to the Abbey were now producing, acting in, directing, marketing and otherwise staging their own works.

Of such work, Amy Conroy's *I Heart Alice Heart I* (2010) stands out, both politically and formally. Ostensibly it is a documentary play about two women, both called Alice, who fall in love during middle age and become a couple. What is remarkable about them is how unremarkable they are: they are well educated, in good jobs, relatively well off – and thus quite similar to the typical Irish theatregoer. As we've seen, most Irish plays aim to create a contrast between the audience and the characters on stage; to repeat Nicholas Grene's phrase, it is 'typically other people' that the Irish audience sees in the theatre (1999: 264). The Alices, in contrast, are not 'other people' in the eyes of the audience – except in one respect, of course, which is their sexuality. Given that there had been so few representations of lesbian characters on the Irish stage, it is notable that Conroy chooses to present her characters not in terms of their differences but rather to assert what they have in common with the audience. That assertion feeds into a political ambition; the play promotes the idea that same-sex marriage is not just desirable but morally imperative.

Where Conroy complicates matters, however, is at her production's conclusion. As they watch the play, the audience form the belief that they are watching the 'real' Alices – not actors recounting their words but the actual people themselves. This is proven to be an illusion, as the two actors (in the original production played by Conroy herself and Clare Barrett) step out of character and explain who they really are, replacing the words 'we will be seen' with 'they will be seen' (in Conway, 2012: 219). This is a very powerful shift from the subjective to the objective, from 'us' to 'them', and it is one that in performance often left the audience confused, if not sorrowful. What had made the action invigorating before that point was our belief that we were hearing from people whose stories we had never heard before: we believe we are experiencing a kind of liberation, the freeing of a narrative that has hitherto been suppressed. By showing us that this liberation has only happened in the world of fiction, Conroy creates in her audience the hunger to ensure that it will happen in the society too.

In common with many of the new generation of theatre-makers, Conroy was certainly engaging with international theatre practice, drawing on techniques from verbatim theatre (relatively common in the UK but almost completely absent from the Irish tradition), as well as the postdramatic technique of blurring the boundaries between authorship, performance and truth. Yet she is also clearly and directly engaged with her own society's needs.

In Northern Ireland, the theatre has likewise experienced problems due to austerity, but there remains a strong tradition of playwriting, especially by women. The work of Tinderbox in promoting new writing is very important in that respect, bringing forward new plays by Abbie Spallen, Lisa McGee, Stacey Gregg, Judith King and Rosemary Jenkinson, among others. Also important are the plays of Owen McCafferty, one of the very few contemporary Northern Irish writers who has consistently managed to stage work in Dublin and London as well in Belfast. His 2003 *Scenes from the Big Picture* remains one of the great works of post-Ceasefire Northern Ireland, dramatizing the life of a society that has been deeply scarred by the Troubles but which refuses to be defined exclusively by that conflict.

The Troubles would also – most unexpectedly – make a return to the London stage when Jez Butterworth's *The Ferryman* (2017) proved an enormous hit, first in the Royal Court and then the West End. A respectful engagement with the legacies of such Irish dramatists as Friel, Murphy and O'Casey, Butterworth's play nevertheless provoked some criticism from commentators with Irish connections (such as the *Guardian*'s Sean O'Hagan), people who worried about the ethics of an English playwright writing an Irish play. But what Butterworth might have been demonstrating is how the Irish play has become a kind of genre internationally, a form of drama that anyone can write in, regardless of whether he or she knows the real country. John Patrick Shanley's *Outside Mullingar* (2014) is another example of this phenomenon: it is an American play set in the Irish town named in the title, but seems to have derived its knowledge of the country mostly from plays by Martin McDonagh. Also relevant was Richard Eyre's decision in 2013 to perform Pirandello's *Liolà* with an all-Irish cast, speaking in their own accents but intended to represent the peasantry of Sicily. The suggestion that Irish and Sicilian identities were interchangeable for Eyre raises questions: do we see this as an example of cultural insensitivity, or was he simply trying to make Pirandello more immediate for his London audience while retaining a sense of its foreignness? What all of this demonstrates is that Irishness continues to be a valued commodity in the marketplaces of the West End and Broadway – but it is a very narrow form of Irishness that has little to do with life in the country itself.

As I bring this book to a conclusion, then, it seems important to suggest that Irish theatre now is undergoing another period of transition, one that is comparable to what it faced in the early 1950s. The relationship between Britain and Ireland dominated the theatre of that earlier period and will undoubtedly continue to be a subject of investigation and contestation – but of more significance is the question of whether theatre in the Republic of Ireland and Northern Ireland will continue to evolve into what are increasingly looking like related but distinctive traditions. This book has tended to avoid making too rigid a distinction between the two jurisdictions, at least insofar as theatre is concerned. But it is likely that future studies will need to do more to consider the differences between them.

So too must we acknowledge that Irish theatre has been at its strongest when engaged with international influences, whether Tennessee Williams in the 1950s or Katie Mitchell in the early 2010s. In his *History of Irish Theatre*, Chris Morash memorably called for an understanding of the country's dramatic output in terms of audiences rather than plays (2002: 3) – but perhaps that statement can now be expanded to state that the term 'Irish theatre' must encapsulate not just plays written by people who happen to have been born on the island, but much more. It must include emerging forms of intercultural performance, but also must allow for a proper appreciation of how Irish artists have staged international plays.

It is also essential to acknowledge how far the theatre in Ireland has travelled in a relatively short time. In 1957, it became the flashpoint for a conflict between Church and state in a dispute about the (non-)appearance of a condom on stage – but by 2014 it would take a leading role in the campaign for same-sex marriage, just as the #WakingTheFeminists campaign that began in 2015 would call for the achievement of equality not just in the theatre but in the nation more broadly. It is a sign of the importance of dramatic literature and theatre practice that it is impossible to understand Ireland since 1950 without understanding Irish theatre since 1950. This is true in many of the areas discussed in this book – secularization, the achievement of peace in Northern Ireland, the liberalization of attitudes to sexuality, the growth of interculturalism, and so on. But there are many other areas that might similarly have been explored, especially in such areas as community drama, theatre for children and young audiences, and work in languages other than English.

This is not to suggest, however, that the value of theatre must be seen only in terms of its societal impact. What I have tried to demonstrate in this book is how Irish actors, writers and directors have contributed to the development of theatrical form and practice, nationally and internationally. This includes innovations in matters of writing, directing, design and acting. But it also includes a willingness to find ways to stage truths that many societies (not just Ireland) had found unpalatable. And in doing so they have given us some of the great plays and productions of this era.

A very large number of Irish plays present a story that does not have a clear beginning, middle and end, but in which an initial event is repeated in some form, often several times. We can map that approach onto the history of the form itself, to show that Irish theatre since 1950 has involved a series of repetitions, many of which were made without knowledge of what had come before. It remains to be seen which of the patterns I have identified here will recur in the future – and which will be broken, allowing for new ways of making and receiving drama. But whatever happens, my aim here has been to show how theatre matters in Ireland: it is a driver of change, a source of consolation and entertainment, and a reflection on the country's best and worst elements.

# CHAPTER 7
# CRITICAL PERSPECTIVES

This book concludes with a collection of critical perspectives by other authors, the aim of which is to identify three roads not taken in the discussion thus far – and, by doing so, to point to the multiplicity of possible approaches to the study of Irish drama and theatre since 1950.

As was argued in Chapter 1, amateur drama has had an important symbiotic relationship with the professional theatre – notably so in the career of John B. Keane, a dramatist whose enormous popularity in Ireland contrasts with the fact that he is virtually unknown outside the country. Finian O'Gorman provides a case study of Keane's *Sive*, demonstrating its importance in and of itself, but also showing how there is a need for considerably greater attention to be paid to the amateur sector more generally.

The status of performance art in Ireland since 1950 is itself a huge subject, and Áine Phillips' important critical study (2015) gives it sustained attention. Her essay in the present volume calls attention to the overlaps between performance art and theatre, showing the two in another kind of symbiotic relationship, and also demonstrating how boundaries between artforms are gradually eroding, in Ireland as elsewhere.

We conclude with Siobhán O'Gorman's work on scenography. I have sought throughout this book to call attention to the importance of actors and directors as well as playwrights – but, as O'Gorman shows, the importance of design must not be disregarded. The interplay between the word and the image is one of the defining characteristics of the theatre – yet scholarship on Irish drama remains disproportionately preoccupied with text. The scholarship of Siobhán O'Gorman – together with critical volumes such as Joe Vaněk's discussion of his own career in *Irish Theatrescapes* (2015b) – acts as an important corrective to that tendency. In the essay, O'Gorman surveys the impact of design on the reception of Irish theatre since 1950, pointing out key moments and showing that much more needs to be known and understood about this subject.

These essays seek to achieve a task set for this book in its entirety – to ask the question of how Irish theatre appears when it is viewed from a long perspective (in the present case, one lasting seventy years). Considered from day to day, or from one annual Arts Council application to another, the rate of change in Irish theatre might seem very slow; viewed from these longer-term perspectives, the speed of development is often startling. While these three essays necessarily only provide snapshots of those developments, their aim collectively is to demonstrate how the narrative presented in the book thus far runs in parallel with a variety of other developments that must also be fully explored.

# JOHN B. KEANE, *SIVE* (1959) AND THE ART OF
# THE AMATEUR

*Finian O'Gorman*

It is not entirely clear why Robert Hogan and Richard Burnham chose *The Art of the Amateur* as the title for the fifth volume of Hogan's seminal series on modern Irish drama. The text does make fleeting references to amateur societies such as the Leeside Players in Cork and the Catholic Rosario Players in Belfast, but the bulk of the material is dedicated to activities at the Abbey. Given the time period they consider (1916–20), perhaps they were indirectly referencing revolutionaries like James Connolly and Patrick Pearse, who not only penned amateur works for the Irish stage but also aspired to the role of amateur statesmen. That usage would resonate with a widely accepted view of amateur theatre, where it is often framed as an embryonic stage in the development of a more advanced professional practice. Accordingly, when asked to list the achievements of amateur theatre in Ireland, most people will name successful professionals who began their careers as amateurs, from Tom Murphy in the 1950s to Liam Neeson in the 1970s. Thus, we might assume that the 'art' of the amateur outlined by Hogan and Burnham is, in actuality, the art of progressing from amateur to professional status.

Along with Murphy and Neeson, John B. Keane is one of the more prominent examples of a practitioner who fits within that framing of amateur and professional practice. The widely publicized story about Keane's early career is that, having been rejected by the Abbey with *Sive* in 1959, the young playwright gave the script to an amateur theatre group in his native town of Listowel in County Kerry. The unprecedented furore that grew around the play and its subsequent success on the competitive amateur festival circuit propelled Keane onward to a career as a professional playwright. A problem with that story is that it casts amateur theatre as an antechamber in which Keane languished before being invited to his rightful place among the professionals. It fails to recognize that with amateur and professional theatre in Ireland, we are presented with two interrelated but nevertheless discrete traditions that evolved at different points in time, and in response to different influences and priorities.

This chapter proceeds on the basis that, through a closer consideration of the separate trajectories of those traditions, we can gain a better understanding of the unique blend of conventions that is evident in *Sive*. While Keane intended *Sive* to be produced by the Abbey, it is not, strictly, an

Abbey play. Rather, it is a hybridized blend of melodrama and realism that owes its form to the regional amateur theatre tradition from which it emerged. My contention is that the performance of *Sive* in a regional amateur context precipitated performance occasions that responded directly to the overt, melodramatic conventions in the play. Conversely, when the play transferred to a professional milieu, those melodramatic conventions were either used as evidence of the play's failings, or ignored completely by metropolitan critics. Thus, while Keane's transition to the professional ranks might be viewed as a gain for the playwright in that it fulfilled his personal ambitions, it might also be seen as a loss for Irish theatre in terms of the stylistic changes that it instigated in his later work. This paper thus offers a retelling of the story of Keane and *Sive*, wherein the play is no longer viewed as the embryonic outpouring of a would-be professional, but as a superlative example of what we might term the art of the amateur.

Following a premiere run of three nights in its home town in February 1959, the Listowel Group won first prize with *Sive* at both the Clare and Limerick drama festivals in March, in the process securing a nomination for the All-Ireland Drama Festival in Athlone. It placed second at the North Cork Drama Festival and first at the Kerry Drama Festival, before advancing to the All-Ireland in late April and winning the award for Best Play. The Listowel Group's All-Ireland success was burnished by an unexpected and unprecedented invitation from the Abbey to present *Sive* in its temporary home in the Queen's Theatre at the end of May. Thus, in the space of three months and via an unconventional route, Keane had risen from obscurity to secure his ambition of having his work performed on the Abbey stage. A chronological account of the Listowel Group's festival successes with *Sive* provides a sense of the very short period in which Keane became a household name in Ireland. However, it does little to capture the fervour that grew around the play as the Listowel Group progressed from regional amateur festivals to the national theatre. As local newspaper reports showed, hundreds of playgoers without tickets were turned away from the Group's appearances at the Limerick and North Cork Drama Festivals, and at least some of the furore around *Sive* can be attributed to the air of controversy that surrounded it. In a curious coincidence, one of the members of the Abbey management that had rejected *Sive*, Tomás Mac Anna, adjudicated the North Cork Drama Festival – which was the only festival in which the Listowel Group did not win the premier award. Although he placed it behind Tuam Theatre Guild's production of Robert Ardrey's *Thunder Rock*, Mac Anna's adjudication of *Sive* was quite positive overall. For example, he described Keane as being 'on

the edge of something that was new and very exciting in the theatre'
(*Kerryman*, 11 April 1959). Nevertheless, Keane took exception to what Mac
Anna had to say about the Abbey's rejection of *Sive*:

> I read this play in the Abbey ... and I was one who said that I did not
> like it all that much. The point was that when I read it, it was not this
> version. It was an earlier version and since that time the re-written
> version has come our way ... Mr. Keane has re-written it in the way we
> suggested.

> (ibid.)

A week later, the *Kerryman* reported that Keane had asked Mac Anna to
withdraw those remarks. He claimed that *Sive* had been returned to him
with 'no comment whatsoever', and that Mac Anna 'should have had the
humility to confess to a deceived public that the Abbey had not given any
consideration to the play at all' (18 April 1959). The conflict with Mac Anna
forged an enduring perception of Keane as a playwright who was
marginalized by the Abbey and metropolitan critics, in spite of his widespread
popularity with the Irish public. A common line of thinking on Keane's
career follows Anthony Roche's contention that, prior to the 1980s when
the Abbey produced *The Field* (1980), *Sive* (1985) and *Big Maggie* (1988),
the playwright was one of a number of 'theatrical outsiders' who had
been 'unjustifiably excluded' from the national theatre (1989: 29). Keane's
exclusion is often somewhat vaguely attributed to a bias against his regional
background and his association with amateur theatre. However, it is worth
returning to Mac Anna's comment that, with *Sive*, Keane was 'on the edge of
something new and very exciting in the theatre'. It is tempting to
retrospectively frame that comment in terms of the contribution that *Sive*
would eventually make to the professional stage, but it is significant that it
was said in the context of a regional, amateur performance of the play.
Through a closer consideration of the particularities of that context we can
arrive at a better understanding of what made the play so potentially 'new'
and 'exciting' for the previously sceptical Mac Anna.

When the curtains opened on *Sive* in 1959, audiences could have been
forgiven for thinking that they would not be presented with anything
particularly new or exciting. The poorly furnished cottage kitchen on stage
matched the ubiquitous setting for many of the Abbey's plays of this period.
Furthermore, in its presentation of a family home as a metonymic

representation of the nation, it was very much in the mould of popular, naturalistic Abbey plays such as Frank Carney's *The Righteous Are Bold* (1946) or Walter Macken's *Home Is the Hero* (1952). However, as the action progressed, regional audiences steeped in a tradition of melodrama would have recognized a familiar pattern to the unfolding events, a pattern that deviated significantly from the tenets of naturalism. In his seminal work *The Melodramatic Imagination* (originally published in 1976), Peter Brooks outlines the structure of what he terms 'classical' melodrama: 'the play typically opens with a presentation of virtue and innocence, or perhaps more accurately, virtue *as* innocence ... And there swiftly supervenes a threat to virtue, a situation – and most often a person – to cast its very survival into question, obscure its identity, and elicit the process of its fight for recognition' (1995: 29).

In the opening scene of *Sive* the audience is presented with the eponymous heroine, a character whose indelible and uncomplicated virtue corresponds to the type of broad characterization that we would associate with melodrama. In keeping with the structure outlined by Brooks, a threat to that virtue soon arrives in the form of the local matchmaker, Thomasheen Sean Rua. Thomasheen proposes marriage to Sive on behalf of Seán Dota, a melodramatically repulsive character whose considerable wealth is matched by his age. The Faustian pact proposed by Thomasheen not only threatens Sive, but also poses a threat to the virtue of her guardians, Mike and Mena, for whom it offers a rare chance to escape the stranglehold of poverty. Brooks points out that the success of the villain in melodrama 'depends largely on the errors of perception and judgement committed by those who should rightfully be the protectors of virtue, especially the older generation of uncles, guardians, and sovereigns' (1995: 33). Accordingly, Mike and Mena succumb to temptation, and their niece Sive must rely on a group of individuals that correspond to the conventional allies of the melodramatic heroine: 'a handmaiden, a fiancé, a faithful (often comic) peasant, or very often ... a child' (ibid.). Liam Scuab proposes marriage to Sive, her grandmother fulfils the role of handmaiden, and a pair of travelling tinkers adopt the role of faithful and musical peasants. In true melodramatic form, Sive's escape hinges on the safe delivery of a letter, and much of the dramatic tension of the final act is based on that letter's proximity to enemies of the heroine. Ultimately, and somewhat unexpectedly, the letter is intercepted by Thomasheen and burned before the audience's eyes. Another unexpected turn is encountered at the play's climax, which denies its audience the happy conclusion so common to melodrama. As Brooks points out, in melodrama

there was usually 'a reforming of the old society of innocence, which ...
[had] now driven out the threat to its existence and reaffirmed its values'
(32). Yes, in *Sive* the heroine's innocence is saved, but at the cost of her life,
and it is not quite clear whether her death symbolizes the preservation or the
destruction of the community's values in the face of an oncoming,
materialistic modernity. The resolution is more in line with the conventions
of tragedy or realism, and it is likely that this added to the play's impact
on audiences. The appearance of Liam Scuab with Sive's drowned body at
the conclusion would have shocked audience members who were keenly
anticipating the happy ending promised by the preceding melodramatic
conventions.

The blending of realism and melodrama in *Sive* is not uncommon:
Thomas Postlewait observes that 'most of the time we can find melodramatic
elements in realistic drama and realistic elements in melodramatic plays'
(1996: 55). However, there is evidence to suggest that regional audiences
of the Listowel Group's production of *Sive* had an acute awareness and
appreciation of its melodramatic conventions. For example, the tinkers
introduce music into the play which, as the 'melo' (derived from 'melody') in
the term suggests, was a key part of the multifaceted entertainment that
classical melodrama offered its audiences. Keane's biographers, Gus Smith
and Des Hickey, describe audiences being 'hypnotised' by the tinkers in
Listowel (1992: 18), and the 'electric' atmosphere instigated by their arrival
on stage at the Clare Drama Festival (55). Similarly, a review of the Listowel
Group's performance in Limerick cited the 'entry of the tinker men' as one of
the 'great moments' of the play (*Limerick Leader*, 18 March 1959). Evidently,
regional audiences had an acute appreciation for the melodramatic
conventions of the play, and that appreciation often extended beyond the
'hypnotism' described by Smith and Hickey and into more overt displays of
emotion. Brendan Carroll, the director of the Listowel production, recalled
people 'weeping' in the audience at the opening night of the play (qtd by
Smith and Hickey, 1992: 19). Smith and Hickey report that during the
performance of the play at the Kerry Drama Festival, 'people laughed in the
wrong places', while others 'applauded during tense moments, as though
unable to control their emotions' (59). Furthermore, to the chagrin of many
within the amateur movement, the normally decorous reception afforded to
adjudicators was repeatedly ruptured at the regional festivals in which the
Listowel Group competed. H.L. Morrow, the adjudicator at the Limerick
festival, could hardly be heard 'amid the euphoria in the auditorium' (Smith
and Hickey, 1992: 57), while there was heckling during Jim Fitzgerald's

adjudicatory speech at the Kerry Drama Festival. Although expressed in support of the Listowel Group, those overt demonstrations were not always welcomed by the cast. For example, Nora Relihan, who played Mena, recalled that the opening night performance at the Queen's Theatre had almost been overwhelmed by the audience reaction: 'Many people applauded in the wrong places, others went wild over the tinkers. They weren't a help at all. And I think I gave a poor performance that night' (qtd by Smith and Hickey, 1992: 69). With people weeping, laughing and applauding in the 'wrong places', *Sive* not only presented a blend of melodramatic and realistic conventions on stage, but also elicited a less harmonious mix of reactions from audiences. Critics of the laughing, stamping audience members were quick to attribute their behaviour to a lack of understanding of what constituted proper conduct in the auditorium. However, those demonstrative displays had antecedents that extended deep into the roots of regional, amateur theatre.

Prior to the flowering of the amateur movement in the twentieth century, the first experience of theatre for many people in regional towns and villages in Ireland was provided by strolling players, or 'fit-up' companies: touring groups that erected or 'fitted up' their own performance spaces. Helen Burke writes that by the end of the eighteenth century 'there was scarcely a town of any size in Ireland that was not provided with theatrical entertainment of this kind' (2005: 120). Fit-ups specialized in a range of entertainments, from variety shows to circus routines, but those that performed drama concentrated almost exclusively on melodrama and farce. The fit-up companies had to service an eclectic range of tastes, even within small communities, and the musical and emotional thrills of melodrama and farce were well suited to that aim. Furthermore, there is evidence to suggest that a key part of the appeal of those performances was the way that the emotion on stage spilled out into the audience. Beginning with examples from the eighteenth century, Ciara O'Farrell shows that 'disruption of fit-up performances through over zealous [*sic*] audiences was still prominent in provincial Ireland right up to the 1950s' (2004: 54). O'Farrell outlines examples of audience members fainting, crying, jumping and even in some cases mounting the stage to join the action (55–6). In O'Farrell's analysis, those audience members 'were totally unexposed to drama, except for these rare fit-up visits, and thus were more likely to take what they saw at face value' (57).

I would argue, however, that there was a performative element to those outbursts that we might view as a precursor to the appearance of regional audience members on stage as part of amateur societies. Furthermore, we should consider Brooks' contention that the dramatic action of melodrama is primarily driven by a Manichaeistic struggle between good and evil (1995: 12). With that in mind, it is plausible that in the small, regional communities described by O'Farrell it was beneficial, and even enjoyable, to perform your allegiance to the side of 'good' while under the watchful eyes of your neighbours.

It would appear that the Listowel Group's tour of *Sive* on the regional festival circuit precipitated occasions that were – to return to Mac Anna's adjudicatory comments – 'exciting' but not quite 'new'. On the contrary, audiences responded according to conventions that had a lineage that significantly predated the relatively recent arrival of dramatic realism and its attendant codes of conduct. That being said, the type of raucous reaction that *Sive* elicited was becoming increasingly rare at amateur festivals by 1959. The exponential growth of amateur groups in Ireland in the early part of the twentieth century contributed significantly to the demise of the fit-up companies. A concurrent development was that amateur groups competing at festivals discarded the predominantly melodramatic repertoire of the fit-ups. The impetus for this move came from critics, commentators and adjudicators who subscribed to what Postlewait identifies and critiques as a 'familiar binarism' that was applied to realism and melodrama in the early decades of the twentieth century: 'On the twentieth-century side of the great divide we find complex and ambitious drama, dedicated artists, and challenging plays about the human condition. On the nineteenth-century side we have derivative entertainment, theatrical artisans, and the constraining values of popular taste' (1996: 42).

In 1940 the author Michael Farrell conducted a survey of regional amateur theatre for the literary magazine *The Bell*. In a despairing tone Farrell noted the continued popularity of melodramas in regional towns and villages, but struck a more positive note in reference to amateur groups producing Abbey plays. For Farrell, the Abbey Theatre – firmly on the twentieth-century side of Postlewait's binarism – had introduced a repertoire which 'set a standard for the country' (1942: 391). Amateur groups competing at festivals adapted their output to the preferences of professional adjudicators and critics such as Farrell, many of whom were associated with the Abbey in some capacity.

However, in spite of the efforts of those reformers, the popularity of melodrama, farce and variety endured in provincial towns and villages and, in response, amateur groups competing at festivals would often produce a melodrama or farce for their home audience. They would then use the proceeds to fund what became known as the 'festival play': a less popular but more 'serious' work of dramatic realism that was usually drawn from the Abbey repertoire. Writing in *The Irish Times* in anticipation of what would be the seventh All-Ireland festival in 1959, Aileen Coughlan lamented the growing ubiquity of the 'festival play' in the competition (11 April 1959). The source of her concern was that, in their quest for prizes, amateur groups were opting for tested and tired 'classics' from the Abbey and other metropolitan theatre houses. She urged amateur societies to risk 'the cold blast of criticism' from adjudicators and audiences rather than continue to be 'comfortably smothered'. Coughlan welcomed *Sive* on the basis that it was a new play, but it is unlikely that she could have anticipated the type of innovation that the play represented. Its naturalistic theme and setting gestured towards the established conventions of the festival play and the attendant code of behaviour that those conventions demanded. However, the play's melodramatic conventions triggered unexpected ruptures that violated that code. Those ruptures, and the occasions that they created, pointed towards the potential for a hybridized theatre experience: an event that combined the participatory, popular appeal of the melodrama with the social engagement and character development of realism or naturalism.

The fulfilment of the hybrid potential of *Sive* in the professional sphere would depend on a positive endorsement of the play's melodramatic conventions by metropolitan critics. However, where those conventions were identified in reviews, they were often used as evidence of the play's failings. For example, when the Listowel Group performed *Sive* at the Queen's Theatre, the *Irish Times* reviewer claimed that the play presented 'melodramatic situations that would have been credible on the stage ... in 1909, but stick slightly in the craw fifty years later' (26 May 1959). Similarly, a review in the *Irish Press* claimed that *Sive* was the type of play that 'tends to undo much of the good work of the past decade in Irish playwriting in banishing the stage Irishman into well-merited oblivion' (26 May 1959). This pattern was not necessarily restricted to the Listowel Group's production of *Sive* in 1959. Scathing reviews in *The Times* of London and in *The Guardian* of a professional production in Hammersmith the following year both cited melodrama in their analyses of weaknesses in the play. Perhaps in reaction to the metropolitan critical response to *Sive*, there was a discernible change in Keane's work in the period between his emergence with *Sive* and what we might term his redemption at the Abbey in the 1980s. The seeds of that change can be found in Keane's collaboration with the director Barry Cassin for *The Highest House on the Mountain* in 1961. *The Highest House* appeared in the Gas Company Theatre and became the longest-running play at the 1960 Dublin Theatre Festival. In many ways Cassin and Keane were a peculiar pairing. Keane was famed as a popular playwright, while in 1951 Cassin had founded the 37 Theatre Club, a basement theatre committed to producing avant-garde plays that would not have been considered for the commercial theatre. Prior to the start of rehearsals, Cassin spent weeks editing the manuscript of *The Highest House* and, at the request of the director, Keane made further revisions once rehearsals began. In his introduction to the published text of the play, Cassin questioned whether the production of *Sive* by amateurs had been truly beneficial for Keane's craft as a playwright. He suggested that 'even an effective writer like Keane needs direction that amateurs are unlikely to provide', and commended the playwright for having 'the good sense and humility to realise that by observing the work of professionals he could improve his own' (Keane, 1961: ix). It would appear that through the process of producing *The Highest House,* Cassin made Keane aware of the fissures between the art of the amateur and the quite different craft of the professional. The result was a play that Seamus Kelly in *The Irish Times* described as Keane's 'best play yet'. Kelly surmised, 'where *Sive* and *Sharon's Grave* were merely repetitive and melodramatic, this latest work undoubtedly is a piece of contemporary theatre' (14 September 1960).

Keane resumed his collaboration with Cassin for both *The Field* (1965) and *Big Maggie* (1969), two of his most critically acclaimed plays. Both are similar to *Sive* in how they explore the effect of modernity on the values and codes of rural communities. However, they are much closer to conventional works of dramatic realism in their characterization. For example, the complex and nuanced portrayal of 'The Bull' McCabe in *The Field* contrasts with that of Mena in *Sive* who, in spite of the sympathy we might hold for her, is ultimately a conduit for the melodramatic battle between good and evil at the heart of the action. I would suggest that with Cassin, Keane had a director and a collaborator who was adept at parsing the naturalistic elements of *Sive* into separate, highly successful works.

However, the popular, melodramatic side of Keane's writing was by no means abandoned. In the same month that *The Field* opened at the Olympia in 1965, Keane's first musical, *The Roses of Tralee*, premiered in the Cork Opera House. By his own admission, Keane had written the musical 'as a kind of light relief' after what he described as the 'heavy demands' of writing *The Field* (qtd by Smith and Hickey, 1992: 147). We might view the almost concurrent showings of those plays as a separation of what was once a unified approach in Keane's writing. With that in mind we could trace an imaginative line between Dublin and Cork in 1965 – between the bitter naturalism of *The Field* and the light-hearted musicality of *The Roses* – and find a meeting point in Athlone in 1959, in the hybridity of *Sive* and the unique kind of occasion that its performance precipitated. We might also view that imaginative meeting point in Athlone as an end point of sorts for amateur theatre in Ireland. The potential for a hybridized form that came to the fore through *Sive*'s performance on the regional amateur circuit was never fully realized. If anything, the play represented the last vestiges of melodrama at amateur drama festivals.

Aileen Coughlan penned a retrospective article for the programme of the twenty-first All-Ireland in 1973. In her analysis, one of the most notable changes that had occurred in two decades of the festival was evident in the audience: 'From being an independent creature capable of snarling its disapproval or yawning its boredom in your face, it has become a gentle gathering of individuals, appreciative and appreciated' (Coughlan and O'Brien, 2002: 47). Coughlan welcomes this development, but not without regret: 'This, when one remembers the old flaming cigarette lighters, the seat-banging, the rustling sweet-papers, is a change very much for the better; yet there are times when, perversely, one would welcome the sound of the old snarl' (47). In the same way that Keane's success as a professional was predicated on a separation of the hybridity evident in *Sive* into its constituent elements, amateur theatre festivals had disavowed the deep tradition of melodrama from which they had emerged. At those festivals in Ireland today, we have smoke-free, silent occasions that are perfectly appropriate for the realistic, esoteric works of drama that are so often presented. As Coughlan suggested in 1973, we are grateful to escape the noise and clamour of modern life: to sit quietly and to listen carefully. But occasionally, in that silence, we might faintly crave the stomping of feet and the banging of seats, and wonder what happened to the art of the amateur.

# AN INCOMPLETE HISTORY OF PERFORMANCE ART IN IRELAND (AND ITS BLOOD RELATIONSHIP TO THEATRE)

*Áine Phillips*

Contemporary performance in Ireland is diverse, porous and often operates across disciplines. In this essay I will explore and discuss why and how interdisciplinarity has developed in performance worlds in Ireland, with a focus on the relationship between theatre and performance art. Performance art is the fulcrum around which my discussion will turn, not because I am placing it in a hierarchy of practice but because of my academic and artistic focus stemming from visual art. To begin I will give a brief background and theory of performance art and go on to discuss its relationship to theatre in Ireland.

Performance art can trace its international lineage back to the Dadaists of the early twentieth century; it was later designated as happenings, action art, body art and currently, in the late 2010s, Live Art. It was influenced in one way by fine artists rejecting the creation of objects for art markets and who therefore turned to their body as the site and material of their practice. Performance art was also impacted by artists who attempted to break the traditions of the circumstance and expectations of theatre. In Ireland artists began making performance art in the 1970s that related to these movements and was also inspired by theatre, storytelling, dance and music. Comparably, Irish theatre with its roots in literature and drama has developed contemporary forms that now reflect visual languages of performance as much as dance, sound art/music and social events or civic activism.

As contemporary theatre in Ireland moved away from a reliance on text and narrative content, there was a movement towards innovation. A creative appropriation of alternative forms and methods typical of performance art was seen to occur. For example, this includes performance in off-site or site-specific contexts, participatory engagements with audiences, durational or looped actions as performance, event-based productions, one-on-one intimate acts, the use of lens-based media and technology, along with the employment of striking visual imagery (in sets, props or costume) to carry an idea or the overarching meaning of the work. Later in this essay I will give examples of early Irish performance art or current Live Art that illustrates how these methods were originally created and presented.

Another factor that has caused this cross-pollination between art forms is that collaboration across artistic areas of practice is particularly strong on the small island of Ireland. There is much diffusion and infiltration of ideas and methods of working due to proximity. Disciplines brush against each other willingly and with pleasure. Performance art in Ireland has been impactful and influential across disciplines due to its formal and conceptual experimentations but also because of its apt representations and expressions of the particular Irish sociopolitical situation and its rehearsal of national identities. I will show in this text how performance, by 'asserting itself in the present', as Peter Brook writes (1968: 111), and inventing new forms of expression, has allowed Irish artists to address and comprehend our times and lives.

In the following sections I will sketch the broad outlines of performance art in the north of Ireland as it developed in correspondence with the Troubles, reflecting and processing the reality of a people living with war. Feminist performance confronted gender inequalities and proposed new identities and empowering ways of being in the world for women and dispossessed minorities. Current Live Art operates across varied contexts and spaces using new languages of representation to engage and intervene in the public sphere. I will mention some notable examples of artists and the works they created to illustrate my examples. In choosing some works I am leaving out others that deserve recognition and tribute, but to include all is beyond the scope of this text. This is an incomplete and miniature history.

## The Troubles: performance art in the north

Performance art in Ireland engaged with political history and popular culture, and it reflected many of the social movements of civil rights and feminism in particular. The development of performance art in Ireland began in the early 1970s with the visit of the German artist Joseph Beuys to Dublin and Belfast to present work and give his famous performative lectures. The encounter with this legendary figure catalysed a number of visual artists into making live actions and performances, especially on the streets and public spaces of Belfast. A war-torn city at the time, Belfast was enduring the Troubles, the civil and military conflict that racked the north until 1998. Artists such as Alastair MacLennan, Tara Babel and André Stitt created performances that addressed the violent conflict and social division of their homeland. In works that functioned as cathartic exercises to help externalize and make visible hidden oppressions and to express unspoken trauma and loss, these artists used performance to involve general public audiences in the healing potential of art.

Conventional visual art and theatre used institutional spaces to represent and narrate stories of the Troubles, but at this time performance artists used public space and inserted their art work into the flow of everyday life. They aimed to depict and personify collective lived experience using the formal and aesthetic 'framing' of a live performative action or set of behaviours. They used ritual and catharsis as a means whereby public artistic testimony, intervention and memorializing were converted into acts of transformation in that conflicted environment.

The work of Alastair MacLennan, who taught at the University of Ulster during the 1970s and 1980s, exemplifies this approach. In *Target* (1977), he walked daily through the streets of Belfast for the duration of one month, on his way to and from work. He wore a graphic target in the form of a large dartboard hanging over his chest, carrying a black zipped holdall with his head covered in a plastic sheath absurdly weighed down at the ends by lengths of bamboo. His bizarre costume rendered him depersonalized as he navigated the barricades and sectarian walls of the city. He was a metaphorical target but also a real target for the armed soldiers and paramilitaries who controlled the militarized zones he moved through.

This simple action was made remarkable by the fact that he could have been viewed as a security breach (transporting a bomb in his bag, perhaps?), and at its extreme consequence he could have actually been shot. Well aware of this potential, he carried a note in his pocket that explained the artistic intention behind this action, also providing his name and address. The work engaged everyone who encountered it, in an intervention disrupting the military control, anxiety and menace of the public space by explicitly subverting it. It was a dangerous but potent and effective action that created a type of tension and energy that the artist was able to manipulate. In doing so he was able to reverse the status and intimidation of the situation. MacLennan has continued to create innovative and deeply moving performances dealing with the troubled reality of the north. Over decades he has often used the names of dead and disappeared citizens, in their thousands, as part of the materials of his actions. He attempts to help us to remember those who have been lost and shows that the context of war is unsupportable. Similarly, to reflect the perpetuation and long endurance of a people at war, his performance methods have incorporated long duration, in works that have lasted up to 144 hours.

Nigel Rolfe, based in Dublin in the 1980s and 1990s, was creating performances that also addressed the northern conflict. In *The Rope that*

*Binds Us Makes Them Free* (1983), Rolfe wrapped his head in creosote-covered twine, representing the smothering, isolation, loss and failure of the Troubles. His work often used materials such as dust and detritus, and pigment as stain, which he would manipulate in his live actions. Rolfe travelled the country during the 1980s presenting his performances in schools and community halls as well as galleries and theatre spaces.

More recently, Sandra Johnson has generated innovative performance work dealing with the trauma of place. She explores how aspects of collective memory connected to specific locations can become altered after violent events, creating layers of stigmatization or, conversely, commemoration. In her seminal doctoral project of 2012, *Beyond Reasonable Doubt*, she investigated doubt, risk and testimony through performance art processes in relation to systems of legal justice. Based in Belfast, the collaborative group Bbeyond continue the early street-based performance methods integral to this art form in the north by coming together at designated public sites once a month to perform simultaneously. Their work addresses the use of public space as a common platform for social and political freedoms of expression and representation.

## Women performing feminism with intent

Performance art addressing social justice and politics continued its labour in the south as feminist artists in the 1980s and 1990s produced new forms of female identity and power with the intention of encouraging a more gender-equitable Irish society. Pauline Cummins, Alanna O'Kelly and Mary Duffy created radical performance that was also a type of embodied politics to make powerful statements and activist art about gender inequalities. O'Kelly presented *Chant Down Greenham* (1985–6), a vocalization sound piece incorporating chanting, calling and keening (a traditional Irish wordless song of lament), blending repetitive chants and sounds of protest with wordless vocal expression. E.L. Putnam writes of this work that 'guttural screams drive into the core of the listener, an echo of suffering and physical exhaustion that reverberates in the soul' (see Phillips, 2015: 154). O'Kelly shifted to creating multimedia works during the 1990s and sound remained a prominent influence in her process.

Mary Duffy worked with her disabled female body as the central live image in her performances dealing with identity, agency and objectification. In *Stories of a Body* (1990), Duffy appears naked, confronting conventional ideals of beauty. A survivor of thalidomide, as a child Duffy was made to wear large, uncomfortable prosthetic arms in an effort to render her body normative. Images of stones were projected onto her body as she verbally recalled memories of hurt and humiliation under the medicalized gaze that divested her subjectivity as a child. Audience expectations of ability and disability were unsettled as Duffy claimed her right to speak. Duffy's work addressed issues of disability rights, and also allowed for disability to be read as a metaphor for the cultural expectations placed on women's bodies in the Ireland of that era. She simultaneously allowed the viewer to comprehend an alternative to these impossible expectations in the form of a fully embodied acceptance of what is now called a queer body – one that transcends the status quo and offers alternative ways of being in the world. Mo White, reviewing Duffy's work in 1995, expresses this in another way:

What Mary Duffy does here, in what becomes a powerful strategy, is an act of circumvention by being at the same time the object of, and the active subject in constructing our gaze. Where her story tells of the gaze that is directed at her, the audience is forced to examine their own gaze, which reproduces exactly the same conditions of looking as she tells of. The space which can exist between the represented and the representational has been collapsed. My gaze, as a member of the audience, is returned and I am implicated in this process of looking. It has revealed something of myself in me. This is why the performance works. It does its own job, right before your eyes.

Contemporary feminist performance in Ireland continues its evolution working with the legacies of these groundbreaking artists. *Labour*, a touring Live Art event featuring eleven Irish women artists in 2012, addressed many of the key issues of the 1980s that continue to be of relevance, such as reproductive rights, domestic labour, gender inequality, sexual violence and women's traumatic invisible history. While being concept driven the performance events were formally structured in communal large, open, white cube spaces with artists performing simultaneously over eight hours to reflect the average working day. *Labour* was interactive in that audiences wandered among the performers, occupying the same territory and proximity. The concurrent performances created active images that cross-referenced and juxtaposed against each other, generating rich and unexpected feelings and meanings.

The performances included Amanda Coogan moving with slow deliberation through the space in a sculptural costume made from layered children's coats while dribbling blue liquid from her mouth. Chrissie Cadman bathed in a bath of ice water. I crawled through the space gradually 'bleeding' black ink through my white garments, carrying a hidden speaker playing testimonial recordings of women who had been incarcerated in Irish Magdalene laundries. Helena Walsh – goddess-like – enacted gestures of filling condoms with laundry washing powder, attempting their insertion into her vagina, subsequently piercing them with knitting needles to create a mound of fragrant powder on a bed of soil. Meanwhile in off-site actions, Pauline Cummins and Frances Mezzetti in a collaborative work, *Walking in the Way*, dressed as mature men and strolled through the city streets, occupying the masculine spaces such as bars and barber shops adjacent to the performance venues in Dublin, London and Derry. Their intention was to inhabit positions that are precluded to them as aging women and to explore their own relationships to maleness. In doing so they created a disturbing and beautiful work, both tender in its love of men and scathing in its exposure of how the ownership of public space is gendered.

## Live Art and socially engaged performance

Live Art, as a recent naming of what artists do with performance, offers an expanded environment for experimentation across art forms, contexts and spaces to open up new artistic models. The potential performance holds to function in the present moment, to generate relationships between people and ideas and to rehearse alternative identities, has been embraced by emerging artists and companies in Ireland. Building on what was previously achieved using performance strategies, new ways of intervening in the public sphere have been explored. The body of the artist as central to performance art has been expanded into a more inclusive approach, with the use of other performing bodies and the bodies of spectators. One theory of performance art I propose is that the performer uses the real to represent the Real (the Lacanian Real which is understood to be that opposed to the imaginary, located outside the symbolic). This theory is brought to an optimal manifestation in much recent Live Art where performers are protagonists that perform or present as themselves, where action takes place in the flow of everyday life or located at sites of actual events.

Two important platforms for Live Art in Ireland have been Live Collision since 2009 and Dublin Live Art Festival (DLAF), founded in 2012. Both festivals have brought innovative international practitioners to Dublin as well as presenting the work of Irish artists. This cross-fertilization has been vital in the development of the sector alongside promoting the creative colliding of artists and ideas across disciplines of theatre, dance and other diverse forms of performance art. The use of heritage sites for performance was explored by Niamh Murphy of DLAF in 2011 with *Right Here Right Now* in historical Kilmainham Gaol, and in 2016 with *Future Histories* to commemorate and question the 1916 Rising, Ireland's revolution against British colonial rule. Appropriating such spaces of institutional authority offers the chance to readdress official chronicles and present alternative understandings of our present times. This tactic has been used most powerfully to redress and reveal the hidden and suppressed histories of women in Ireland by theatre-maker Louise Lowe and ANU Productions with the work *Laundry* (2011), which was presented as a live performative installation in an inner-city Dublin Magdalene Laundry a site haunted by the mass incarceration of women up to 1996.

Live Art and performance is at the forefront of socially engaged practices dealing with social justice, often with the participation of communities. *Proximity Mouth 2015* by Dominic Thorpe was located in another institutional building, the former children's court at Dublin Castle. The performance was conducted by guides with personal experience of the current Direct Provision asylum system in Ireland. Audience members were brought into the room one at a time holding the hand of their tour guide, who told them the history of the court room interspersed with testimonies from their own experience of seeking asylum to be legally recognized as a refugee. Performative and interactive actions between a young girl and the audience/participant poetically charged the scene to create a situation of heightened reality and insight into the conditions of those in Direct Provision. Thorpe, in collaboration with this community, planned the performance meticulously, with sensitivity to his responsibilities as the author of work dealing with other people's lives. He has discussed this controversial approach in his 2015 text 'Working with Stories of Other People's Traumatic Experiences' and suggests 'art offers possibilities to open up necessary, wide-ranging and honest forms of interaction and discourse' (n.d. [2015]: para 1). This type of work asserts the possibility that art can have a healing function and help ameliorate social ills. Performance is particularly useful for this purpose; as discussed earlier, it reproduces unmediated relationships between people, it exists in the time and space we all occupy and it provokes emotional, intellectual and physical connections.

Constructive and affecting work has also been made with these methodologies by Fiona Whelan. In her multipart project *Policing Dialogues*

(2010), which developed over three years, she worked with young people in Rialto Dublin and the local Garda Síochána (Irish police force) to generate mutually beneficial dialogues and exchange. She established a collaborative grouping – What's the Story? Collective – to devise the project, which also included youth workers, educators and academics, to democratically generate an active exploratory space committed to exploring and testing social power relationships.

The collective gathered anonymous personal stories of power and powerlessness by young people. Most of these stories related to policing, and a common theme emerged of being judged and unjustly treated by gardaí. A proposal was made to the chief superintendent of Dublin South Central District and following months of negotiation, a participatory reading event, *The Day in Question*, was held in the Irish Museum of Modern Art, with a large group of gardaí, the young writers of the personal but uncredited stories, and an invited group of witnesses. The event had two parts. Individual gardaí read the stories aloud. Having filmed the readings, cameras were turned off and an hour-long discussion ensued between the collective and the gardaí on the issues arising. To conclude, a group of invited 'witnesses' were invited to respond, which included community workers, sociologists, artists and young people who had actively watched and listened to the readings and dialogue.

The reading event functioned as a mediation tool enabling the two social groups to share and understand power and powerlessness as it impacted their lives and occupations. As a live performance it represented opposing experiences of power in a symbolic reversal of identity, authorship or voice and social roles. This reversal engaged the audience participants emotionally and meaningfully in an authentic response to a real-life situation. Whelan, from a visual art background, also makes performative work across disciplines, collaborating with Brokentalkers theatre company at the Project Arts Centre Dublin in 2016 with *Natural History of Hope*, a further evolution of *Policing Dialogues* based on hundreds of testimonies of women and performed by an intergenerational cast of Rialto women exploring gender, class inequality and the complexity of women's lives.

## A blood relationship to theatre

The conventional contrasts often cited with theatre are that performance art rejects narrative, employs random or chance elements and makes direct appeal to audiences, among others I have discussed above. It is clear that contemporary theatre employs all these tactics too and that performance art or Live Art similarly puts narrative to use, which is often planned, rehearsed and presented within the framing of the proscenium arch, white cube gallery or museum. An abundance of hybridity occurs between these fields currently.

In this essay, I have shown how performance art in Ireland since the 1970s has reflected and expanded many alternative forms of political expression and, as an art form, it has been at the centre of Irish cultural and artistic change. In these functions, it holds much commonality with Irish theatre. I believe the appropriation of long-established performance art methods helped transform contemporary theatre and push it into the avant-garde strategies that have been so developmental to the sector. Visual performance has bestowed visuality, aesthetics and conceptual art structures onto theatre that have allowed practitioners to find alternatives to dramatic and narrative conventions. I also regard as true that performance art in Ireland evolved from theatre, with its great cultural influence that extends into all Irish arts, its overlaps with political examination and critique, and its set of principles that have rehearsed our lives and society.

In Irish theatre the use of text and literature has been primary and this is one area of contrast. Textuality in performance art or Live Art resides in the images that are created as part of the work. As Roland Barthes has shown, almost all images, in all contexts, are accompanied by some sort of linguistic message. The difference between performance art and theatre lies mainly in the forms of language employed. A linguistic act of communication certainly takes place across both art forms.

Another diminishing difference between these fields is that performance art, historically, tempts failure. It is the potential and enchantment of failure always existent in performance that often holds artists and audiences alike with such a grip. Emotionally, intellectually, imaginatively we are mesmerized by the cliff-edge of actions that are unstructured and extemporaneous. In theatre there is some assurance that a show will 'succeed'. In performance and Live Art an expectation that the work will resolve in a predictable or even comfortable way is groundless. That is its beauty and fascination, I believe. Tempting failure is fearful but offers the possibility of transcendence, which is another potentially liberating state of being, close to transformation and empowerment.

Performance, Live Art and experimental or applied theatre, with its core pro-social function, are blood relatives. Each attempts to operate beyond discipline or subject boundaries, to break down established modes and expand into new territories of meaning and action, exchange and communication. Cultural activism is often the driving force behind making such work, with transformation and empowerment for those who encounter this work being seen as desirable. However, we must ask what political purpose this effect might bring? Performance art and theatre often converge, blending into one another, and perhaps the naming doesn't matter much. What really matters is that the work is excellent, with beauty and impact, and it provokes good change to happen in the body of the audience or the wider body politic.

# STAGE DESIGN SINCE 1950

*Siobhán O'Gorman*

Stage design in Ireland has long been overshadowed by the cultural and academic prominence of Irish theatre's literary traditions. The value of those traditions had been enshrined in the 1897 founding manifesto of the Irish Literary Theatre, leading to the opening of the Abbey in 1904; both were key events in the development of the cultural nationalism that drove Ireland towards liberation from British rule. However, recent studies suggest that scenography also contributed significantly to Ireland's postcolonial nation-building. Joan FitzPatrick Dean, for example, in her groundbreaking book *All Dressed Up: Modern Irish Historical Pageantry* (2014) examines how public spectacles – complete with live music, costumes and fireworks – presented Irish identities as large-scale performances. Stage sets were also central to the Irish Literary Theatre's efforts to conjure a distinctively Irish authenticity, for example with the placing of Douglas Hyde's *Casadh an tSúgáin* (1901) entirely within the one-room, domestic space of the rural peasant class. Following this, similar box sets portraying cottage interiors were regularly reused at the Abbey, both to depict the peasant settings prevalent in Irish drama and 'with a minimum of adaptation to make up the one room on view in O'Casey's first two tenement plays' (Grene, 1999: 132). Set builder Seaghan Barlow oversaw 'the customary rearrangement of "basic" scenic elements' at the Abbey from 1911 until 1949 (Vaněk and O'Donoghue, 2005: 19). By the mid-twentieth century the cottage kitchen set was 'embarrassingly ubiquitous' (Morash, 2002: 121). Nevertheless, such stage images were made iconic to a large extent through processes of repetition and recycling.

Yet, despite scenography's role in the construction of Ireland as lived on the stage, its documentation is relatively fragmented and the country has participated only twice (in 2007 and 2015) in the world's largest exhibition of scenography, the Prague Quadrennial, or PQ. The core of PQ, since its founding in 1967, has consisted of displays showcasing representative scenographies from a growing number of countries and regions around the world, presenting recent trends in the field within largely national exhibition formats. As John Bury wrote in the catalogue for the UK's exhibition at the PQ in 1983, 'theatre design is not just an academie [*sic*] subject but reflects the cultural and artistic heritage of a nation' (PQ archive). John Comiskey, curator of Ireland's 2007 entry, admitted that it was 'ridiculous' that Ireland had not participated before then, but he was hopeful that participation would improve future documentation of Irish stage design: 'It is hard for people to keep that model box if they have no reason to keep it. PQ will give their documentation a purpose, a reason to keep their material' (qtd in Keating, 2007). Key archival collections such as the Pike Theatre Papers at Trinity College Dublin, the Gate Papers at Northwestern, and the Abbey Digital Archive at NUI Galway all help to resource the composition of stage design histories, even though scenographic remains are scattered across a range of collections.

In spite of the fact that many Irish productions have not left 'a publicly documented legacy' (McMullan, 2016: 103), urgent questions need to be considered. In what ways has scenography reflected Ireland's cultural and artistic heritage, particularly following the establishment of the Irish Republic in 1949? Broadly, what trends might be seen to have characterized design for theatre and performance in Ireland within and beyond the latter half of the twentieth century?

Dean links postcolonial nation-building with distinct 'flurries' of Irish historical pageantry that took place in the decade after the founding of the Irish Free State, and again during the 1950s following the establishment of the Irish Republic (2009: 20–1). From the 1950s, however, these and other Irish scenographies can be seen also to engage with nation-*branding*, contextualized following the European Recovery Programme and the Organisation for European Economic Co-operation (both 1948), when the Irish state began to consider the nation in terms of international, economic competitiveness. The formation of outward-looking initiatives centred on place-marketing followed: these include An Tóstal and Dublin Theatre Festival in the area of culture, as well as the foundation of Bord Fáilte (the tourist board) in 1955 (as discussed in Chapter 2). As Ireland has become increasingly affected by the forces of global capitalism, Irish theatre design has engaged in a range of ways with increasingly commodified conceptions of place. The evocation of place is often one of scenography's key processes; as stage design historian Christin Essin argues, 'designs convey meaning guided by *but* beyond that specified by playwrights' intentions and directors' concepts, particularly in their representations of place' (2012: 55). This critical commentary examines how Irish theatre has employed scenography variously to create, celebrate, interrogate, host and ghost various national constructions of place.

Realist box sets, largely depicting peasant cottage kitchens, began to achieve their iconic status under Yeats' influence at the Abbey – partly as a result of that practitioner's intense dislike of painted backdrops, which he associated with the artificiality and excesses of British staging practices. In spite of Yeats' efforts at nation-building via the built environment of the stage, by 1950 a flourishing convention of scenic painting had taken hold. Box sets could represent effectively indoor, but not outdoor, spaces, which meant that even the early-twentieth-century Abbey at times had to resort to using suggestively painted flats – and occasionally even backdrops – to convey outdoor scenes or to offer a more stylized realism. Irish scenography, resulting from developments in the kinds of places it needed to represent, was largely characterized by a tradition of scenic painting from the 1950s to the 1980s. These practices have continued into contemporary work, incorporated into the output of such designers as Frank Conway for *The Bird Sanctuary* (Abbey, Dublin, 1994), Sonia Haccius for *The Hen Night Epiphany* (Focus, 2011) and Owen MacCarthaigh for *A Skull in Connemara* (Decadent, 2013); talented scenic painters such as Ger Sweeney continue to carry out such work, for example in *Frank Pig Says Hello* (Galway International Arts Festival, 2012). Despite continued use of scenic painting in the theatre industry, though, it often is viewed as an outdated practice; moreover, its association with 'backgrounds' perhaps has contributed to the subordination of designers' contributions to theatre events. Conway, who has designed theatre in Ireland since the mid-1970s, laments what he sees as the ongoing subordination of the work of designers (who, he suggests, should be designated more aptly as 'scenographers'). Often, he argues, the work of designers is reduced to 'doing the backgrounds' rather than theatre-making (Conway, 2012: 15). He contends that the specific role of designers continues in the discourses of Irish theatre to be 'undervalued, undermined even, a casualty of an outdated, unchallenged nineteenth-century perception that is still pervasive in the industry' (34). Yet 'doing the backgrounds' has often offered practical solutions to issues of place-making – as well as opportunities to engage with broader national and international visual-cultural trends, to achieve artistry or even to join artistic communities – in Irish theatre design throughout much of the twentieth century.

German expressionist art began to influence design practices at the Peacock and Gate theatres during the 1920s. Elaine Sisson has made an important contribution to Irish theatre design scholarship by discussing this trend, tracing its roots to the establishment of the Dublin Drama League in 1918; the Dublin Drama League sought specifically to provide a more European vision of national life beyond the cottage or the tenement (2011: 39). Increasing international influences, productions of European plays and demands for expressionist approaches to staging plays produced by such

Irish playwrights as Seán O'Casey (culminating in *The Silver Tassie*, famously rejected by the Abbey in 1928) saw painted backdrops, wing-pieces and curtains being essential to convey a range of abstract, dream-like and other variously non-realistic places and spaces. The Gate continued regularly to employ expressionist approaches, especially through the interplay of lighting effects on suggestively painted backcloths. Mac Liammóir was an accomplished draughtsman, costume designer and scenic painter; Edwards was a skilled lighting designer and a proponent of inventive techniques in stagecraft. As Dean rightly asserts, Mac Liammóir also was heavily involved in designing the century's most successful public spectacles of Irish history, for example different versions of *The Pageant of St Patrick* which were staged in Dublin as part of the national Tóstal festivals of the 1950s (2009: 33).

From the late 1940s on, small theatre clubs including Globe, Studio, 37 Club, Pike, Orion, Gemini, Pocket, Garrick, Lantern and Focus popped up around Dublin. Many sought to challenge the seemingly tired images of Irishness played out on the Abbey's stage. One of the most famous was the Pike Theatre, which, as discussed elsewhere in this book, was renowned for premiering work by Behan and Beckett – and for the *Rose Tattoo* controversy. However, it was the Pike's late-night revue series called *Follies* that kept the club financially afloat throughout its existence (O'Gorman, 2016: 134). The *Follies* provided light entertainment and at times biting humour. Fittingly, the scenic design for these variety shows made no attempt at realism, often featuring cloth backdrops painted in abstract or expressionistic designs by artists including Pauline Bewick and, later, when Bewick turned her talents to performing, Reginald Gray. Moreover, through practices such as costuming, the *Follies* satirized emerging place-marketing endeavours that were being carried out through the decoration of Dublin city for An Tóstal. The most popular sketch for *The Follies of Herbert Lane*, which premiered in December 1953, was a satire on the first Tóstal, launched the previous April. Its subject was 'The Bowl of Light', a public sculpture that Dublin Corporation had instituted in an effort to decorate O'Connell Bridge. Although the sculpture had been intended as a permanent structure, members of the public boisterously protested its ugliness not long after its unveiling, and it was destroyed by vandalism within weeks of being erected. The Pike's sketch presented Milo O'Shea as a personification of the Bowl of Light as it had been in all of its glory. Playing the 'Ghost of the Tóstal flame', and surveying Tóstals past and future, he wore a 'flaming' headdress to represent the large octagonal basin containing multicoloured, plastic flames of which 'The Bowl of Light' had consisted. As such, the Pike used costume (in conjunction with satirical text) to lampoon An Tóstal's efforts to entice visitors to Dublin, disrupting ideals of place-as-brand also by calling attention to public discontent and vandalism.

Yet, as I have contended elsewhere, the Pike later could be seen to be in mutual co-optation with the outward-looking, modernizing agendas of such government-sponsored initiatives as An Tóstal and Bord Fáilte, through which place-marketing via visual culture was harnessed to improve Ireland's performance within an increasingly international cultural economy (O'Gorman, 2014: 38). The painted backdrop for the Pike's 1955 production of Beckett's *Waiting for Godot* is a case in point. Images of the West of Ireland soon became central to Bord Fáilte's branding and, as Swift reveals, the Pike deliberately pointed to the west through its design for *Godot*:

> We used clothes, but painted in a mixture of browns and greens in blobs and sponges which, when lit, gave the effect of a continuous vista of what might be a bog, with a pathetic little willow in the foreground, its growth weakened and warped, as it would be in such a place, with nothing to shield it from the force of the west wind carrying rain clouds from the Atlantic.
>
> (Swift, 1985: 190)

Trish McTighe aptly places the Pike's production of *Waiting for Godot* 'in the context of a time when Ireland's tourism industry was at a very nascent stage, at the beginnings in Ireland of a determined and focused strategy of rural place and landscape marketing' (2013a). Indeed, by 1957 the Pike 'had become the darling of Bord Fáilte, sponsors of the [Dublin Theatre] Festival, who kept ringing to request seats for distinguished foreign journalists' (Swift, 1985: 247). McTighe elsewhere claims that the Gate's 1991 Beckett Festival ignited a process of reclaiming Beckett for Ireland, linked to 'the relationship of his work to place' (2013b: 169). The beginnings of that process could be traced back to the Pike's set for *Godot*. Essin's views on scenography and place are apt: 'By bringing their own impressions of landscape to a production, designers imbue dramatic texts with meaning not necessarily present before being translated to the stage' (2012: 55). Through its evocation of the west, the Pike imbued *Godot* with Irishness at a time when the concept of Irishness as associated with the landscape was becoming commodified.

At the Abbey, there were genealogies of scenic paintings depicting dewy, romantic impressions of the west, and it is likely that such regularly recycled stage images influenced the Pike's *Godot* and perhaps even Bord Fáilte's marketing. For example, settings for Synge's *The Well of the Saints* (1905), originally designed by Edy Craig and Pamela Coleman Smith, were replaced in 1908 by a design that Charles Ricketts created, which required Seaghan Barlow to 'smudge over the work with a sponge to give the impression of a misty, rain-washed landscape' (Cave, 2004: 104). When the original Abbey was destroyed by fire in 1951, however, many of the sets that had been reused over the years, in addition to costumes and props, were destroyed. The Abbey opened at the Queen's Theatre with a production of *The Silver Tassie*, which would have required scenic painting to convey expressionist outdoor scenes, such as the battlefront during World War One. Yet, the Abbey was without a resident designer for much of its tenure there, finally hiring Brian Collins for the role in 1964. Collins, as the Abbey's resident designer, maintained 'standards of excellence in scene painting and design up until 1983' (Vaněk and O'Donoghue, 2005: 19). This allowed the tradition of scenic painting to live on.

Scenographer Christopher Baugh, who contributed to the design of several Abbey productions from the late 1960s to the late 1970s, vividly recalls how a range of designers and technicians working within and beyond the Abbey were engaged in maintaining a tradition of scenic painting; importantly, he remembers that painted backcloths depicting pseudo-impressionistic architecture or Connemara landscapes still seemed to prevail during the period in which he worked at Ireland's national theatre (Baugh, 2015). I interviewed Baugh – along with designers Sabine Dargent and Joe Vaněk, and director Joe Devlin – as part of a documentary film that accompanied Ireland's entry to the PQ in 2015, which was curated by the Dublin-based arts organization MART with the support of Culture Ireland. Baugh's contribution is particularly useful for understanding how the Abbey habitually operated, particularly in terms of design, in its early years at (what was then) its new theatre building. My subsequent discussions of Baugh's work at the Abbey draw on that interview. Alan Barlow and Hugh Hunt, both of whom had strong connections with the Abbey, were Baugh's tutors when he studied at the University of Manchester. Baugh's own opportunity at the Abbey came when he took over from Barlow for a 1967 production of Frank O'Connor and Hugh Hunt's *The Invincibles* (1937). Baugh worked only from Barlow's rough model; his practice involved composing ground plans and scale drawings, as well plenty of physical making and scene painting up on the paint-frame with 'the legendary Brian Collins' (Baugh, 2015). A year later, Baugh assisted Barlow on Boucicault's *The Shaughraun*, a production adorned with 'spectacular painted cloths and detailed "local colour"' (Vaněk and O'Donoghue, 2005: 43).

Scene painting remained central to the Abbey's evocations of place till the mid-1980s, but more inventive ways of placing scenes were also emerging. Baugh's other projects in 1967 included assisting on productions of O'Casey's *Red Roses for Me* and Frank McMahon's *Borstal Boy*; both were directed and designed by Tomás Mac Anna. Part of Baugh's work on *Red Roses for Me* consisted of painting a backcloth comprising 'the classic, mythic scene of Dublin' that he identifies as stylistically resembling many other backcloths in use at the time (Baugh, 2015). He describes that painted scene as follows: 'It was a view down the Liffey, the Four Courts [. . . and] these sort of tenements, slums, impressionistic architecture and the river running away down the centre' (Baugh, 2015). *Borstal Boy* gave opportunities for more scenographic innovation, with actors moving scenery in full view of the audience; this was an aesthetic decision that Baugh remembers as being met with resistance from the actors. The production team also made use of scenic units containing painted flats and furniture on trucks that wheeled in three-dimensional scenes, such as a bedroom or a prison, as appropriate. For the first time at the new Abbey building that had been opened in 1966, the production team removed all the wings and masking to reveal the actual back wall of the theatre, which itself became the backdrop. With Collins, Baugh worked to make the back wall of the then-new Abbey appear old and decaying through the use of dirty paint slapped across the wall itself, in addition to the exposed radiators and pipes. In front of this novel background there hung a huge monochrome portrait of Behan that Baugh had painted.

Baugh assisted on a number of other productions, and is officially credited with designing the Abbey's professional premiere of George Fitzmaurice's *The Enchanted Land* in 1976, which, due to a setting based on Irish mythology and located largely underwater, drew on Ireland's now long-established tradition of scenic painting. Traditional scenic painting continued in conjunction with alternative approaches offered by new designers who began working professionally in Ireland between the late 1960s and the late 1970s. These included Conway, along with Bronwen Casson, Wendy Shea and Monica Frawley.

Many of these professionals promoted practices that increased the authority of designers and their generative contribution to theatre-making processes – developments that may be seen as central to the modernization of design in Irish theatre. Frawley trained at the Central School of Art and Design, London, where she was taught by Pamela Howard, author of the seminal *What Is Scenography?* (2009). In 1983, Frawley worked with designer and mask-maker Gabby Dowling to produce an almost wordless promenade piece called *Forbidden Fruit* which took place at Temple Bar Studios. Supported by an Arts Council 'Special Theatre Project' grant, the production mainly was devised through scenographic practice. Frawley remains a key figure in Irish scenography.

Conway and Casson both trained under the innovative design team, Motley, at Sadler's Wells in London. There, designers were positioned as key collaborators in the theatre-making process. By 1983, Casson had made her name having designed a range of productions, including over sixty for Ireland's national theatre. That year she joined a team of practitioners, including writer Tom MacIntyre, director Patrick Mason and actor Tom Hickey, to work on the very physical, imagistic and linguistically sparse *The Great Hunger*, a reimagining of Patrick Kavanagh's eponymous poem on the Peacock stage. *The Great Hunger* was penned by MacIntyre on the basis of collaborative rehearsal room practices combining adaptation, improvisation, devising and design. As such, it made design a partner in the theatre-making process, foregrounding the visual, aural and material aspects of theatre. Regrettably, Casson's collaboration in the process often goes unacknowledged. Morash and Swift were perceptive in revealing the lack of recognition for the immense contribution of designers in Irish theatre, using Casson's work on MacIntyre's plays as an example. Although these works, as these writers point out, drew on collaborative practice and pointed up the visual aspects of theatre, they were presented as the creation of a dramatist, a director and an actor (Hickey) 'but not, significantly, a scenographer' (Morash and Swift, 1994: 489).

Casson worked on a series of productions encompassing the same key practitioners and embracing similar collaborative approaches to theatre-making, including *The Bearded Lady* (1984), *Rise Up Lovely Sweeney* (1985) and *Dance for Your Daddy* (1987). Conway worked on Druid's momentous productions of Tom Murphy's *Bailegangaire* and *Conversations on a Homecoming* in 1985. When Druid's founding director, Garry Hynes, took on artistic directorship of the Abbey in 1991, Conway worked that year with her on an inventively stark production of *The Plough and the Stars* and, in 1993, he collaborated with Hynes and actor Fiona Shaw on *The Hamlet Project*, a devised initiative characterized by a lack of hierarchy: 'just the democracy of intense hard work, imagination and play' (Conway, 2012: 20). These experiences, which authorized (rather than subordinated) the designer's contribution, may have aided Conway's confidence to offer such an iconoclastic design for Garry Duggan's *Shibari* in 2012, in which an upended traditional Irish kitchen hung over the stage throughout the duration of the actors' performances. As Ian Walsh points out regarding this production, Conway 'literally turned the old design of the Abbey on its head' (2016: 452).

Frawley also has contributed to a range of subversive approaches to iconic images of Ireland, some of which have themselves become iconic – such as her design for the Abbey's world premiere of Marina Carr's *By the Bog of Cats* (1998). Almost ten years earlier, she designed Michael Harding's *Una Pooka* (Peacock, 1989). The play is a farcical take on the Pope's 1979 visit to Ireland; it probes restrictions on Irish sexuality maintained through the enduring authority of the Church at the time of the production. Visually encapsulating themes of limitation and myopia, Frawley's set offered a distorted, tunnel perspective that squeezed the acting space and appeared to restrict the performers' movements. With Dave Nolan's sound setting the scene by juxtaposing a recording of the declaration of a new pope with frantic church bells at the beginning, and Tony Wakefield's lighting casting obtrusive shadows throughout, the design team worked together to make palpable appropriately claustrophobic environments. Frawley's approach to *By the Bog of Cats* had quite the opposite effect to *Una Pooka*'s set. For Carr's blend of poetic naturalism and surrealism within a midlands' bog setting, Frawley's set extended towards the backdrop and sides in non-uniform horizontal strata that appeared to be covered in snow and that evoked a bog, sliced up and iced over; her design offered an edgeless quality that seemed to bleed into the audience space. As *By the Bog of Cats* progressed to become Carr's most internationally renowned play, Frawley's approach of maintaining a bleak, snow-covered set throughout the performance became iconic – influencing many designers who worked on future productions, including Joe Vaněk in his design for the San José Repertory Theatre production in 2001, directed by Timothy Near. Enrica Cerquoni examines different scenographies of *By the Bog of Cats*, comparing the Abbey's original production, the San José Repertory' production and the Irish Repertory production in Chicago (2001), directed by Kay Martinovich and designed by Michelle Habeck. The latter was characterized by 'an utterly empty expanse of monochrome greyish flatness' in which shafts of 'light partially infused the stage surface with the snowy and frozen appearance of a winter landscape' (Cerquoni, 2003: 194). Although Frawley returned to the text to conceptualize her design for a new Abbey production of the play in 2015, she again produced the appearance of a vast, frozen expanse, supplemented with an occasional use of video projections on a background screen.

Designers and directors often choose period settings for *By the Bog of Cats*: San José Repertory's production set the play between the late 1960s and early 1970s, while the Abbey's 2015 production was set in the 1990s. Yet the frozen landscapes, initiated by Frawley and enduring throughout most productions, tend instead to suggest futuristic dystopias that imagine Ireland as a bleak wasteland, or evoke what Vaněk calls 'the frozen wastes of [the protagonist] Hester's world' (2015b: 60). Prevailing concerns regarding climate change intensified the possibility of such meanings for the Abbey's 2015 production.

Vaněk's approach to *By the Bog of Cats* was underpinned by significant research into the nature of the Irish midlands, including a study of the Bog of Allen that is documented in his book (2015b: 58–60). Since he began working professionally in Ireland during the mid-1980s, his scenographic research repeatedly has been embedded in the 'sweeping land and seascapes' of the Irish countryside (2015b: 9). Such trends in seeking increased authenticity in Irish scenography's relationship to place flourished in the 1980s, and have proliferated in more recent practice. Druid, for the 1985 Galway Arts Festival, offered a special promenade performance of *Conversations on a Homecoming* at Rabbits Bar in the city centre. Mike Pearson characterizes the operation of scenography within site-based work using a host/ghost alliance, consisting of 'two basic sets of architectures', including the chosen site (the host) and 'the constructed scenography or the ghost, that which is temporarily brought *to* site' (2010: 35–6). The pub served as host to *Conversations on a Homecoming* by providing an apt setting, framed and ghosted by temporary performance and scenography, making the venue 'an active component of performative meaning, rather than a neutral space of exposition' (36).

International trends such as 'environmental design' also influenced efforts to situate Irish theatre within environments comprising real materials and drawn from real places. John Barrett, writing in 1983, identified a spate of recent Irish productions employing 'environmental design', which he defines as 'a type of design that aims to create an atmosphere of authenticity in the theatre' (2010). Barrett's list included: a 1983 Project Arts Centre production of Tom Murphy's *The Morning After Optimism*, collaboratively designed by Michael Scott, Brian Power and Barbara Bradshaw to incorporate silver birch trees and a floor covered with 'tons of peat moss'; Fergus Linehan's adaptation of Seamus Murphy's *Stone Mad* (Peacock, 1982), designed by Casson to create an authentic stonemason's yard 'with dust, dirt and real stone'; and finally *The Great Hunger*, for which Casson's design required 'a quarter ton of clay' to be brought on stage and to be worked laboriously 'into potato drills' (Barrett, 2010). Central to *The Great Hunger*'s set were a number of key objects including a gate, a tabernacle and a wooden effigy to represent the protagonist's mother (crafted by designer Frank Hallinan Flood), which Casson describes as 'a cross between a bog oak Madonna and a piece of kitchen furniture' (Casson, 2015: 87). These bare bones of set were brought to a cowshed in Annaghmakerrig, Co. Monaghan for two nights as part of *The Great Hunger*'s tour. Like Druid's Galway Arts Festival production of *Conversations on a Homecoming*, these performances of *The Great Hunger* ghosted the more permanent architecture of an aptly chosen existing place with what can be considered the 'ephemeral architecture' of scenography (Pantouvaki, 2012: 43).

These efforts to achieve increased authenticity through the composition and, at times, specifically located positions of Irish scenographies have culminated in the contemporary site-specific work of companies such as ANU Productions. Co-directed by visual artist Owen Boss and director Louise Lowe, ANU was established in 2009. Since then, the company has been prolific in creating site-specific theatre concerning Irish social history; in addition to further embedding theatre practice within significant places, the collaboration of a visual artist and a director in making such work signals the increasing proliferation of scenography as a mode of theatre-making in contemporary practice. ANU's most famous work forms the Monto tetralogy (2010–14), which offered four productions that mined historically significant places within an economically deprived, former red-light district known as the Monto in Dublin's inner city. Brian Singleton aptly locates the company's work within an Irish recession era (since 2008), with a tendency towards moving away from theatre buildings 'and towards a reclaiming of unbounded social and unsocial space, particularly but not exclusively in the spaces of Dublin's urbanization' (2016a: 169). As such, ANU's work might be seen to challenge urbanization by calling attention to sites that have been excluded from urbanization's perceived benefits. Elsewhere, Singleton applies Pearson's host/ghost alliance to ANU's work, but notes that while the company's chosen 'micro-sites have a material host architecture, they also have ghosts of sometimes absent narratives that the company seek to recover' (2013: 23). Nevertheless, ANU's site-based works can be seen to foreground scenography in ways already established by companies that emerged in the 1990s, companies that continue to centralize the collaborative work of designers and directors. Examples include Blue Raincoat, which, though led by director Niall Henry, often collaboratively workshop plays by drawing on the skills of such directors as Kellie Hughes and designers including Jo Conway, Joseph Hunt and Michael Cummins. Also important is Pan Pan, which, especially in the work of its co-founder Aedín Cosgrove, showcases scenography's potential to maximize the intermedial possibilities of adaptation in productions from *Mac-Beth 7* (2004) to *The Tempest* (2017).

Comiskey, discussing Ireland's PQ07 entry, noted with optimism that, despite the dominance of writing in Irish theatre, 'design is becoming integrated at a much earlier stage' within production processes (qtd in Keating, 2007). Indeed, Baugh notes that, within contemporary theatre and performance practice, 'scenography is no longer primarily the servant of dramatic performance; it has floated free and may create from within its own practices and research' (2013: 239). Such approaches, however, have deep genealogies in Irish theatre and performance, particularly in their relationships to place. G.A. Hayes-McCoy and Captain John Dowling also might be seen to have experimented collaboratively with site-based work, for example in an outing of *The Pageant of St Patrick* (1954), which represented fifteen-century-old scenes from the story of St Patrick at several places significant to that story dotted throughout the Boyne Valley in Co. Louth. These and other genealogies of contemporary practice merit deeper mining and further interpretation, by unearthing and gathering together scattered scenographic documentation. Securing the ongoing documentation of contemporary Irish scenography involves bringing designers together to formally advocate for stage design's importance and to share scenographic resources. Baugh's interview interestingly reveals the presence of an informal cooperative of designers and technicians that was active across Dublin city during the 1960s and 1970s; the individuals involved would visit each other at their places of work, sharing skills and general conversation. Mac Liammóir, for example, taught Baugh a technique for painting a back- and front-lit gauze to represent Kilmainham Gaol in the style of a nineteenth-century engraving for *The Invincibles*. According to Baugh, Mac Liammóir knew Collins 'and they would help each other out'; there were 'technicians going from theatre to theatre – from the Olympia to the Gate etc. all the time' (2015). It is unfortunate that this community of designers and technicians did not form a more official guild in order to more regularly present and – as such – ensure the more careful documentation of their work for national and international interest groups. As late as 2007, Comiskey bemoaned the lack of a formalized community for theatre design in Ireland: 'We don't even have a forum for talking to ourselves, let alone talking to other people' (qtd in Keating, 2007). The establishment of such organizations as the Association of Irish Stage Technicians (AIST) and the Irish Society of Stage and Screen Designers (ISSSD) bodes well for the curation, documentation and interpretation of current and future Irish scenographies. However, there is also a need to more fully retrieve, understand and celebrate the achievements of designers in Ireland since (at least) the beginning of the twentieth century.

# NOTES

## Introduction

1. Quotations from the #wakingthefeminists event are taken from video material available at http://wakingthefeminists.org/.
2. This remark was made in an interaction between me and Katy Hayes on social media, which is publicly accessible here: https://twitter.com/Katy_Hayes/status/477197727793958912.

## Chapter 1

1. I am grateful to my former student Joseph McCarrick, whose 2017 MA dissertation on religion at the amateur theatre festival documents the importance of key religious figures: 'Clerical Influence in Amateur Drama', National University of Ireland, Galway.

## Chapter 5

1. This information is derived from the Irish Playography.
2. Available at: https://www.youtube.com/watch?v=WXayhUzWnl0.

# REFERENCES AND FURTHER READING

Barrett, John (2010), 'Environmental Design in the Dublin Theatre', in Bernadette Sweeney and Marie Kelly (eds), *The Theatre of Tom Mac Intyre: 'Strays from the Ether'*, Kindle edn, Dublin: Carysfort.

Baugh, Christopher (2013), *Theatre, Performance and Technology: The Development of Scenography in the Twentieth Century*, Basingstoke: Palgrave Macmillan.

Baugh, Christopher (2015), interviewed by Siobhán O'Gorman in *Performing Scenographic Sense Memories*, documentary produced by Siobhán O'Gorman and Noelia Ruiz; directed by Steve O'Connor and Manus Corduff, Dublin: MART.

Beckett, Samuel (2006), *Complete Dramatic Works*, London: Faber and Faber.

Beckett, Samuel (2009), *Letters Volume 1*, London: Faber and Faber.

Behan, Brendan (1978), *The Complete Plays*, London: Methuen.

Behan, Brendan (1981), *Poems and a Play in Irish*, Dublin: Gallery.

Blythe, Ernest (1963), *The Abbey Theatre*, Dublin: Abbey Theatre.

Brady, Deirdre (2017), ' "Writers and the International Spirit": Irish PEN in the Postwar Years', *New Hibernia Review*, 21 (3): 116–30.

Brannigan, John (2002), *Brendan Behan: Cultural Nationalism and the Revisionist Writer*, Dublin: Four Courts.

Brook, Peter (1968), *The Empty Space*, London: Penguin.

Brook, Peter (1988), *The Shifting Point: Forty Years of Theatrical Exploration, 1946–87*, London: Methuen.

Brooks, Peter (1995), *The Melodramatic Imagination: Balzac, Henry James, Melodrama, and the Mode of Excess*, New Haven, CT: Yale University Press.

Brown, Terence (2004), *Ireland: A Social and Cultural History*, London: Harper.

Burke Brogan, Patricia (2008), *Eclipsed*, Galway: Wordsonthestreet.

Burke Brogan, Patricia (2014), *Memoir with Grykes and Turloughs*, Galway: Wordsonthestreet.

Burke, Helen (2005), 'Eighteenth-Century Theatrical Touring and Irish Popular Culture', in Nicholas Grene and Chris Morash (eds), *Irish Theatre on Tour*, 119–38, Dublin: Carysfort.

Burke, Mary (2009), '*Tinkers': Synge and the Cultural History of the Irish Traveller*, Oxford: Oxford University Press.

Byrne, Ophelia (1997), *The Stage in Ulster from the Eighteenth Century: Selected from the Theatre Archive of the Linen Hall Library*, Belfast: Linen Hall Library.

Caldwell, Lucy (2016), *Three Sisters*, London: Faber and Faber.

Caldwell, Lucy (2017), 'On Writing *Three Sisters*', in Linda Anderson and Dawn Miranda Sherratt-Bado (eds), *Female Lines: New Writing by Women from Northern Ireland*, 1116–124, Dublin: New Island.

## References and Further Reading

Callow, Simon (2015), *Orson Welles: One-Man Band*, London: Vintage.

Carlson, Marin (2003), *The Haunted Stage: The Theatre as Memory Machine*, Ann Arbor, MI: University of Michigan Press.

Carney, Frank (1951), *The Righteous Are Bold*, Dublin: Duffy.

Carr, Marina (1999), *Plays 1*, London: Faber and Faber.

Carr, Marina (2009), *Plays 2*, London: Faber and Faber.

Carr, Marina (2015), *Plays 3*, London: Faber and Faber.

Carr, Marina (2016), *Anna Karenina*, London: Faber and Faber.

Casson, Bronwen (2015), ' "Environmental Design" and the Plays of Tom Mac Intyre in the Dublin Theatre', in Bernadette Sweeney and Marie Kelly (eds), *The Theatre of Tom Mac Intyre: 'Strays from the Ether'*, Kindle edn, Dublin: Carysfort.

Cave, Richard Allen (2004), 'On the Siting of Doors and Windows: Aesthetics, Ideology and Irish Stage Design', in Shaun Richards (ed.), *The Cambridge Companion to Twentieth-Century Irish Drama*, 93–108, Cambridge: Cambridge University Press.

Cerquoni, Enrica (2003), ' "One Bog, Many Bogs": Theatrical Space, Visual Image, and Meaning in Some Productions of Marina Carr's *By the Bog of Cats*', in Cathy Leeney and Anna McMullan (eds), *The Theatre of Marina Carr: 'before rules was made'*, 172–99, Dublin: Carysfort.

Chambers, Lilian, Ger Fitzgibbon and Eamonn Jordan (eds) (2001), *Theatre Talk: View of Irish Theatre Practitioners*, Dublin: Carysfort.

CICA (Commission to Inquire into Child Abuse) (2004), 'Transcript, 21 June 2004', Dublin: Government of Ireland. Available online: http://www. childabusecommission.ie/public_hearings/documents/04/Transcript-21June2004.PDF.

Coffey, Fiona Coleman (2016), *Political Acts: Women in Northern Irish Theatre, 1921–2012*, Syracuse, NY: Syracuse University Press.

Conway, Frank (2012) 'The Sound of One Hand Clapping', in Rhona Trench (ed.), *Staging Thought: Essays on Irish Theatre, Scholarship and Practice*, 15–34, Oxford: Peter Lang.

Conway, Thomas (2011), *The Oberon Anthology of Contemporary Irish Plays*, London: Oberon.

Cooney, John (2003), *John Charles McQuaid: Ruler of Catholic Ireland*, Dublin: O'Brien Press.

Coughlan, Aileen and Gearoid O'Brien (2002), 'From the Inside: A Short Chronicle', *All-Ireland Drama Festival Athlone 1953–2002*, Athlone: All-Ireland Festival Committee.

Dean, Joan FitzPatrick (2004), *Riot and Great Anger: Stage Censorship in Twentieth-century Ireland*, Irish Studies in Literature and Culture, Madison, WI: University of Wisconsin Press.

Dean, Joan FitzPatrick (2009), 'Rewriting the Past: Historical Pageantry in the Dublin Civic Weeks of 1927 and 1929', *New Hibernia Review*, 13 (1): 20–41.

Dean, Joan FitzPatrick (2014), *All Dressed Up: Modern Irish Historical Pageantry*, Syracuse, NY: Syracuse University Press.

Delaney, Paul (2000), *Brian Friel in Conversation*, Ann Arbor, MI: University of Michigan Press.

Devitt, John (2012), *Shifting Scenes: Irish Theatre-Going 1955–1985*, Dublin: Carysfort [ebook].

Dixon, Ros (2008), 'West Meets East: Russian Productions at the Dublin Theatre Festival, 1957–2006', in Nicholas Grene and Patrick Lonergan (eds), *Interactions: Dublin Theatre Festival 1957–2007*, 75–92, Dublin: Carysfort.

Donohue, Brenda, Ciara O'Dowd, Tanya Dean, Ciara Murphy, Kathleen Cawley and Kate Harris (2017), *Gender Counts: An Analysis of Gender in Irish Theatre 2006–2015*, Dublin: #WakingTheFeminists.

Dowling, Vincent (2001), *Astride the Moon: A Theatrical Life*, Dublin: Wolfhound.

Dukes, Gerry (2004), 'Englishing "Godot"', *Samuel Beckett Today / Aujourd'hui*, 14: 521–31.

Edwards, Hilton (1958), *Mantle of Harlequin*, Dublin: Progress House.

Essin, Christin (2012), *Stage Designers in Early Twentieth-Century America: Artists, Activists, Cultural Critics*, New York: Palgrave Macmillan.

Farrell, Michael (1942), 'The Country Theatre', *The Bell*, 3 (5): 386–91.

Feeney, William J. (1984), *Drama in Hardwicke Street: History of the Irish Theatre Company*, Plainsboro, NJ: Associated University Presses.

Fitzgerald, F. Scott (1998), *The Great Gatsby*, Oxford: World's Classics.

Fitzpatrick, Lisa (2012), *Representing Systemic Violence: The Example of* Laundry *by ANU Productions*, Warwick Politics and Performance Network Working Papers Vol 1: 4, University of Warwick. Available online: http://uir.ulster.ac.uk/25268/1/vol1_issue_4_lisa_fitzpatrick.pdf.

Fitz-Simon, Christopher (2008), 'An Tóstal and the First Dublin Theatre Festival: a Personal Memoir', in Nicholas Grene and Patrick Lonergan (eds), *Interactions: Dublin Theatre Festival 1957–2007*, 205–22, Dublin: Carysfort.

Foley, Imelda (2003), *The Girls in the Big Picture: Gender in Contemporary Ulster Theatre*, Belfast: Blackstaff Press.

Friel, Brian (1996), *Plays 1*, London: Faber and Faber.

Friel, Brian (1999), *Essays, Diaries, Interviews: 1964–1999*, London: Faber and Faber.

Friel, Brian (2008), *Three Sisters*, Oldcastle, Co. Meath: Gallery Press.

Gregory, Lady Augusta (1972), *Our Irish Theatre: A Chapter of Autobiography*, Gerrards Cross: Colin Smythe.

Grene, Nicholas (1999), *The Politics of Irish Drama: Plays in Context from Boucicault to Friel*, Cambridge: Cambridge University Press.

Grene, Nicholas (ed.) (2002), *Talking About Tom Murphy*, Dublin: Carysfort.

Grene, Nicholas and Patrick Lonergan (2008), *Interactions: Dublin Theatre Festival 1957–2007*. Dublin: Carysfort.

Hall, Peter (2002), 'Sleaze Nation', *The Guardian*, 2 October. Available online: https://www.theguardian.com/stage/2002/oct/02/theatre.artsfeatures.

Harrington, John P. (1991), *The Irish Beckett*, New York: Syracuse University Press.

Harrington, John P. (2004), 'Samuel Beckett and the countertradition', in Shaun Richards (ed.), *The Cambridge Companion to Twentieth-Century Irish Drama*, 164–76, Cambridge: Cambridge University Press.

Harrington, John P. (2007), *Modern and Contemporary Irish Drama*, New York: W.W. Norton.

## References and Further Reading

Harris, Claudia (ed.) (2006), *The Charabanc Theatre Company: Four Plays – Inventing Women's Work*, Gerrards Cross: Colin Smythe.

Hederman, Mark Patrick and Richard Kearney (1977), 'Editorial', *The Crane Bag Book of Irish Studies*, 1 (1): 3–5.

Hickey, Des and Gus Smith (1972), *A Paler Shade of Green*, London: Frewin.

Hill, Shonagh (2015), ' "Popular Feminisms" and the Radical Within', in Eugene McNulty and Tom Maguire (eds), *The Theatre of Marie Jones: Telling Stories from the Ground Up*, 163–80, Dublin: Carysfort.

Hogan, Robert (1968), *After the Irish Renaissance: A Critical History of the Irish Drama Since 'The Plough and the Stars'*, London: Macmillan.

Hogan, Robert and Richard Burnham (1984), *The Art of the Amateur, 1916–1920*, Dublin: Dolmen.

Howard, Pamela (2009), *What Is Scenography?*, Abingdon: Routledge.

Inglis, Tom (2002), 'Sexual Transgression and Scapegoats: A Case Study from Modern Ireland', *Sexualities*, 5 (1): 5–24.

Jones, Marie (2000), *Stones in His Pockets: Two Plays, Also Featuring A Night in November*, London: Nick Hern.

Jones, Marie (2008), *The Blind Fiddler*, London: Samuel French.

Keane, John B. (1959), *Sive: A Play in Three Acts*, Dublin: Progress House.

Keane, John B. (1961), *The Highest House on the Mountain*, Dublin: Progress House.

Kearney, Eileen and Charlotte Headrick (2014), *Irish Women Dramatists 1908–2001*, Syracuse, NY: Syracuse University Press.

Keating, Sara (2007), 'All the World's a Set Design', *The Irish Times*, 12 June. Available online: https://www.irishtimes.com/culture/all-the-world-s-a-set-design-1.1210022.

Kennedy, Seán (2010), *Beckett and Ireland*, Cambridge: Cambridge University Press.

Kilroy, Thomas (1959), 'Groundwork for an Irish Theatre', *Studies: An Irish Quarterly Review*, 48 (190): 192–8.

Kilroy, Thomas (1992), 'A Generation of Playwrights', *Irish University Review*, 22 (1): 135–41.

Kilroy, Thomas (2008), 'A Playwright's Festival', in Nicholas Grene and Patrick Lonergan (eds), *Interactions: Dublin Theatre Festival 1957–2007*, Dublin: Carysfort.

Kinahan, Deirdre (2014), *Spinning*, London: Nick Hern.

Knowlson, James (1997), *Damned to Fame: The Life of Samuel Beckett*, London: Bloomsbury.

Leeney, Cathy (2010), *Irish Women Playwrights 1900–1939: Gender and Violence on Stage*, New York: Peter Lang.

Leeney, Cathy (2016), 'Women and Irish Theatre Before 1960' in Nicholas Grene and Chris Morash (eds), *The Oxford Handbook of Modern Irish Theatre*, 269–85, Oxford: Oxford University Press.

Littlewood, Joan (2016), *Joan's Book*, London: Methuen.

Lojek, Helen Heusner (2011), *The Spaces of Irish Drama: Stage and Place in Contemporary Plays*, Basingstoke: Palgrave Macmillan.

Lonergan, Patrick (2009), *Theatre and Globalization: Irish Drama in the Celtic Tiger Era*, Basingstoke: Palgrave Macmillan.

Lonergan, Patrick (2012), *The Theatre and Films of Martin McDonagh*, London: Methuen.

Lonergan, Patrick (2015), 'Shakespearean Productions at the Abbey Theatre, 1970–1985', in Donald E. Morse (ed.), *Irish Theatre in Transition: From the Late Nineteenth to the Early Twenty-First Century*, 149–61, Basingstoke: Palgrave Macmillan.

Lowe, Louise (2013), 'You Had to Be There', in Fintan Walsh (ed.), *'That Was Us': Contemporary Irish Theatre and Performance*, London: Oberon Books.

Luke, Peter (ed.) (1978), *Enter Certain Players: Edwards-Mac Liammoir and the Gate, 1928–78*, Dublin: Dolmen Press.

Mac Liammóir, Micheál (1964), *Theatre in Ireland*, Dublin: Cultural Relations Committee.

Macken, Ultan (2009), *Walter Macken: Dreams on Paper*, Cork: Mercier Press.

Maguire, Tom (2006), *Making Theatre in Northern Ireland: Through and Beyond the Troubles*, Exeter: University of Exeter Press.

Manning, Mary (1957), *The Voice of Shem*, London: Faber and Faber.

McDonagh, Martin (1996), *The Cripple of Inishmaan*, London: Methuen.

McDonagh, Martin (1997), *Plays 1*, London: Methuen.

McDonnell, Bill (2008), *Theatres of the Troubles: Theatre, Resistance and Liberation in Ireland*, Exeter: University of Exeter Press.

McGrath, Aoife (2011), *Dance Theatre in Ireland: Revolutionary Moves*, Basingstoke: Palgrave Macmillan.

McGuinness, Frank (1996), *Plays 1*, London: Faber and Faber.

McIvor, Charlotte (2016), *Migration and Performance in Contemporary Ireland: Towards a New Interculturalism*, Basingstoke: Palgrave Macmillan.

McIvor, Charlotte and Matthew Spangler (2014), *Staging Intercultural Ireland: New Plays and Practitioner Perspectives*, Cork: Cork University Press.

McMullan, Anna (2016), 'Staging Beckett in Ireland: Scenographic Remains', in Trish McTighe and David Tucker (eds), *Staging Beckett in Ireland and Northern Ireland*, 103–19, London: Bloomsbury Methuen.

McNulty, Eugene and Tom Maguire (eds) (2015), *The Theatre of Marie Jones: Telling Stories from the Ground Up*, Dublin: Carysfort.

McPherson, Conor (2004), *Plays 2*, London: Nick Hern.

McPherson, Conor (2006), *The Seafarer*, London: Nick Hern.

McTighe, Trish (2013a), 'Landscapes and Literary Tourism: The Pike's *Godot* and the Commodification of Place in Ireland', conference paper given at the Annual Conference of the Irish Society for Theatre Research, Birkbeck College, University of London, 1–2 November.

McTighe, Trish (2013b), ' "Getting Known": Beckett, Ireland and the Creative Industries', in Fintan Walsh (ed.), *'That Was Us': Contemporary Irish Theatre and Performance*, 157–213, London: Oberon Books.

McTighe, Trish and David Tucker (2016), *Staging Beckett in Ireland and Northern Ireland*, London: Bloomsbury.

Merriman, Brian (2011), *The Midnight Court / Cúirt an Mheán Oíche*, ed. Brian Ó Conchubhair, Syracuse, NY: Syracuse University Press.

Moore, Dermod (2010), 'The Lunatics in the Basement: Madness in Mac Intyre', in Bernadette Sweeney and Marie Kelly (eds), *The Theatre of Tom Mac Intyre: 'Strays from the Ether'*, Kindle edn, Dublin: Carysfort.

Morash, Christopher (2002), *A History of Irish Theatre, 1601–2000*, Cambridge: Cambridge University Press.

Morash, Christopher (2010), *A History of the Media in Ireland*, Cambridge: Cambridge University Press.

Morash, Christopher and Carolyn Swift (1994), 'Ireland', in Don Rubin (ed.), *The World Encyclopaedia of Contemporary Theatre: Volume 1, Europe*, 467–95, London: Routledge.

Morin, Emilie (2009), *Samuel Beckett and the Problem of Irishness*, Basingstoke: Palgrave Macmillan.

Murphy, Paul (2009), *Hegemony and Fantasy in Irish Drama, 1899–1949*, Basingstoke: Palgrave.

Murphy, Tom (1993), *Plays 2*, London: Methuen.

Murphy, Tom (1994), *Plays 3*, London: Methuen.

Murphy, Tom (2006), *Plays 4*, London: Methuen.

Murphy, Tom (2009), *The Last Days of a Reluctant Tyrant*, London: Methuen.

Murray, Christopher (1999), *Twentieth-Century Irish Drama: Mirror up to Nation*, Syracuse, NY: Syracuse University Press.

Murray, Christopher (2004), *Seán O'Casey: A Biography*, Dublin: Gill and Macmillan.

Murray, Christopher (2006), *Samuel Beckett: 100 Years*, Dublin: New Island.

Murray, Christopher (2016), 'Foreword', in Trish McTighe and David Tucker (eds), *Staging Beckett in Ireland and Northern Ireland*, xv–xx, London: Bloomsbury Methuen.

Ní Chinnéide, Máiréad (2006), *An Damer: Stair Amharclainne*, Dublin: Gael Linn.

Ní Ghráda, Máiréad (2003), *An Triail*, Dublin: An Gum.

Ó hAodha, Micheál (1994), *Siobhán: A Memoir of an Actress*, Dingle: Brandon.

O'Casey, Seán (1975), *Letters 3*, London: Macmillan.

O'Farrell, Ciara (2004), *Louis D'Alton and the Abbey Theatre*, Dublin: Four Courts Press.

O'Gorman, Siobhán (2014), 'Scenographic Interactions: 1950s' Ireland and Dublin's Pike Theatre', *Irish Theatre International*, 3 (1): 25–42.

O'Gorman, Siobhán (2016), '"Hers and His": Carolyn Swift, Alan Simpson, and Collective Creation at Dublin's Pike Theatre', in Kathryn Mederos Syssoyeva and Scott Proudfit (eds), *Women, Collective Creation and Devised Performance*, 129–44, New York: Palgrave Macmillan.

O'Gorman, Siobhán (2018), 'Ireland: A Designer's Theatre', in Eamonn Jordan and Eric Weitz (eds), *The Palgrave Handbook of Contemporary Irish Theatre and Performance*, Basingstoke: Palgrave Macmillan.

O'Gorman, Siobhán (2019), *Theatre, Performance and Design: Scenographies in a Modernizing Ireland*, Basingstoke: Palgrave Macmillan.

O'Hagan, Sean (2001), 'The Wild West', *The Guardian*, 24 March, 32. Available online: https://www.theguardian.com/lifeandstyle/2001/mar/24/weekend. seanohagan.

O'Leary, Philip (2017), *An Underground Theatre: Major Playwrights in the Irish Language 1930–1980*, Dublin: UCD Press.

O'Malley, Aidan (2011), *Field Day and the Translation of Irish Identities*, Basingstoke: Palgrave Macmillan.

O'Neill, Rory (2015), *Woman in the Making*, Dublin: Hachette.

O'Rowe, Mark (1999), *Howie the Rookie*, London: Nick Hern.

O'Rowe, Mark (2011), *Plays 1*, London: Nick Hern.

O'Sullivan, Michael (1999), *Brendan Behan: A Life*, Boulder, CO: Roberts Rinehart.

O'Toole, Emer (2017), 'Guerrilla Glamour: The Queer Tactics of Dr. Panti Bliss' *Eire-Ireland*, 52 (3/4): 104–21.

O'Toole, Fintan (1994), *Tom Murphy: The Politics of Magic*, Dublin: New Island.

O'Toole, Fintan (2000), 'Irish Theatre: State of the Art', in Eamonn Jordan (ed.) *Theatre Stuff*, Dublin: Carysfort [ebook].

O'Toole, Fintan (2006), 'A Mind in Connemara: The Savage World of Martin McDonagh', *The New Yorker*, 6 March: 40–7.

O'Toole, Fintan (2008), 'The Dublin Theatre Festival: Social and Cultural Contexts', in Nicholas Grene and Patrick Lonergan (eds), *Interactions: Dublin Theatre Festival 1957–2007*, 189–204, Dublin: Carysfort.

Pantouvaki, Sofia (2012), 'A Space Within a Space: Contemporary Scenographic Approaches to Historical Theatre Spaces', in Adèle Anderson, Filipa Malva and Chris Berchild (eds), *The Visual in Performance Practice: Interdisciplinary Perspectives*, 43–54, Oxford: Inter-Disciplinary Press.

Parker, Stewart (2000), *Plays 2*, London: Methuen.

Parr, Connal (2017), *Inventing the Myth: Political Passions and the Ulster Protestant Imagination*, Oxford: Oxford University Press.

Pearson, Mike (2010), *Site-Specific Performance*, Basingstoke: Palgrave Macmillan.

Pelletier, Martine (2000), ' "Creating Ideas to Live By": An Interview with Stephen Rea', *Sources*, 9: 48–65.

Phillips, Áine (2015), *Performance Art in Ireland: A History*, London: Intellect.

Pilkington, Lionel (2001), *Theatre and the State in Twentieth-Century Ireland: Cultivating the People*, London: Routledge.

Pilkington, Lionel (2010), *Theatre & Ireland*, London: Palgrave Macmillan.

Pilkington, Lionel (2016), 'The Little Theatres', in Nicholas Grene and Chris Morash (eds), *The Oxford Handbook of Modern Irish Theatre*, 286–305, Oxford: Oxford University Press.

Pine, Emilie (2010), *The Politics of Irish Memory: Performing Remembrance in Contemporary Irish Culture*, Basingstoke: Palgrave Macmillan.

Pine, Richard (1999), *The Diviner: The Art of Brian Friel*, Dublin: UCD Press.

Postlewait, Thomas (1996), 'From Melodrama to Realism: The Suspect History of American Drama', in Michael Hays (ed.), *Melodrama: The Cultural Emergence of a Genre*, 39–60, London: Macmillan.

Poulain, Alexandra (2008), 'Tom Murphy's *The Sanctuary Lamp* at the Dublin Theatre Festival, 1975 and 2001', in Nicholas Grene and Patrick Lonergan (eds), *Interactions: Dublin Theatre Festival 1957–2007*, 93–104, Dublin: Carysfort.

Rebellato, Dan (1999), *1956 and All That: The Making of Modern British Theatre*, London: Routledge.

## References and Further Reading

Rees, Catherine (2017), *Adaptation and Nation: Theatrical Contexts for Contemporary English and Irish Drama*, Basingstoke: Palgrave Macmillan.

Reid, Christina (1997), *Plays: 1*, London: Methuen.

Richtarik, Marilynn (2001), *Acting Between the Lines: The Field Day Theatre Company and Irish Cultural Politics*, Washington DC: Catholic University of America Press.

Richtarik, Marilynn (2012), *Stewart Parker: A Life*, Oxford: Oxford University Press.

Roche, Anthony (1994), *Contemporary Irish Drama: From Beckett to McGuinness*, Dublin: Gill and Macmillan.

Roche, Anthony (2009), *Contemporary Irish Drama*, Basingstoke: Palgrave Macmillan.

Roche, Anthony (2011), *Brian Friel: Theatre and Politics*, Basingstoke: Palgrave Macmillan.

Roche, Anthony, John B. Keane and Ben Barnes (1989), 'John B. Keane Respectability at Last!', *Theatre Ireland*, 18: 29–32.

RTÉ (1974), 'Interview with Joan Littlewood'. Available online: http://www.rte.ie/archives/exhibitions/925-brendan-behan/317556-brendan-behan-the-writer-the-rebel-and-the-rollicking-boy/ (accessed 3 September 2018).

Ryan, Phyllis (1996), *The Company I Kept: Revelations from the Life of Ireland's Most Distinguished and Independent Theatrical Manager*, Dublin: Town House and Country House.

Ryan Report (2009), *Commission to Inquire into Child Abuse*, Dublin: Government of Ireland. Available online: http://www.childabusecommission.ie/rpt/.

Schneider, Rebecca (2011), *Performing Remains: Art and War in Times of Theatrical Reenactment*, Abingdon: Routledge.

Sihra, Melissa (ed.) (2007), *Women in Irish Drama: A Century of Authorship and Representation*, Basingstoke: Palgrave Macmillan.

Simpson, Alan (1962), *Beckett and Behan and a Theatre in Dublin*, London: Routledge.

Singleton, Brian (2013), 'ANU Productions and Site-Specific Performance: The Politics of Space and Place', in Fintan Walsh (ed.), *'That Was Us': Contemporary Irish Theatre and Performance*, London: Oberon.

Singleton, Brian (2016a), *ANU Productions and the Monto Cycle*, London: Palgrave Pivot.

Singleton, Brian (2016b), 'Staging Beckett in Ireland: Scenographic Remains', in Trish McTighe and David Tucker (eds), *Staging Beckett in Ireland and Northern Ireland*, 169–84, London: Bloomsbury Methuen Drama.

Sisson, Elaine (2011), 'Experimentalism and the Irish Stage: Theatre and German Expressionism in the 1920s', in Linda King and Elaine Sisson (eds), *Ireland, Design and Visual Culture: Negotiating Modernity, 1922–1992*, 169–84, Cork: Cork University Press.

Smith, Gus and Des Hickey (1992), *John B.: The Real Keane – A Biography*, Cork: Mercier Press.

States, Bert O. (1985), *Great Reckonings in Little Rooms: On the Phenomenology of Theater*, Berkeley, CA: University of California Press.

Sweeney, Bernadette (2008), *Performing the Body in Irish Theatre*, Basingstoke: Palgrave Macmillan.

Swift, Carolyn (1985), *Stage by Stage*, Dublin: Poolbeg.

Synge, J.M. (1982) *Plays 2*, Gerrards Cross: Colin Smythe.

Szabo, Carmen (2007), *'Clearing the Ground': The Field Day Theatre Company and the Construction of Irish Identities*, Newcastle upon Tyne: Cambridge Scholars.

Taylor, Charles (2007), *A Secular Age*, Cambridge, MA: Harvard University Press.

Thorpe, Dominic (n.d. [2015]), 'Working with Stories of Other People's Traumatic Experiences: Questions of Responsibility as an Artist', *Arts and Health*. Available online: http://www.artsandhealth.ie/perspectives/working-with-stories-of-other-peoples-traumatic-experiences-questions-of-responsibility-as-an-artist/.

Toibin, Colm (1995), 'On the Literary Wing', *Times Literary Supplement* [London, England], 28 April, 10.

Trotter, Mary (2008), *Modern Irish Theatre*, Cambridge: Polity Press.

Vaněk, Joe (2015a), interviewed by Siobhán O'Gorman in *Performing Scenographic Sense Memories*, documentary produced by Siobhán O'Gorman and Noelia Ruiz; directed by Steve O'Connor and Manus Corduff, Dublin: MART.

Vaněk, Joe (2015b), *Irish Theatrescapes: New Irish Plays, Adapted European Plays and Irish Classics*, Cork: Gandon.

Vaněk, Joe and Helen O'Donoghue (2005), *Scene Change: One Hundred Years of Theatre Design at the Abbey* [exhibition catalogue], Dublin: Irish Museum of Modern Art.

Wall, Richard (1987), 'Introduction', in Brendan Behan, *An Giall* and *The Hostage*, Washington DC: Catholic University of America Press.

Wallace, Clare (2005), ' "Pastiche Soup": Bad Taste, Biting Irony and Martin McDonagh', *Litteraria Pragensia: Studies in Literature and Culture*, 15 (29): 3–38.

Walsh, Enda (2006), *The Walworth Farce*, London: Nick Hern.

Walsh, Enda (2012), *Once: The Musical*, London: Nick Hern.

Walsh, Fintan (ed.) (2010) *Queer Notions: New Plays and Performances from Ireland*, Cork: Cork University Press.

Walsh, Fintan (2014), *Queer Performance and Contemporary Ireland: Dissent and Disorientation*, Basingstoke: Palgrave Macmillan.

Walsh, Ian R. (2012), *Experimental Irish Theatre After W.B. Yeats*, Basingstoke: Palgrave Macmillan.

Walsh, Ian R. (2016), 'Directors and Designers Since 1960', in Nicholas Grene and Chris Morash (eds), *The Oxford Handbook of Modern Irish Theatre*, 443–58, Oxford: Oxford University Press.

Watt, Stephen (2009), *Beckett and Contemporary Irish Writing*, Cambridge: Cambridge University Press.

Welch, Robert (1999), *The Abbey Theatre 1899–1999: Form and Pressure*, Oxford: Oxford University Press.

West, Michael (2010), *Freefall*, London: Methuen.

Whelan, Gerard with Carolyn Swift (2002), *Spiked: Church–State Intrigue and the Rose Tattoo*, Dublin: New Island Books.

## References and Further Reading

White, Mo (1995), 'Mary Duffy, the Factory, Belfast, March 1995' [Review], *Circa*, 72: 52.

White, Victoria (1989), 'Towards a Post-Feminism?', *Theatre Ireland*, 18: 33–5.

Wills, Clair (2007), *That Neutral Island: A History of Ireland During the Second World War*, London: Faber and Faber.

Woodward, Guy (2014), *Across the Boundaries: Talking About Thomas Kilroy*, Dublin: Carysfort.

Yeats, W.B. (2001) *The Collected Works of W.B. Yeats Volume II: The Plays*, Basingstoke: Palgrave Macmillan.

# NOTES ON CONTRIBUTORS

**Finian O'Gorman** is an IRC Government of Ireland Scholar at the Centre for Drama, Theatre and Performance in NUI Galway. His 2018 PhD dissertation is entitled 'Ireland's Theatre of Nation: The Amateur Theatre Movement, 1952–1982'. His published work has featured in *New Hibernia Review, Hungarian Journal of English and American Studies, Irish Theatre Magazine* and *The Theatre of Enda Walsh*.

**Siobhán O'Gorman** is a Senior Lecturer at the School of Fine and Performing Arts, University of Lincoln. She co-edited with Charlotte McIvor *Devised Performance in Irish Theatre: Histories and Contemporary Practice* (2015). Her forthcoming monograph, *Theatre, Performance and Design: Scenographies in a Modernizing Ireland*, is based on archival study funded by the Irish Research Council at Trinity College Dublin (2013–15). In addition to publishing her research in a number of journals and edited collections, she was part of the team representing Ireland at the Prague Quadrennial 2015. She is a member of the executive committee of the Irish Society for Theatre Research and the editorial board of *Studies in Costume and Performance*.

**Áine Phillips** is one of Ireland's most established performance artists and the editor of *Performance Art in Ireland: A History* (2015). She has presented multimedia performance works internationally since the late 1980s and has created work for diverse contexts: public art commissions and communities, the street, club events and gallery/museum exhibitions. Her work has been shown across five continents, in places such as Tokyo, Ljubljana, New York, Uganda and Brisbane, and she has given talks on her work at Tate Britain and IMMA. She has worked extensively as a curator of performance events in Ireland and the UK, is the Head of Sculpture at Burren College of Art, and lectures at the O'Donoghue Centre for Drama, Theatre and Performance in NUI Galway.

# INDEX

# Index

# Index

# Index